Decentralizing Power

Paul Goodman, circa 1970

Decentralizing Power

Paul Goodman's Social Criticism

Edited by Taylor Stoehr

BLACK ROSE BOOKS

Montréal/New York
London

3367140

NUV - 9 2016

BLACK ROSE BOOKS No. X218
Hardcover ISBN 1-551640-09-0
Paperback ISBN 1-551640-08-2

Canadian Cataloguing in Publication Data

Main entry under title:

Decentralizing Power: Paul Goodman's social criticism

ISBN: 1-551640-09-0 (bound) —
ISBN: 1-551640-08-2 (pbk.)

1. Goodman, Paul, 1911-1972. 2. United States — Civilization — 1945   .
3. Social problems — United States. 4. Social institutions — United States.
I. Stoehr, Taylor, 1931   .

HN65.D35   1994   306'.0973   C94-900628-9

Cover Design: Rasa Pavalanis

Mailing Address

BLACK ROSE BOOKS
C.P. 1258
Succ. Place du Parc
Montréal, Québec
H2W 2R3 Canada

BLACK ROSE BOOKS
340 Nagel Drive
Cheektowaga, New York
14225 USA

Printed in Canada
A publication of the Institute of Policy Alternatives of Montréal
(IPAM)

Contents

Acknowledgements

I wish to thank previous publishers, the Houghton Library of Harvard University, and Sally Goodman for permission to print Goodman's social criticism. I also thank, for their comments and assistance, the following persons: David De Leon, Geoffrey Gardner, Naomi Goodman, Sally Goodman, Susan Goodman, and Ruth Perry.

Introduction

Paul Goodman's years of public prominence coincided with the youth movement in America. From *Growing Up Absurd* (1960) to *New Reformation* (1970) the young gave him his subject, his audience, his troops. But if youth provided perspective, his angry eye ranged the entire social order, and his proposals for other ways of growing up covered not only schooling, work, and family life, but also religion, psychotherapy, the standard of living, media, community planning, racial justice, political activism — the list could go on. He had already written books in several of these areas.

Growing Up Absurd came at the right moment to heighten the self-consciousness of a new political constituency and help shape its program. He told the young that they were right to rebel against a society that did not give them meaningful work, sexual freedom, a community to be proud of, and food for the spirit. He reminded them that it had not always been that way. Part of the thrill in reading him was the recognition that we have a past to be worthy of — splendid ideas and works of art, stirring acts, glorious human beings. Much to deplore too, of course, though it hardly matched the "super power" or the nuclear warhead. Indignation and hope were the feelings he roused in the young.

Another side of Goodman's appeal was that he was so evidently not a member of the establishment, neither in grey flannels nor tweed jacket. He was a scruffy interloper who had somehow gotten hold of the microphone and was "telling it like it is." Some hostile reviewers were scandalized by his sympathy for roughnecks making free with other people's property, or his championing of sexual freedom for teenagers — but these were the very things that won him disciples. The young needed an adult world that reflected their experience of growing up, but also — and this was what Goodman gave them — permission to *be* young and enjoy it. Paradoxically, it also took many older readers aback to find Goodman writing so unabashedly about traditional ideals. Again and again he was described as "old-fashioned" and even "old-fashionedly moral," because he spoke of honor and faith and a sense of vocation. Indeed, the values he loved to mention — prudence, thrift, honesty, patriotism, temperance — sounded like the Boy Scout Oath, except that he included lust, curiosity, and a spirit that was ready to break the rules for the sake of an evident good.

These were Goodman's own habits and ideals, the fruit of fifty years of bohemian life in his beloved New York City. Raised fatherless in a home full of women (his father abandoned them before he was born, and his brother Percy left at 13), Goodman had been a pampered, brainy kid, given the best free education the city could provide. The family was Jewish, but not part of the wave of immigration from Eastern Europe. On the mother's side — and it was the matriarchal line that always held things together — they were Sephardim, from the low countries, already in the United States for over a century, and relatively prosperous before the father ran off. Despite their poverty they had petty bourgeois values and a proprietary air as they walked the streets of Washington Heights.

Graduating from City College in the early years of the Depression, Goodman lived with his older sister, who supported him while he attempted a literary career. He published a few stories, poems, essays, a play — one of which won a prize — and he even got some fan mail, but very little money.

In 1936, he was offered an assistantship at the University of Chicago, and he began work on his doctorate in philosophy. There he married and had his first child. But being bisexual, Goodman continued to cruise the parks and bars for young men. Although his wife did not object, university officials finally did. He was fired when he would not promise to keep his amorous pursuits off campus.

He might have kept his job if he had been willing to knuckle under, but by 1939, Goodman was homesick, and quite ready to return to Manhattan where the literary avant garde had at last "discovered" him. He finished his dissertation in a hurry (published fourteen years later as *The Structure of Literature*) but could not find a teaching job to support his little family.

Then came Pearl Harbor. When the editors of *Partisan Review* realized that their new film critic was not only a flagrant queer but also advocated draft dodging, his work stopped appearing in their pages. A few places kept publishing him, but soon he was relying on friends with little presses of their own to bring out his books. By 1950, *The Dead of Spring*, probably his best single work of fiction, had to be printed by subscription in David Dellinger's anarchist shop. Meanwhile, his wife had left him, he had remarried and fathered another child. (Neither of his marriages was legally ratified by the State.) They lived below the poverty line on his wife's wages as a secretary, augmented by what he could make teaching in the night school at New York University and one summer at Black Mountain College.

Goodman's antimilitarism brought him in touch with the anarchist groups of New York. He wrote for *Why?* and *Retort* as well as for Dwight Macdonald's *Politics,* the most important of the radical magazines grappling with the disintegration of the Old Left. Parts of both *Communitas* and "The May Pamphlet," Goodman's major political writing of the forties, first appeared in the anarchist press. During this period, he also had his fleeting contact with Wilhelm Reich, an event which launched him on his own self-psychoanalysis. An article that he wrote on Reich for *Politics* brought him in touch with Frederick and Lore Perls, and their friendship led in turn to the founding of the Gestalt therapy movement. It was Goodman rather than Perls who actually wrote the theoretical portion of *Gestalt Therapy* (1951), though the book was a genuine collaboration of ideas — just as *Communitas* (1947) had been with his brother Percival, who furnished the architectural expertise.

Up to this time, Goodman considered himself primarily an artist, but stories and poems poured out of him much faster than they got published. Although he had acquired a dedicated little audience, and was even nominated (by W. H. Auden) for an award from the American Academy of Arts and Letters, Goodman finally gave up trying to blast his way into New York's literary establishment. He turned to psychotherapy as a way of making a living and for the next decade took private patients, ran groups, and held training sessions for the Gestalt Therapy Institute.

Yet he could not keep from writing. Four of Goodman's plays were produced in the fifties by the Living Theatre, for whom he was a kind of guru. *The Empire City,* a long comic epic that was doubtless the greatest achievement of his thirty years as a novelist, finally found a mainstream publisher in 1959, through the efforts of two young editors who ended up losing their jobs over it. But none of this brought money or fame. Meanwhile he contributed to the new political magazines *Dissent* and *Liberation* as well as to student publications like Harvard's *i.e., The Cambridge Review* that were beginning to crop up. By the end of the decade, he had become an unofficial editor of *Liberation,* welcomed by A. J. Muste, David Dellinger, Bayard Rustin, and other pacifist and civil rights leaders. Then came the invitation to write the book on juvenile delinquency that became *Growing Up Absurd.*

At the same time that his new book appeared, Goodman's publishers brought out a paperback edition of *Communitas,* the decentralist manual of community planning that he and his brother had written in the forties. In *Communitas* can be found the main

strands of what might be called his "anarchist ecology," elaborated
further in the sixties but not essentially modified: abhorrence of
waste and revulsion from American's commodity-ridden standard of
living, rethinking the balance of urban and rural values, and insistence that decisions about technology be made on other than crudely
commercial criteria.

Before long, it was apparent that Goodman's anarchism of the
forties was precisely the New Left politics demanded by the young of
the sixties. He reissued "The May Pamphlet" under the title *Drawing
the Line,* adding an assessment of the current "Crisis and New Spirit."
Written when he faced the draft during the Second World War, these
fifteen-year-old essays wrestled with questions that were to face the
young during the Vietnam War: At what point must the free citizen
resist the violence of the State? What was the nature and force of the
moral law that took precedence over the laws of society? In a crisis of
legitimacy, what was the duty of the citizen?

Henceforth Goodman would publish at least a book a year —
sometimes two or three — and he spoke on several campuses every
week. It took four or five publishers to keep up with his social commentary and to drain the backlog of fiction, poems, diaries, plays, and
literary criticism. Although he continued to give his work to *Liberation, Dissent,* and the "little magazines," he could now be read in
many mainstream publications catering to liberal opinion. He was
making money; his wife quit work and had another baby.

He became the first visiting fellow of the Institute for Policy
Studies, the radical think-tank founded in 1963 to lobby policymakers
in Washington. After that, he also made several semester-long visits to
various universities, where he acted as gadfly-in-residence. When the
"Free Speech Movement" erupted on the Berkeley campus, Goodman
flew out to have a look for himself, and was invited to speak at one of
its mass meetings. He was surprised by the anarchist character of the
movement — its grassroots communication network, its "leaderless"
steering committee, its sophisticated use of the general strike — and
for a moment, he thought the situation, at least in Berkeley, was
genuinely revolutionary. For the next few months, he was likely to
receive phone calls at four a.m. from his "crazy young allies" wanting
to discuss tactics with him.

But even at this point in the movement, early 1965, there were
signs that his love affair with the students would not last. There can
be little doubt that the "free university" experiments, at Berkeley and
elsewhere, were largely inspired by Goodman's *Community of Scholars*
(1962), just as his book on elementary level schooling, *Compulsory Mis-*

education (1964), heavily influenced the "free school" movement. Yet his harping on the historical lessons that were to be found in the model of the medieval university, and his badgering students to create alternative institutions on that model instead of simply "bringing down" the Ivory Tower, raised suspicions of bourgeois individualism in some quarters. Nonetheless, in the Spring of 1966, he became the first student-hired professor in the Experimental College at San Francisco State University.

Goodman summed up the case for such decentralized counter-institutions in the book he wrote at the Institute for Policy Studies, *People or Personnel* (1965), a compendium of practical proposals for down-scaling and humanizing the Organized System. He was no social Luddite, and there was nothing doctrinaire about his Utopia. "Decentralization is not lack of order or planning, but a kind of coordination that relies on different motives from top-down direction, standard rules, and extrinsic rewards like salary and status." Yet his argument was not based on a romantic view of human nature. On the contrary, "My experience is that most decentralists are crotchety and sceptical and tend rather to follow Aristotle than Rousseau. We must avoid concentration of power precisely because we *are* fallible; *quis custodiet custodes?* Democracy, Aristotle says, is to be preferred because it is the 'least evil' form of government, since it divides power among many."

By the middle of the sixties the Vietnam War had escalated enough to bring the rebelling campuses into direct confrontation with the government. Goodman's next book was *Like a Conquered Province: The Moral Ambiguity of America* (1966), which originated as a series of lectures for the Massey Lectures heard on the Canadian Broadcasting System. Goodman never focused exclusively on the Cold War or the conflict in Southeast Asia, but rather raised questions about the society that made such things possible: "It should be obvious by now that the vital conflict today is not between one bloc and another bloc, nor between Left and Right, but between a worldwide dehumanized system of things and human decency and perhaps survival. Yet only the young seem to recognize this — in remarkably identical language from Berkeley or Prague or Warsaw or Madrid. The people of my generation cannot see the woods for the trees. ... We do not know how to cope with the new technology, the economy of surplus, the fact of One World that makes national boundaries obsolete, the unworkability of traditional democracy. We must invent new forms."

By the spring of 1967, the radical young on the campuses had become the shock troops of the antiwar movement, which now included many thousands of adult activists. Goodman's fellow editor at *Liberation,* Dave Dellinger, was co-ordinator of a series of protest marches and demonstrations. In April, at a huge rally in New York's Central Park the first mass burning of draft cards took place, organized by a group of Cornell University students including Goodman's son Mathew. Goodman joined Grace Paley and Karl Bissinger in forming the New York branch of Resist, which gave adult support and counsel to draft dodgers. One of the five indicted for such activity (in the famous Dr. Spock case) was his friend, Marc Raskin, at the Institute for Policy Studies, and Goodman was prepared for a similar fate.

His son Mathew's own prosecution for draft refusal seemed imminent that summer. Mathew had never registered, and the FBI was investigating his case. Father and son talked it over at the old farmhouse in northern New Hampshire which Goodman had purchased with the first proceeds from *Growing Up Absurd.* He hoped Mathew would choose to go into exile in Canada, as many draft resisters were doing, but that seemed unlikely. His son's character was a very stubborn one. Then, on August 8th, during a hiking and blueberry-picking party up one of the local peaks, Mathew was killed in an accidental fall.

Nothing Goodman did after that had the same meaning for him. A new recklessness entered his antiwar work, and he seemed to be courting arrest and jail through "aiding and abetting" the draft resisters.

As the 1968 elections approached, Goodman began to speak of a "crisis of legitimacy," and of a "new populism" in response to it, a wave of disgust sweeping over ordinary people, not just the young or the blacks or the poor. "Throw the rascals out!" was the mood he sensed. Perhaps so, though the country elected Richard Nixon. But it was not just the mood of the common man that was getting ugly, nor Goodman who was ready for a reckoning. Many young radicals who had come to the fore in the movement were now calling for violence to meet violence.

Goodman still hoped the "populist" masses were moving toward a new consensus, and tried to use his leverage in the media to encourage the Jeffersonianism that was America's native anarchist tradition. To the movement's vanguard this seemed nothing but a liberal ploy to blunt revolutionary zeal. His speeches began to be heckled and his writings vilified. When the New York *Times* published Goodman's little survey called "The Black Flag of Anarchism," which distinguished anarchist and Leninist strands in the SDS protests at Columbia, Murray Bookchin snapped at him, "How long do we have to endure …

your senile posturing as the Establishment's 'spokesman' for anarchism in the United States?" (Bookchin later apologized.)

Goodman delighted in *ad hominem* polemics. It never threw him
off his stride to be heckled, but he was angry and depressed as he saw
the movement whipping itself up into romantic fantasies of insurrection. Even *Liberation* magazine had adopted this desperate rhetoric, so
much so that Goodman decided to resign. Aside from Dellinger (and
Sid Lens in Chicago) none of the original editors were left, and no one
in the production collective even recognized him. They were busy
pasting the next issue together when Goodman walked in and said he
wanted his name off the masthead. Someone handed him a razor
blade and told him to do it himself.

However deluded they were about the "revolutionary situation,"
Goodman did not cease hectoring the young about their historical
moment. From the very beginning he had spoken of it as a religious
phenomenon, in the tradition of Luther's denunciation of the Whore
of Babylon. Goodman's last book of social commentary bore the title,
New Reformation: Notes of a Neolithic Conservative (1970). Once again, he
deplored the failure of scientists and professionals to live up to their
responsibilities, but the young too were at fault. Their apocalyptic
struggles to bring down the heavens were not justified by the times.
He ended by telling the story of his son's brief pacifist career —
modest, earnest, practical — so different from the ambitions of the
new cadres of violence.

Goodman was nearing the end of his own life. He seemed to
know this even before his first heart attack in 1971, and from now on
each of his books ended with a little *apologia pro vita sua*. The "Notes of
a Neolithic Conservative" were such, as was the "Defence of Poetry"
in his next book, *Speaking and Language* (1971). He was summing up his
work.

Speaking and Language culminated many years' work. He began
collecting material for it in 1960 and had used several of his teaching
semesters to think it through. A critique of the linguistic positivists on
the one hand and the media mongers on the other, it was more important to him as a scholar and an artist than most of his social commentary. He was disappointed when both the literary and the academic
establishment ignored his treatise — but what did he expect from the
very persons he had attacked?

His last book brought these personal testimonies to their climax.
In *Little Prayers and Finite Experience* (1972) a series of short poems were
printed on the *verso* pages, while on the *recto* pages facing them appeared three essays on "how I think," reflections on his way of being

in the world — as one of its creatures, as a citizen, and as a spiritual being. The "little prayers" were poems he had written for himself in moments of crisis over a period of thirty-five years, coping "with the despair, horror, joy, or confusion of my existence." The essays distilled for others the lessons of that existence.

His "peasant anarchism," as he now called it, seemed to lie deep in his character. He hadn't changed his political ideas since he was a boy. No doubt this was partly because, in his own words, "I don't learn anything, but it is partly because political truth is so simple that a boy can see it with a frank look, namely: Society with a big S can do very little for people except to be tolerable, so they can go on about the more important business of life."

In his younger days — even a mere ten years earlier — he had breathed fiery thoughts. Were they the same thoughts today?

They seemed less hot to handle. "I am bemused," he wrote, "as I spell out this politics of mine, at the consistent package of conservative biases, the ideology of a peasant or a small entrepreneur who carries his office and capital under his hat":

> Localism, ruralism, face-to-face organization, distrust of planning, clinging to property, natural rights, historical privileges and immunities, letters to the editor that view with alarm, carrying on the family craft, piecemeal reforms, make do, and let me alone.
>
> No. It is not a possessive peasant nor a threatened small entrepreneur, but a small child who needs the security of routine. There is no father. Mother is away all day at work. He is self-reliant because he has to be. It is lonely, but nobody bugs him, and the sun is pouring through the window.
>
> ... Politically I want only that the children have bright eyes, the river be clean, food and sex be available, and nobody be pushed around. There must not be horrors that take me by the throat, so I can experience nothing; but it is indifferent to me what the Growth Rate is, or if some people are rich and others are poor, so long as they are *pauvres,* decently poor, and not *misérables* (Péguy's distinction). I myself never found that much difference between being very poor and modestly rich.
>
> Idolatry makes me uneasy. I don't like my country to be a Great Power. I am squeamish about masses of people enthusiastically building a New Society.

The great conservative solutions are those that diminish tension by changing 2 percent of this and 4 percent of that. When they work, you don't notice them. Liberals like to solve a problem by adding on a new agency and throwing money at it, a ringing statement that the problem has been solved. Radicals like to go to the root, which is a terrible way of gardening, though it is sometimes sadly necessary in dentistry.

Such were his thoughts in the middle of his sixty-first year. He finished his book in April 1972, but it did not appear until after his final heart attack in August. Goodman was working on his *Collected Poems* when he died.

He had already published four volumes of poetry during the sixties, as well as two books of stories, a novel, three plays, and his journals. Of these only the novel and about half of the poems were actually written during the decade, but even so, combined with ten books of social thought, it was a tremendous output.

Perhaps it will be the poems, a few of the stories, and *The Empire City* that future generations will read, major works that will hold their own against time and fashion. But at this moment in our history, we need his decentralist ideas more than ever. In this new collection of his most acute and durable political writing, readers will recognize the spirit of indignation and hope Goodman first roused in 1960 with *Growing Up Absurd*, the book that set so much of the agenda for the Youth Movement. Many of Goodman's ideas are now part of our common political heritage, in the line from Jefferson through Garrison and Thoreau to Randolph Bourne — truths of human nature we remember and rethink at moments of impasse and crisis. We need to harken once again to his call for decentralization and local autonomy based in community life; to his urging a more livable balance of urban and rural values; to his reminder that technology properly belongs to moral philosophy, and not to the research and development teams of the corporations or the Pentagon; and to his critique of the lock-step educational system and the art-killing mass media, both so devoted to our wasteful standard of living. Whether we call these ideas radical or conservative, Goodman was right when he said that States and institutions interfere too much in people's lives, undermining initiative for the sake of soulless order and mindless material growth. We still have much to learn from him.

Taylor Stoehr
Cambridge, Massachusetts,
October 1994

Selected Bibliography

Major Works by Goodman

Art and Social Nature, New York: Vinco, 1946.

Kafka's Prayer, New York: Vanguard, 1947.

Communitas (with Percival Goodman), Chicago: University of Chicago, 1947. (New edition, New York: Columbia University Press, 1990.)

Gestalt Therapy (with F.S. Perls and Ralph Hefferline), New York: Julian Press, 1951.

The Structure of Literature, Chicago: University of Chicago Press, 1954.

The Empire City, Indianapolis and New York: Bobbs-Merrill, 1959.

Growing Up Absurd, New York: Random House, 1960.

The Lordly Hudson, New York: Macmillan, 1962.

Drawing the Line, New York: Random House, 1962.

The Community of Scholars, New York: Random House, 1962

Utopian Essays and Practical Proposals, New York: Random House, 1962.

The Society I Live In Is Mine, New York: Horizon, 1962.

Making Do, New York: Macmillan, 1963.

Compulsory Mis-education, New York: Horizon, 1964.

People or Personnel, New York: Random House, 1965.

Five Years, New York: Brussel and Brussel, 1966.

Like a Conquered Province: The Moral Ambiguity of America, New York: Random House, 1967.

New Reformation: Notes of a Neolithic Conservative, New York: Random House, 1970.

Speaking and Language, New York: Random House, 1971.

Little Prayers and Finite Experience, New York: Harper and Row, 1972.

Edited by Taylor Stoehr

Collected Poems, New York: Random House, 1973.

Drawing the Line: Political Essays;

Creator Spirit Come! Literary Essays;

Nature Heals: Psychological Essays;
  New York: Free Life Editions, 1977.

Collected Stories and Sketches, 4 vols., Santa Barbara: Black Sparrow Press, 1978-1980.

Don Juan: or, The Continuum of the Libido, Santa Barbara: Black Sparrow Press, 1979.

Parents' Day, Santa Barbara: Black Sparrow Press, 1985. (Original publication, Saugatuck, Conn.: 5 X 8 Press, 1951.)

Format and Anxiety: Paul Goodman's Critiques of the Media, Brooklyn: Autonomedia, 1994.

Crazy Hope and Finite Experience: Final Essays of Paul Goodman, San Francisco: Jossey-Bass, 1994.

Works About Goodman

Hayden Carruth, "Paul Goodman and the Grand Community," *American Poetry Review,* 12 (September/October 1983), 22-32.

George Dennison, "The Ways of Nature," *Inquiry Magazine,* 1 (March 6, 1978), 20-22. (This issue also contains pieces on Goodman by Michael Rossman, Lewis Perry, and Emile Capouya. See also Dennison's "Memoir" in Goodman's *Collected Poems.*)

Lewis Fried, *Makers of the City,* Amherst: University of Massachusetts Press, 1990. (Chapter 4, "Paul Goodman: The City as Self," pp. 159-206.)

Geoffrey Gardner, "Citizen of the World, Animal of Nowhere," *New Letters,* 42 (Winter/Spring 1976), 216-227. (Special issue devoted to *The Writings of Paul Goodman* along with essays and memoirs.)

Richard King, *The Party of Eros: Radical Social Thought and the Realm of Freedom,* Chapel Hill: University of North Carolina Press, 1972. (Chapter 3, "Paul Goodman," pp. 78-115.)

Tom Nicely, *Adam and His Work: A Bibliography of Sources by and about Paul Goodman,* Metuchen, N.J.: The Scarecrow Press, 1979.

_____, "Adam and His Work: A Bibliographical Update," in *Artist of the Actual: Essays on Paul Goodman,* edited by Peter Parisi, Metuchen, N.J.: The Scarecrow Press, 1986. (This volume includes essays and interviews by a variety of hands.)

Leo Raditsa, "On Paul Goodman—and Goodmanism," *Iowa Review,* 5 (Summer 1974), 62-79.

Theodore Roszak, *The Making of a Counter Culture,* Garden City: Anchor, 1969. (Chapter 6, "Exploring Utopia: The Visionary Sociology of Paul Goodman," pp. 178-238.)

Taylor Stoehr, "Paul Goodman and the New York Jews," *Salmagundi,* No. 66 (Winter/Spring 1985), 50-103.

_____, "Adam and Everyman: Paul Goodman in his Stories," in *Words and Deeds: Essays on the Realistic Imagination,* New York: AMS, 1986, pp. 149-164.

_____, "Paul Goodman, The Living Theatre, and the Great Despair," *Theater*, 21 (Winter/Spring 1990), 17-22.

_____, "*Growing Up Absurd*—Again: Rereading Paul Goodman in the Nineties," *Dissent*, 37 (Fall 1990), 486-494.

_____, "Graffiti and the Imagination: Paul Goodman in his Short Stories," *Harvard Library Bulletin* (1994).

_____, *Here Now Next: Paul Goodman and the Origins of Gestalt Therapy*, San Francisco: Jossey-Bass, 1994.

Colin Ward, *Influences: Voices of Creative Dissent*, Bideford, Devon: Green Books, 1991. (Chapter 6, "Patrick Geddes and Paul Goodman," pp. 103-146.)

Kingsley Widmer, *Paul Goodman*, Boston: Twayne, 1980.

David Wieck, "Paul Goodman: *Drawing the Line*," *Telos*, 35 (Spring 1978), 199-214.

The first essay in this collection, "Social Criticism," was found in Goodman's papers after his death, and has never been published. It was written in 1963, just before Goodman began his period in Washington as senior fellow of the new Institute for Policy Studies. He seems to have decided not to publish it because he now had hopes that social criticism—his own—might make a difference after all. Moreover, his essay had as one of its themes the question: "If things are as bad as the social critics say, why is there no widespread rebellion?," and just as he was finishing it, the upheaval of the sixties was beginning in earnest. The question was moot.

The other items have been published in various books and magazines, some of them rare and most of them long unavailable. Although they have been slightly edited in removing them from their original contexts, there has been no attempt here to update or streamline them.

"Introduction": essay by Taylor Stoehr on "Paul Goodman" in *Leaders from the 1960s: A Biographical Sourcebook of American Activism*, ed. David De Leon, Westport, CT.: Greenwood Press, 1994, pp. 509-516.

"Social Criticism": 1963, previously unpublished. Printed by permission of the Houghton Library of Harvard University, where most of Goodman's papers are deposited.

"The Anarchist Principle": published as "Reflections on the Anarchist Principle," *Anarchy* 62 (April 1966), 115-16.

"Anarchism and Revolution": in *The Great Ideas of Today*, ed. Robert Hutchins and Mortimer Adler, Chicago: Encyclopaedia Britannica, 1970, pp. 44-65.

"Freedom and Autonomy": published as "Just An Old Fashioned Love Song," *WIN*, 8 (February 1972), 20-21. (Extracts from *Little Prayers and Finite Experience* along with new material.)

"Children's Rights": Introduction to the American edition of Paul Adams et al., *Children's Rights*, New York: Praeger, 1971, pp. 1-8. (The version printed here appeared as "What Rights Should Children Have?" in the *New York Review of Books*, 17 (September 1971), 20-22.)

"The Present Moment in Education": first published in the *New York Review of Books*, 12 (April 10, 1969), 14ff. The version printed here was published in *Summerhill: For and Against,* New York: Hart Publishing Co., 1970, pp. 205-222.

"The Unteachables": *Orientation/1964* (Nashville) (July 1964), 20-24. (A version of material in *Compulsory Mis-education.*)

"The Human Uses of Science": First published in *Commentary,* 30 (December 1960); the version printed here was published in *Utopian Essays and Practical Proposals* as "'Applied Science' and Superstition," pp. 23-48.

"Prudent Technology": from *New Reformation,* pp. 7-20.

"A Causerie at the Military-Industrial": *New York Review of Books,* 9 (November 23, 1967), 14-19. (A speech Goodman gave for the National Security Industrial Association's *Symposium on National Research and Development for the 1970s,* October 19, 1967, in the State Department Auditorium in Washington, D.C., the same week as the March on the Pentagon.)

"Format and Colloquial Speech": from *Speaking and Language,* pp. 200-209.

"The Limits of Local Liberty": *New Generation* (formerly *American Child*), 51 (Summer 1969), 13-17.

"Racism, Spite, Guilt, and Non-Violence": published as "Reflections on Racism, Spite, Guilt and Non-Violence," *New York Review of Books,* 10 (May 23, 1968), 18-23.

"Civil Disobedience": published as "Reflections on Civil Disobedience," *Liberation,* 13 (July/August 1968) 11-15. (Originally prepared for a conference on civil disobedience at Kenyon College, this essay is an early version of material in *New Reformation.*)

"Some Prima Facie Objections to Decentralism": *Liberation,* 9 (December 1964), 5-11. (Early version of opening chapter of *People or Personnel.*)

"The Sentiment of Powerlessness": published as "The Sentiment of Powerlessness in American History," chapter 11 of *People or Personnel.*

"Confusion and Disorder": *Earth,* 2 (August 1971), 57-61.

"Notes of a Neolithic Conservative": *New Reformation,* pp. 191-208.

Social Criticism

1

In the past decade, there has accumulated a whole literature of sweeping critique of American institutions that has come to be called Social Criticism, and I shall try to locate some specific properties of this genre. I think it has peculiarities, different from other literature of protest, polemic, and satire. Much of it has been excellent and acute as sociology and moral philosophy; much of it has been immensely popular, including some pretty meretricious performances. There is no doubt that it has had an important influence on the cultural tone of the present, yet very little influence on apparent social and political behavior. This certainly merits examination. In this essay, I shall avoid mentioning particular works and authors, but just think of the ground covered, the multiplicity of targets! — the lonely crowd, the manufactured taste, the wasteful production, the tailfin cars, the pseudo-news, suburban emptiness, career anxiety, the paper-economy, the disillusionment of youth, the administered colleges, the conformist executive, the bureaucratic labor-union, the inhuman housing, the perverted use of sociology and psychology, the garrison state, the power-elite, the damaging motherhood, the poisoned land, the insidious advertising, the devolution of democracy. I stop at twenty.

In some of the authors, the peculiar "social criticism" quality, desperate sweeping attack on the general cultural tone, is part of a more specialist scientific analysis, including constructive suggestions, in economics and technology, sexology and pedagogy, ecology and city-planning, etc. And the criticism naturally aims at traditional objects of political and moral reform, at race-prejudice, poverty, political graft, bureaucratic stupidity, the arms race. Nevertheless we must explore how Social Criticism is different from scientific analysis and reform politics.

Conversely, there is nothing new about Social Criticism itself. Especially since the First World War, in such diverse writers as Benda and Ortega, or Mumford and Borsodi, or Freud, the tone is often very like our contemporary critique. In the preceding century, since the Industrial Revolution, much moral philosophy and even most of sociology, sounds somewhat like Social Criticism, in Coleridge, Ruskin,

Proudhon, Marx, Veblen. Earlier, the tone is, if anything, more unmis-
takable, among the satirists and *philosophes,* Voltaire, Swift, Rousseau,
Mandeville, and so back to Erasmus and the Reformation, Rabelais
and Cervantes, and the Millenarians and proto-reformers of the Middle Ages. The sentiment that it is not this-or-that that is wrong, but all
of the way men go about living. But it is just in this historical perspective that we can notice how the present literature is unique.

2

Let's make a quick survey of other literatures of social protest.
First there is the satire and invective of a Loyal Opposition. It is loyal
in the sense that it accepts the existing social structure or State, but attacks the government or party in power. In muck-raking, however,
this opposition is more outraged and desperate, for it is felt that the
abuse includes all the available parties, not merely the one ostensibly
in power. Muck-raking therefore verges easily into frankly revolutionary propaganda; it wants to subvert the State and change the social institutions. The question is, which institutions? How profound a
change is necessary? Economy and politics? Law? Technology? Family and Morals? Science and Religion? Education and Child-Care?

In theory, frank revolutionists like Marx and Proudhon wanted
rather total change, and they reasoned that changes in productive
and legal relations would encompass all the other necessary changes.
In fact, however, they assumed that enlightened men — enlightened
according to the contemporary standard — industrialized or
craftsmanlike, were solid stuff to make a revolution with. They really
did not question the education, science, aesthetics, family morals, or
technology of the times. The problem was, as Engels said, to replace
the government over people by an administration of things.

But if we go back to the French Revolutionary writers, Voltaire,
Rousseau, de Sade, we meet a more thoroughgoing dismay and a tone
in some ways more like our own. For they felt that not only was the
regime corrupt but it had corrupted the entire nature of man. But the
nature of man was not corrupt; mankind was not inhuman but vi-
cious; and the cure was Enlightenment itself, to make men rational,
wholesome, and free. Accordingly, there was, until 1787, almost no
overtly "revolutionary" writing (perhaps Paine); rather, the writers
are busy with primitive anthropology, permissive pedagogy, the
religion of reason, politics as a science, natural economics. The
revolution was bound to occur; they were looking to a post-revolu-
tionary reconstruction. It was as if, on the one hand, the thorough-

going critique of regime and of mankind corrupted by it made any attempt at political power seem irrelevant, if not wicked; but, on the other hand, the power of the regime itself was largely illusory, because it was grounded in superstition and was morally bankrupt, whereas men were potentially reasonable and good and would simply be stronger. We can see exactly this strain persisting through the nineteenth and twentieth centuries in the radical anarchist writers, who look to total revolution and reconstruction by pedagogy, civil liberty, and decentralization in industry and administration.

But there was finally, in the eighteenth century and earlier, back through the Reformation, a rather different strain of critique that also interestingly resembles our own. Men — so Swift or Erasmus felt — are really impossible by nature, and nothing can be done. The tone is dismayed but detached and often humorous (except when it becomes pious, as in Bunyan). Our humanity is, has been, and will be a disaster. Luckily, God keeps things going. In this vein, Social Criticism merges on one side with general moral satire and on the other side with eschatological religion.

3

How does our Social Criticism resemble and differ from these older strains? Our writers too are variously politically and morally outraged, revolutionist, Utopian, apocalyptic, or humorously complacent. What constitutes their writing as a genre is a peculiar combination of these attitudes that, naturally, closely answers our contemporary social plight.

(1) They express a fairly global dismay. Each critic tends to choose a particular target for his informed protest, but it is clear that he considers it as part of a pervasive evil. As we have seen, urbanism, economy, work-attitudes, administration, education, etc. are each singled out as being in intolerably bad shape. Taken together, they make up pretty much the whole of social life. But significantly, unlike in former times, there is not much complaint about basic subsistence, health, exploitation of labor, cruelty to children; though of course there are angry books on poverty, poisoning, and nuclear war. This is significant because the great revolutionary motivation of physical pain and immediate distress is, in America, diminished; the biological dangers that are cried up require imagination to understand.

(2) The criticism is not only global but irrefutable. The writers polemically exaggerate, but by and large the readers feel that their books make articulate what everybody has dumbly known anyway.

And there is almost no rebuttal, except snide insults in *Time* or peevish reviews that point out inaccuracies but concede that there is much in the main burden. One has the impression that the authors of the Establishment dare not rebut or are morally bankrupt; and indeed, that the powers-that-be are so strong, or think they are, that they do not need moral justification, but will continue just as they please no matter what is said. There is no doubt that the overbearing centralization, war-budgeting, commercialism are continually both more ruthless and blander.

(3) Nevertheless, similar to the lull before the French Revolution, there is little expression of revolutionary spirit, certainly not in the form of an organized counter-program, nor even — except in the apocalyptic poets — of an emotional plea for withdrawal or rebellion commensurate with the evil. It is as if there were no "total" alternative. Partly, I think, this is because of the conviction that under contemporary conditions any sweeping revolution, whether brought about by violent or political means, would end up with the very same evils and maybe worse. Partly, it is that there is a lack of social imagination *of* alternatives to the way of life. As I have frequently argued, this lack of imagination, the sentiment that "Nothing Can Be Done," is self-causing and self-proving in the very conditions that the critics attack.

(4) Rather, eerily, in the face of admitted general evils and continuing debasement that men do not strive to change, it is not a common feeling among the critics that *Man* is to be despaired of. This kind of issue is hardly raised, except among professional theologians who, in the manner of Niebuhr, are smug about it and condone even the Cold War. Among the critical, even nuclear annihilation is not regarded religiously but as a kind of objective apocalypse that does not spring from human corruption or divine wrath. (Among ordinary people there is a kind of disgusting panic at crises like the Cuban crisis of last fall, including frantic inquiries about tickets to New Zealand; but a week later business goes on as usual. So also the Jews went to the gas-chambers.) In brief, although social life is criticized as quite generally intolerably unworthy and possibly suicidal — and though the criticism is not refuted — yet men are not moved, nor urged, to change their ways. Even more strange, this human callousness or apathy is not itself challenged as the evil. Not much is said about either despairing of, or changing, "human nature." Indeed, "changes in human nature," for example, by drugs or conditioning, are correctly taken as the province of the Establishment itself, at its worst.

4

Such is the paradoxical combination of attitudes of Social Criticism. It is not hard to see the underlying conditions of modern life that call for such a combination. Simply, that industrialization, urbanization, political growth, and the technological applications of accumulating physical science have occurred under the auspices of centralizing power, for the purposes of profits and aggrandizement, and in a logistic and bureaucratic style that suited the discipline of national armies, the collection of taxes, and the production of standard commodities in an economy of scarcity. But diminishing initiative and creating fundamental stupidity. To revert to Engel's formula, we have an administration of things of such a sort that men have become things. In advanced countries immediate physical hardship has diminished, and people are by and large allowed, or even encouraged, to cower into private life for human comfort; but meanwhile top-down public administration controls functions of daily behavior, common sense, taste, education, communication, and science that were formerly either spontaneous or traditional.

In recent decades, the abuse has galloped. Advanced countries have become over-capitalized, over-organized and wrongly organized, over-educated and wrongly educated to a degree that the capitalization and organization, and their thought and style, seem to run like an automatic machine, by its own motivation and for its own sake. The running is valueless and dangerous, but the critics of it, while registering their dismay, do not blame the persons who "run" it or are run by it, and they do not rally people against it, for people have become brainwashed. They cannot act otherwise than as parts of the machine. There is no thinkable alternative, and any suggestion of one rouses anxiety. Any revolutionary action, it is deeply believed, must use the same methods and must come out with the same results as being parts of a very similar machine.

In my opinion, the brainwashing and the timid conformity are not technological or moral, but are caused by confusion, stupidity, and anxiety. People would not be so much influenced by mass-communications, bureaucratic routines, and the pressures of garrison states, if they were in a more normal mental state to begin with. Normally it does not take long reflection to make a little sense, and the mutual encouragement of a few people leads to the beginning of action. But under the best circumstances, the industrial, urban, and technological revolutions involve immense new learning and adjustment; they should have taken place in moderate doses to meet real needs, with plenty of reasoning and voluntary choice, instead of pell-mell and compelled by irrelevant power and profit considerations. Just as industrially backward people are cast into tribal and cultural chaos by the beginnings of industrialism which they have not developed in their own style, so more slowly industrialized societies have been unready for the later stages. Surplus productivity and the plethora of goods and leisure become themselves problematic. Add the fairly sudden diminishing of religious and other traditions without replacement by any comparable interpretations of human experience; and the rapid development of the world community hampered, distorted, and disordered by Nation-States and Great Powers, imperialism and neo-imperialism. These sources of confusion would themselves create enormous public anxiety. But again add to them brute fear, of vast wars and civil policing, and the anxiety has deepened to actual paralysis of initiative and blacking out of social invention. Certainly at present we cannot hope for any generally useful thought or social experiment till we get rid of the Cold War; yet how to do that under the present auspices? People feel that they cannot afford to risk any change, at the same time that they know they are doomed if they continue as at present.

It is this contemporary plight that Social Criticism is about. Though the different critics pursue different quarries, there is one global cluster of complaints. Our society is out of human scale, mechanical, stupid, venal, base, biologically dangerous, massified and socialized without community, regimenting and brainwashing, dedicated to procedure and format rather than function and meaning. Its moral justification is really a self-proving superstition; it "solves" in its own style problems that it has created itself; its research is incestuously staffed from its own bureaucrats who work for their own aggrandizement and cannot see anything else.

5

Given the underlying reality, such criticism is inevitable. As I have said, it is rarely rebutted, but the critics themselves are called Luddite, snobbish, bucolic, eighteenth-century, sixteenth-century, Utopian. These charges simply mean that people are so brainwashed that they cannot, or do not want to, conceive of technology, city-planning, and politics, or even advertising and the TV, managed otherwise than at present. Another charge is that the critics are oblivious to the realities of power, *Realpolitik*, the profit-system, the power elite; one cannot change the system by decrying it, one must get power.

Since the very machinery of getting into power and wielding power is at present a chief cause of the trouble, it is pointless to ask us to affirm "realities" that defeat our purposes. (In his last period, by the way, C. Wright Mills was entranced by the need to get into power. In *The Causes of World War Three* he has a paean to the great *advantage* of unified top-down decision-making, since the boss can then solve all at one stroke! — Max Weber's bureaucracy and charisma gone mad.) People are trapped in a system admittedly absurd, but the critics do not offer any alternatives.

A more serious charge is that the criticism is merely destructive. Literally, this is rarely true. Many of the critics sketch out alternatives to what they are criticizing, sometimes knowledgeably, sometimes amateurishly. Intellectual men do not oppose something without some vague concrete image of what would replace it; the thought of how things should be done is what makes one dissatisfied with how they are done. (Needless to say, nothing comes of these positive suggestions, which are "Utopian.") Furthermore, many things in our society hardly need to be replaced. What may be called for is *not* doing, or fulfilling the function in a simpler or more direct way. If a society suffers from glut, ritual, and greed, destructive ridicule *is* positive.

But this is the real weakness of Social Criticism, as of all moral satire. It disregards the fact that people *cannot* do otherwise than they do, and especially if the message is simply to stop, survey the scene, and make easier sense. This rouses intense anxiety, for people would have to fill the void with their own initiative, which is just what they are afraid of. It is easier to sell other complicated expedients or the "posture of sacrifice," as the President has called it. Social Criticism is ineffectual not because it does not explain how to get power and administer its ideals, but because it does not awaken initiative, the source of power. Despite the prevalent superstition to the contrary, there could be alternative ways of modern life, and some of the critics propose them, but the point is for people to feel themselves differently than they do. I suppose that, for this, we require not critics but prophets. Or, as Wilhelm Reich kept telling us, psychiatrists.

6

Paying attention to the products of the social machine and the inane workings of the machine itself, Social Critics have mostly ignored the underlying social psychology, obvious as it is. Their cultural dismay is genuine, but they take much too lightly the absence of initiative, morale, or commitment; their tone has neither indignation nor Utopian aspiration; they seem to be reconciled to people having no *souls*, in Aristotle's simple sense that the soul is self-moving and initiating and goes toward its good. Perhaps they are misled by the absence of immediate physical suffering (the authors who deal with insanity, police brutality, juvenile delinquency are far more passionate and political); certainly they misread the psychology of the middle-class. They take the conformity as unpleasant complacency rather than resignation; they do not understand that the smiling and togetherness cover anxiety; in the apathy about nuclear war, they do not recognize paralysis caused by the repression of explosive masochism, ready for panic.

In this misunderstanding, our critics are inferior to their predecessors. The social-revolutionaries, for example, Marx or Bakunin, correctly relied on physical deprivation to rouse action (they did not foresee that in the advanced economy the standard of living would rise). The *philosophes*, even when they were mechanists, were sure that people had initiating souls and would resist indignity if once they were disenchanted of their superstitions. Among the older moralists, those who were more good-natured, like Erasmus, Montaigne, and Mandeville, were not cynical about the impossible animal Man, because they knew that man's inevitable vices and follies were natural and gave real satisfaction; and those who were bitter or fiery, like Swift or Luther, took vice and hypocrisy as belonging to men fallen, something to despise or contest with the Devil. By contrast, what does the tone of our contemporary critics mean, whether witty, sensational, cynical, or "objective"?

Evidently, the Social Criticism is part of the system that it criticizes. As one who writes it myself, let me mention several human feelings that it expresses. Most weakly, we are indulging in a kind of griping, not much different from dissatisfied soldiers in any regiment. So society lets off steam, while the real war rolls on. More important (in my own case) it is a kind of spite, the vitality of the powerless, the attempt to make the powerful feel bad, guilty, cheap, foolish, as they roll on.

An obvious virtue of some Social Criticism — part and parcel of the social mores — is to one-up one's fellows. For instance, everybody on Madison Avenue is doing a certain song and dance, but the social critic knows it and points it out, to their disgrace; he himself, to be sure, continues to perform on Madison Avenue, but he can pose, or perhaps feel himself, as a superior individual, a critic. A more desperate and honorable nuance of the same — which feels more like myself — is the defiant cry of lonely reason in a city of unreason, literarily bearing witness. I have seen a gentleman from one of the Foundations burst into tears because proposals of mine were so right and so useless. They were Paradise Lost.

Alas, it is this very witness-bearer who is most useful, perhaps indispensable, for the system he is attacking. He is their court jester, who keeps clear before them the true, the good, and the beautiful as they do otherwise. He helps articulate and work off whatever self-contempt they feel. He provides the excellent entertainment of conversation-pieces. Great national magazines print one such piece of trenchant honesty every fourth issue. It can be said, indeed, that it is precisely the excellent Social Criticism that has hastened the brazenness of the powers-that-be as they roll on, and has made them more ruthless. For now the more sensitive and intelligent *know* they are morally bankrupt and they proceed like pure hipsters. It is only the utter stuffed shirts and horse's asses who can make public speeches with a good conscience, as they roll on. (This is the chief difference between Democrats and Republicans.)

To be sure, these fools are rolling themselves, and perhaps the country, to destruction. As writers, we are only writers; and everybody knows, these days, that writing can be taken in stride. It has no relation to action, or even, sometimes, it contains suggestive ideas that can be misused out of context. Nevertheless, what we critics say is largely true; it has that property, though no influence.

7

Arthur Schlesinger, the sage of the White House, has publicly urged us dissenters (especially me) to continue our indispensable role of dissent. And my own experience has, indeed, been the following: I am invited to be part of the left wing at national *conferences* and *panel-discussions,* too numerous to mention; I have not been invited to sit down on a decision-making board; and the decisions of the actual boards are *not* such as we critics could approve.

Even more interesting is the relation of Social Criticism to the social sciences. Some of us writers are almost universally praised, even in the learned journals, for the insight that we have as "generalists," disregarding disciplinary boundaries; the "fresh look" that we have by not wearing professional blinders; and the forthrightness of our propositions that are not written in Choctaw. All this means, usually, is that we point to something relevant that is obvious, but that professionals are carefully trained to overlook. I have not heard nor personally experienced, however, that we writers are called on to help in scientific work on practical problems. Thus, since there is no social science that is not pragmatic and experimental, our own knowledge remains dilettantish; while professional social science continues as it has been, with social engineering for the *status quo* or academic boondoggling.

Such experiences impress one neither with the honor or practicality of the established powers; nor with the practical relevance of Social Critics.

Anarchism

The Anarchist Principle

Anarchism is grounded in a rather definite proposition: that valuable behavior occurs only by the free and direct response of individuals or voluntary groups to the conditions presented by the historical environment. It claims that in most human affairs, whether political, economic, military, religious, moral, pedagogic, or cultural, more harm than good results from coercion, top-down direction, central authority, bureaucracy, jails, conscription, States, preordained standardization, excessive planning, etc. Anarchists want to increase intrinsic functioning and diminish extrinsic power. This is a social-psychological hypothesis with obvious political implications.

Depending on varying historical conditions that present various threats to the anarchist principle, anarchists have laid their emphasis in varying places: sometimes agrarian, sometimes free-city and guild-oriented; sometimes technological, sometimes anti-technological; sometimes communist, sometimes affirming property; sometimes individualist, sometimes collective; sometimes speaking of Liberty as almost an absolute good, sometimes relying on custom and "nature." Nevertheless, despite these differences, anarchists seldom fail to recognize one another, and they do not consider the differences to be incompatibilities. Consider a crucial modern problem, violence. Guerilla fighting has been a classical anarchist technique; yet where, especially in modern conditions, any violent means tends to reinforce centralism and authoritarianism, anarchists have tended to see the beauty of non-violence.

Now the anarchist principle is by and large true. And far from being "Utopian" or a "glorious failure," it has proved itself and won out in many spectacular historical crises. In the period of mercantilism and patents royal, free enterprise by joint stock companies was anarchist. The Jeffersonian bill of rights and independent judiciary were anarchist. Congregational churches were anarchist. Progressive education was anarchist. The free cities and corporate law in the feudal system were anarchist. At present, the civil rights movement in the United States has been almost classically decentralist and anarchist. And so forth, down to details like free access in public libraries. Of course, to later historians, these things do not seem to be anarchist, but in their own time they were all regarded as such and often literally called such, with the usual dire threats of chaos. But this relativity of the anarchist principle to the actual situation is of the essence of anarchism. There *cannot* be a history of anarchism in the sense of establishing a permanent state of things called "anarchist." It is always a continual coping with the next situation, and a vigilance to make sure that past freedoms are not lost and do not turn into the opposite, as free enterprise turned into wage-slavery and monopoly capitalism, or the independent judiciary turned into a monopoly of courts, cops, and lawyers, or free education turned into School Systems.

Anarchism and Revolution

In anarchist theory, the word *revolution* means the process by which the grip of authority is loosed, so that the functions of life can regulate themselves, without top-down direction or external hindrance. The idea is that, except for emergencies and a few special cases, free functioning will find its own right structures and co-ordination.

An anarchist description of a revolutionary period thus consists of many accounts of how localities, factories, tradesmen, schools, professional groups, and communes go about managing their own affairs, defending themselves against the central "system," and making whatever federal arrangements among themselves that are necessary to weave the fabric of society. An anarchist history of the French Revolution is not much concerned about Paris and the stormy assembly but concentrates on what went on in Lyons — how the bakers carried on the production and distribution of bread though everything seemed to be in chaos, how legal documents were burned up, and how a hastily assembled militia fought off an invader. And of course general history is concerned, not with kings, statesmen, warriors, and politics, but with molecular social conditions, cultural and technical innovation, and the long-range development of religious attitudes and social "movements."

From this point of view, Western history has had some pretty good anarchist successes; anarchy is not merely Utopian dreams and a few bloody failures. Winning civil liberties, from Runnymede to the Jeffersonian Bill of Rights; the escape of the townsmen from feudal lords, establishing guild democracy; the liberation of conscience and congregations since the Reformation; the abolition of serfdom, chattel slavery, and some bonds of wage slavery; the freeing of trade and enterprise from mercantilism; the freedom of nations from dynasties and of some nations from imperialists; the development of progressive education and the freeing of sexuality — these bread-and-butter topics of European history are never called "anarchist," but they are. The anarchist victory was won by human suffering and often at the cost of blood; it has somewhat persisted; and it must be vigilantly defended and extended. Any new political revolution, even if it calls itself liberation, cannot be relied on to care for these ancient things. In fact, we see that some liberators impatiently brush them aside — civil liberties go overboard, labor unions are castrated, schooling becomes regimentation, and so forth. But even this is not so annoying as to hear defenders of the present status quo with its freedoms call those who want to extend freedom aimless anarchists.

With regard to freedoms, even "eternal vigilance" is not enough. Unless freedoms are extended, they are whittled away, for those in power always have the advantage of organization and State resources, while ordinary people become tired of battle and fragmented. We may vigilantly defend constitutional limitations and privileges that we have won, but new conditions arise that circumvent them. For instance, new technology like wiretapping and new organizations like computerized Interpol must be offset by new immunities, public defenders, etc.; otherwise the adversary system of Runnymede is nullified. Labor leaders become bureaucrats and are co-opted and union members do not attend meetings unless new demands revitalize the labor movements — in my opinion, the labor movement can at present only be revitalized by turning to the idea of workers' management. Triumphant science, having won the battles of Galileo and Darwin, has become the new orthodoxy. We see that ecological threats have created a brand new freedom to fight for — the right to have an environment.

On the positive side, the spirit of freedom is indivisible and quick to revive. A good fight on one issue has a tonic effect on all society. In totalitarian countries it is very difficult to control a "thaw," and we have seen how contagious populist protest has been in recent years in the United States. In Czechoslovakia an entire generation was apparently controlled since 1948, but — whether because of native human wildness or the spirit of Hus, Comenius and Masaryk — the youth acted in 1968 as if there were no such thing. And in the United States, twenty-five years of affluent consumerism and organization mentality have not seemed to dampen the youth of the present decade.

Anarchists rely on the inventiveness, courage, and drive to freedom of human nature, as opposed to the proletarian industrialized mentality of Scientific Socialism, which takes it for granted that people are essentially and totally socialized by their historical conditions. But anarchist philosophers disagree sharply on the conditions that encourage freedom. (Characteristically, disagreements among anarchists are taken by them as "aspects" of some common position, rather than as "factions" in a power struggle, leading to internecine strife.) Bakunin, for instance, relies on the unemployed, the alienated, the outcasts, the criminal, the uprooted intelligentsia — those who have nothing to lose, not even their chains. But Kropotkin, by contrast, relies on the competent and independent, the highly skilled —

small farmers with their peasant community traditions, miners, artists, explorers, architects, educators. Student anarchism at present tends to be Bakuninist because, in my opinion, the students are inauthentically students; they are exploited and *lumpen* in principle — kept on ice. "Students are niggers." But hopefully the Movement is now beginning to have a more Kropotkinian tendency — authentic young professionals in law, medicine, and ecology. The March 4 (1969) movement of the young scientists at the Massachusetts Institute of Technology is significant of the new trend.

Revolution and Counter-revolution

In ordinary usage, of course, including both liberal and Marxist usage, the word *revolution* has meant, not that controls cease to operate and hinder function, but that a new regime establishes itself and reorganizes the institutions according to its own ideas and interests. (To anarchists this is precisely the counter-revolution, because there is again a centralizing authority to oppose. The counter-revolution occurred with Robespierre, not during Thermidor or with Napoleon.) Liberal historians describe the abuses of the tyrant that made the old regime illegitimate and unviable, and they show how the new regime instituted necessary reforms. Marxists show how in changed technological and social conditions, the class conflict between the dominant and exploited classes erupts: the old dominant group is no longer competent to maintain its power and ideology, the system of belief that gave it legitimacy. Then the new regime establishes institutions to cope with the new conditions, and from these develop a "superstructure" of belief that provides stability and legitimacy. Agitational Marxism, Leninism, works to *make* the old regime unable to cope, to make it illegitimate and to hasten its fall; it is then likely to take power as a minority vanguard party which must educate the masses to their own interest. In this stringent activity, any efforts at piecemeal improvement or protecting traditional freedoms are regarded as mere reformism or tinkering, and they are called "objectively counter-revolutionary." After the takeover by the new regime, there must be a strong and repressive administration to prevent reaction; during this period (indefinitely prolonged) anarchists fare badly.

Of the political thought of the past century, only Anarchism or, better, anarcho-pacifism — the philosophy of institutions without the State and centrally organized violence — has consistently foreseen the gross dangers of present advanced societies, their police, bureaucracy, excessive centralization of decision making, social engineering, processing, schooling, and inevitable militarization — "War is the health of the State," as Randolph Bourne put it. The bourgeois State of the early nineteenth century may well have been merely the instrument of the dominant economic class, as Marx said, but in its further development its gigantic statism has become more important than its exploitation for profit. It and the socialist alternatives have not developed very differently. All have tended toward fascism — statism pure and simple. In the corporate liberal societies, the Bismarckian welfare State, immensely extended, does less and less well by its poor and outcast. In socialist societies, free communism does not come to be, labor is regimented, surplus value is mulcted and reinvested, and there is also a Power Elite. In both types, the alarming consequences of big-scale technology and massive urbanization, directed by the State or by baronial corporations, make it doubtful that central authority is a workable structure.

It could be said that most of the national States, once they had organized the excessive fragmentation of the later Middle Ages, outlived their usefulness by the seventeenth century. Their subsequent career has been largely their own aggrandizement. They have impeded rather than helped the advancing functions of civilization. And evidently in our times they cannot be allowed to go on. Perhaps we could be saved by the organization of a still more powerful supranation; but the present powers being what they are, this would require the very war that would do us in. And since present central powers are dangerous and dehumanizing, why trust superpower and a central international organization? The anarchist alternative is more logical — to try to decentralize and weaken top-down authority in the nation States, and to come to international organization by piecemeal functional and regional arrangements from below, in trade, travel, development, science, communications, health, etc.

Thus, for objective reasons, it is now quite respectable to argue for anarchy, pacifism, or both, whereas even a generation ago such ideas were considered odd, absurd, Utopian, or wicked. I do not mean that anarchy answers all questions. Rather, we have the dilemma; it seems that modern economies, technologies, urbanism, communications, and the diplomacy demand ever tighter centralized control; yet this method of organization patently does not work. Or even worse: to cope with increasingly recurrent emergencies, we need unified information, central power, massive resources, repression, crash programs, hot lines; but just these things produce and heighten the emergencies. There is real confusion here, shared by myself.

Anarchism and the Young

In any case, now hundreds of thousands of young people, perhaps millions, call themselves anarchist — more so in Europe, of course, where there has been a continuing tradition of anarchist thought. It is hard to know how to assay this. There are isolated phrases with an anarchist resonance: "Do your thing!" "Participatory democracy," "I scoff at all national flags" (Daniel Cohn-Bendit). These do not get us far, but certain attitudes and actions are more significant. The young are severely uninterested in Great Power politics and deterrence "strategy." They disregard passport regulations and obviously want to do without frontiers. Since they are willing to let the Systems fall apart, they are not moved by appeals to Law and Order. They believe in local power, community development, rural reconstruction, decentralist organization, town-meeting decision making. They prefer a simpler standard of living and try to free themselves from the complex network of present economic relations. They balk at IBM cards in the school system. Though their protests generate violence, most tend to non-violence. But they do not trust the due processes of administrators, either, and are quick to resort to direct action and civil disobedience. All this adds up to the community anarchism of Kropotkin, the resistance anarchism of Malatesta, the agitational anarchism of Bakunin, the anarchist progressive education of France, the guild socialism of William Morris, the personalist politics of Thoreau. Yet in the United States at least, except for Thoreau (required reading in Freshman English), these thinkers are virtually unknown.

The problematic character of youthful anarchism at present comes from the fact that the young are alienated, have no world for them. Among revolutionary political philosophies, anarchism and pacifism alone do not thrive on alienation — unlike, e.g., Leninism or fascism. They require a nature of things to give order, and a trust in other people not to be excessively violent; they cannot rely on imposed discipline to give the movement strength, nor on organized power to avert technological and social chaos. Thus, historically, anarchism has been the revolutionary politics of skilled artisans (watchmakers or printers) and of farmers — workers who do not need a boss; of workmen in dangerous occupations (miners and lumbermen) who learn to trust one another; of aristocrats who know the inside story and can economically afford to be idealistic; of artists and explorers who venture into the unknown and are self-reliant; among professionals, progressive educators and architects have been anarchist.

We would expect many students to be anarchist, because of their lack of ties, their commitment to the Republic of Letters and Science, and their camaraderie; and so it was, among many European students of the classical type — just as others were drawn to elitist fascism. But contemporary students, under the conditions of mass education, are in their schedule very like factory proletariat, and they are not authentically involved in their studies. Yet their camaraderie is strong, and in some respects they are like aristocrats *en masse*. The effects are contradictory. They are daring in direct action, and they resist party discipline; they form communities; but they are mesmerized by the charisma of administration and Power, and since they only know going to school, they are not ready to manage much.

In both Europe and America, the confusion of alienated youth shows up in their self-contradictory amalgam of anarchist and Leninist thoughts and tactics, often within the same group and in the same action. In my biased opinion, their frank and clear insight and their spontaneous gut feeling are anarchist. They do not lose the woods for the trees, they feel where the shoe pinches, they have a quick and naive indignation and nausea, and they want freedom. What they really hate is not their countries, neither repressive communism nor piggish capitalism, but how Modern Times have gone awry, the ubiquitous abuse of technology and administration, and the hypocritical distortion of great ideals. But their alienation is Leninist, bent on seizing Power. Having little world for themselves, they have no patience for growth; inevitably frustrated, they get quickly angry; they want their turn on top in the Power structure, which is all they know; they think of using their youthful solidarity and fun-and-games ingenuity to make a *putsch*.

As anarchists, they should be internationalist (and regionalist) and create an international youth movement; but in the United States, at least, their alienation betrays them into the stupidity of simply fighting the Cold War in reverse, "smashing capitalism" and "building socialism." Of course, this does not ally them with the Soviet Union, which in obvious ways looks uncomfortably like their own country and worse; about Russia, they tend to say nothing at all. They say they are allied with the underdeveloped socialist countries — China, Cuba, North Korea, North Vietnam — and all anticolonial liberation movements. This is generous impulse, and it provides them a relevant activity that they can work at, trying to thwart American imperialist intervention. But it is irrelevant to providing models or theory for their own problems in the United States. I am afraid that an advantage of the "Third World" is that it is exotic, as well as starving;

one does not need to know the inner workings. Certainly their (verbal) alliance with it has given the Leninist militants some dubious bedfellows — Nkrumah, Nassar, Kim Il Sung, Sukarno, Che Guevara in Bolivia, etc. In the more actual situation of the Vietnam war protest, where young militants might have had some influence on American public opinion, I have always found it impossible to have a serious discussion with them whether it was to the advantage of the South Vietnamese farmers to have a collective communist regime or just to get rid of the Americans and aim at a system of small landowners and co-operatives, as the radical Buddhists seemed to favor. To the Leninists it was more satisfactory to chant "Ho Chi Minh, the NLF is going to win"; but anarchists might prefer the Buddhist solution, since, as Marxists scornfully point out, "Anarchism is a peasant ideology," and pacifists cannot help but see the usual consequences of war, the same old story for ten thousand years.

Historically, the possibility of an anarchist revolution — decentralist, antipolice, antiparty, antibureaucracy, organized by voluntary association, and putting a premium on grass-roots spontaneity — has always been anathema to Marxist communists and has been ruthlessly suppressed. Marx expelled the anarchist unions from the International Workingmen's Association. Having used them to consolidate their own minority power, Lenin and Trotsky slaughtered the anarchists in the Ukraine and at Kronstadt. Stalin murdered them in Catalonia during the Spanish Civil War. Castro has jailed them in Cuba, and Gomulka in Poland. In the Western press, anarchy is the term for chaotic riot and aimless defiance of authority; in official Marxist statements, it appears in the stereotype "bourgeois revisionists, infantile leftists, and anarchists." They are bourgeois revisionists because they want civil liberties, a less restricted economy, and a better break for most farmers. They are infantile leftists because they want workers' management, less bureaucracy, and less class distinction.

Youth and Power

The American young are not really interested in political economy. Their "socialism" is a symbolic slogan, authentic in expressing disgust at the affluent standard of living and indignation at the existence of so many poor people. Historically, anarchists have been noncommittal or various about socialism, in the sense of collective ownership and management. Corporate capitalism, State capitalism, and State communism have all been unacceptable to anarchists, because they trap people and push them around; and there can easily be too much central planning. But pure communism, the pie-in-the-sky future of Marxists, connoting voluntary labor and free appropriation operating by community spirit, is an anarchist ideal. Yet Adam Smith's free enterprise, in its pure form of companies of active owner-managers competing in a free market, without monopoly, is also congenial to anarchists and was called anarchic in Smith's own time. There is an anarchist ring to Jefferson's agrarian notion that a man need enough control of his subsistence, or tenure in his work, to be free of irresistible political pressure. Small community control — kibbutzim, workers' management in factories, producers' and consumers' co-operatives — is congenial to anarchism. Underlying all anarchist thought is a hankering for peasant independence, craft guild self-management, and the democracy of the village meeting or of medieval Free Cities. It is a question how all this can be achieved in modern technical and urban conditions, but in my opinion we could go a lot farther than we think if we set our sights on decency and freedom rather than on delusory greatness and suburban affluence.

If young Americans really consulted their economic interests, instead of their power propaganda or their generous sentiments, I think they would opt for the so-called Scandinavian or mixed economy, of big and small capitalism, producers' and consumers' co-operatives, independent farming, and State and municipal socialism, each with a strong influence. To this I would add a sector of pure communism, free appropriation adequate for decent poverty for those who do not want to make money or are too busy with nonpaying pursuits to make money (until society gets around to overwhelming them with the coin of the realm). Such a sector of pure communism would cost about 1 percent of our Gross National Product and would make our world both more livable and more productive. The advantage of a mixed system of this kind for the young is that it increases the opportunities for each one to find the milieu and style that suits him, whereas both the present American cash nexus and socialism necessarily process them and channel them.

Despite their slogans of "Student Power" and "Power to the People," I do not think that the young want "power," but just to be taken into account and to be able to do their thing — just as, despite the bloodthirsty rhetoric, the most militant seem to be pacifist: with meticulous planning, they blow up a huge Selective Service headquarters and meticulously see to it that nobody is injured. (The slogan "Black Power" has more substance, since it means getting absentee landlords and foreign social workers, cops, and schoolteachers off the backs of the black communities; but here again, despite the bloodthirsty rhetoric, there has been little personal violence, except that instigated by the police.)

The young indeed want a revolutionary change, but not by the route of "taking over." So except for a while, on particular occasions, they simply cannot be manipulated to be the shock troops of a Leninist coup. If a large number of young people go along with actions organized by Trotskyites or the Progressive Labor party or with some of the delusions of the various splinters of Students for a Democratic Society, it is because, in their judgment, the resulting disruption does more good than harm. And let me say that, compared with the arrogance, cold violence and occasional insanity of our established institutions, the arrogance, hot-headedness, and all too human folly of the young are venial sins.

My real bother with the non-Leninist wing of the New Left is that its abortive manipulation of lively energy and moral fervor for a political revolution that will not be, and ought not to be, confuses the piecemeal social and cultural change that is brightly possible. This puts me off — but of course it is their problem, and they have to do it in their own way. In my opinion, it is inauthentic to do community development in order to "politicize" people, or to use a good do-it-yourself project as a means of "bringing people into the Movement." Good things should be done for their own sake and will then generate their own appropriate momentum. The amazing courage of sticking to one's convictions in the face of the police is insulted when it is manipulated as a means of "radicalizing." The loyalty of youth to one another is extraordinary, but it can turn to disillusionment if they perceive that they are being had. Many of the best of the young went through this in the thirties, and it was a bad scene.

In an important sense, the present bandying about of the word *revolution,* in its usual connotations, is counter-revolutionary. It is too political. It seems to assume that there could be such a thing as a Good Society or Body Politic, whereas, in my judgment, the best that is to be hoped for is a tolerable society that allows the important activities of life to proceed — friends, sex, arts and sciences, faith, the growing up of children with bright eyes, and the air and water clean.

I myself have a conservative, maybe timid, disposition; yet I trust that the present regime in America will get a lot more roughing up than it has: from the young who resent being processed; from the blacks who have been left out; from housewives and others who buy real goods with hard money at inflationary prices, hiked by expense accounts and government subsidies; from professionals demanding the right to practise their professions rather than be treated as personnel of the front office; not to speak of every live person in jeopardy because of the bombs and chemical-biological warfare. Our system can stand, and profit by, plenty of interruption of business as usual. It is not such a delicate Swiss watch as all that. The danger is not in the loosening of the machine but in its tightening up by panic repression.

It is true that because of massive urbanization and interlocking technologies, advanced countries are vulnerable to catastrophic disruption, and this creates intense anxiety. But there is far more likelihood of breakdown from the respectable ambitions of Eastern Air Lines and Consolidated Edison than from the sabotage of revolutionaries or the moral collapse of hippies.

In a modern massive complex society, it is said, any rapid global "revolutionary" or "Utopian" change can be incalculably destructive. I agree. But I wish people would remember that we have continually introduced big rapid changes that have in fact produced incalculable shock. Consider, in the past generation, the TV, mass higher schooling, the complex of cars, roads, and suburbanization, mass air travel, the complex plantations, government subsidies to big planters, chain grocers, and forced urbanization, not to speak of the meteoric rise of the military industries. In all these there has been a big factor of willful decision; these have not been natural processes or inevitable catastrophes. And we have not yet begun to compound with the problems caused by these Utopian changes. Rather, in what seems an amazingly brief time, we have come to a political, cultural, and religious crisis, and talk of "revolution." All because of a few willful fools.

A decade ago it was claimed that there was an end to ideology, for the problems of modern society have to be coped with pragmatically, functionally, piecemeal. This seems to have been a poor production, considering the deafening revival of Marxist-Leninist rhetoric and Law and Order rhetoric. Yet it was true, though not in the sense in which it was offered. The ideological rhetoric is pretty irrelevant; but the pragmatic, functional, and piecemeal approach has not, as was expected, consigned our problems to the expertise of administrators and engineers but has thrown them to the dissenters. Relevant new thought has not been administrative and technological, but existentialist, ethical and tactical. Pragmatism has come to be interpreted to include the character of the agents as part of the problem to be solved; it is psychoanalytic; there is stress on engagement. (Incidentally, it is good Jamesian pragmatism.) Functionalism has come to mean criticizing the program and the function itself, asking who wants to do it and why, and is it humanly worth doing, is it ecologically sound.

Piecemeal issues have gotten entangled with the political action of people affected by them. Instead of becoming more administrative as expected, every problem becomes political. The premises of expert planning are called into question. The credentials of the board of trustees are scrutinized. *Professional* and *discipline* have become dirty words. Terms like *commitment, dialogue, confrontation, community, do your thing* are indeed anti-ideological — and sometimes they do not connote much other thought either — but they are surely not what The End of Ideology had in mind.

The Crisis of Authority

Our revolutionary situation is not a political one, and yet there is a crisis of authority. This is peculiar.

There is a System and a Power Elite. But Americans do not identify with the ruling oligarchy, which is foreign to our tradition. A major part of it — the military-industrial and the CIA, and FBI — even constitute a "hidden government" that does not thrive on public exposure. The daily scandals in the press seem to indicate that the hidden government is coming apart at the seams. Politicians carefully cajole the people's sensibilities and respect their freedom, so long as these remain private. And we have hit upon the following accommodation: in high matters of State, War, and Empire, the oligarchy presents *faits accomplis;* in more local matters, people resent being pushed around. Until 1969, budgets in the billions were not debated, but small sums are debated. From a small center of decision, it has been possible to spend a trillions dollars for arms, employ scores of millions of people, transform the universities, distort the future of science without public murmur; but where a regional plan might be useful — e.g., for depollution or better distribution of population — it fails because of a maze of jurisdictions and private complaints.

In such a case, what is the real constitution? The social compact becomes acquiescence to the social machine, and citizenship consists in playing appropriate roles as producers, functionaries, and consumers. The machine is productive; the roles, to such as have them, are rewarding. In the galloping economy, the annual tax bite, which ordinarily strikes home to citizens everywhere, has been tolerable. (Only the draft of the young hits home, but this was noticed by few until the young themselves led the protest.) Then, human nature being what it is, the Americans have accepted the void of authentic sovereignty by developing a new kind of allegiance to the rich and high-technological style itself, which provides the norm of correct behavior for workmen, inspires the supermarkets, and is used to recruit soldiers.

A typical and very important class is the new professionals. Being essential to tend the engine and steer it, they are high-salaried and prestigious. An expensive system of schooling has been devised to prepare the young for these roles. At the same time, these professionals are mere personnel. There is no place for the autonomy, ethics and guild liberty that used to characterize professionals as persons and citizens. *Mutatis mutandis,* the same can be said of the working class. It reminds one of the development of the Roman Empire, when personal rights were extended under the *jus gentium,* but the whole world became one prison.

On the other hand, large groups of the population are allowed to drop out as socially useless — farmers, racial minorities, the incompetent and deviant, the old, many of the young. When these are not altogether neglected, they are treated as objects of social engineering and are also lost as citizens. This too is like Rome.

In an unpolitical situation like this, it is hard for good observers to distinguish between riot and riotous protest, between a juvenile delinquent, a rebel without a cause, an inarticulate guerrilla, a protestant for legitimacy. Student protest may be adolescent identity crisis, alienation, or politics. On a poll, to say "I don't know" might mean one is judicious, a moron, or a cynic about the questions or the options. Conversely, good behavior may be rational assent, apathy, obsessional neurosis, or a dangerous prepsychosis about to murder father, mother, and four siblings.

With this background, we can understand the rash of "civil disobedience," "lawlessness," and the general crisis of authority. What happens politically in a country like the United States when the government steers a disastrous course? There is free speech and assembly and a strong tradition of democracy; it is false that these do not exist, and — with some grim exceptions — they have been pretty well protected. But the traditional structures of remedy have fallen into desuetude or become phoney, or are terribly rusty. Critical professionals, bourgeois reformers, organizations of farmers and industrial workers, political machines of the urban poor have been largely co-opted. Then, inevitably, protest appears at a more primitive or inchoate level.

"Civil disobedients" are nostalgic patriots without available political means. The new "lawless" are the oppressed without political means. Instead of having a program or party, protesters have to try, as Mario Savio said, to "throw themselves on the gears and levers to stop the machine." Scholars think up ways to stop traffic. Professionals form groups to nullify a law. Middle-class women go by trainloads to Washington to badger senators and are hauled off to jail for disorderly conduct. The physically oppressed burn down their own neighborhoods.

The promising aspect of it is the revival of populism — sovereignty reverting to the people. One can sense it infallibly during the big rallies, the March on Washington in '63 or the peace rallies in New York and at the Pentagon in '67 and in Washington in '69. Except among a few Leninists, the mood is euphoric, the heady feeling of the sovereign people invincible —for a couple of hours. The draft-card burners are proud. The children of Birmingham attacked by dogs look just like Christians. Physicians who support Dr. Levy feel Hippocratic, and professors who protest classified research feel academic right back to Abelard. On the other hand, the government with the mightiest military power in the history of the world does not hasten to alter its course because of so much sweet determination. The police of the cities have prepared arsenals of antiriot weapons. Organized workmen beat up peace demonstrators. Judge Hoffman does not allow relevant evidence to be heard in court. Tear gas is dropped on the Berkeley campus because some people have planted trees.

I do not think this conflict is much the result of evil motives, though there are some mighty stupid people around. There are a few "pigs" as well as a few "subversives" and plenty of patriots on both sides. And I have not heard of any institutional changes that would indeed solve the inherent dilemmas of Modern Times. The crisis of legitimacy is a historical one. Perhaps "social contract," "sovereignty," and "law" in any American sense are outmoded concepts.

The Crisis of Belief

Among the young especially, the crisis is a religious one, deeper than politics. The young have ceased to "believe" in something, and the disbelief occurs at progressively earlier years. What is at stake is not the legitimacy of American authority but of any authority. The professions, the disciplines, reasoning about the nature of things — and even if there is a nature of things — these are all distrusted.

Thus, for instance, the dissenting scientists and professors of MIT and Harvard, who want to change the direction of research and alter the priorities of technology, do not seem to me to understand the profound change in popular feeling. (They often seem just to be griping that the budget for basic Research has been reduced.) Put it this way: modern societies have been operating as if religion were a minor and moribund part of the scheme of things. But this is unlikely. Men do not do without a system of meanings that everybody puts his hope in even if, or especially if, he doesn't know anything about it — what Freud called a "shared psychosis," meaningful simply because shared, and with the power that resides in dream. In advanced countries it is science and technology themselves that have gradually and finally triumphantly become the system of mass faith, not disputed by various political ideologies and nationalisms that have been religious. Marxism called itself "scientific socialism," as against moral and Utopian socialisms, and this has helped it succeed.

For three hundred years, science and scientific technology had an unblemished and justified reputation as a wonderful adventure, pouring out practical benefits and liberating the spirit from the errors of superstition and traditional faith. During the twentieth century, science and technology have been the only generally credited system of explanation and problem-solving. Yet in our generation they have come to seem to many, and to very many of the best of the young, as essentially inhuman, abstract, regimenting, hand in glove with Power, and even diabolical. Young people say that science is anti-life, it is a Calvinist obsession, it has been a weapon of white Europe to subjugate colored races, and manifestly — in view of recent scientific technology — people who think scientifically become insane.

The immediate reasons for this shattering reversals of values are fairly obvious — Hitler's ovens and his other experiments in eugenics, the first atom bombs and their frenzied subsequent developments, the deterioration of the physical environment and the destruction of the biosphere, the catastrophes impending over the cities because of technological failures and psychological stress, the prospect of a brainwashed and drugged 1984. Innovations yield diminishing returns in enhancing life. And instead of rejoicing, there is now widespread conviction that beautiful advances in genetics, surgery, computers, rocketry, or atomic energy will surely only increase human woe.

In such a crisis it is not sufficient to ban the military from the universities, and it will not even be sufficient, as liberal statesmen and many of the big corporations envisage, to beat the swords into ploughshares and turn to solving problems of transportation, desalinization, urban renewal, garbage disposal, cleaning up the air and water, and perfecting a contraceptive. If the present difficulty is religious and historical, it will be necessary to alter the entire relationship of science, technology, and human needs, both in fact and in men's minds.

I do not myself think that we will turn away from science. In spite of the fantasies of hippies, we are going to continue to live in a technological world; the question is, is that viable?

The closest analogy I can think of is the Protestant Reformation, a change of moral allegiance: not giving up the faith, but liberation from the Whore of Babylon and a return to the faith purified.

Science, the chief orthodoxy of modern times, has certainly been badly corrupted, but the deepest flaw of the affluent societies that has alienated the young is not, finally, imperialism, economic injustice, or racism, bad as these are, but the nauseating phoneyness, triviality, and wastefulness, the cultural and moral scandal that Luther found when he went to Rome in 1510. And precisely science, which should have been the wind of truth to clear the air, has polluted the air, helped to brainwash, and provided weapons for war. I doubt that most young people today have even heard of the ideal of the dedicated researcher, truculent and incorruptible, and not getting any grants — the "German scientist" that Sinclair Lewis described in Arrowsmith. Such a figure is no longer believable. I don't mean, of course, that he doesn't exist; there must be thousands of him, just as there were good priests in 1510.

The analogy to the Reformation is even more exact if we consider the school system, from educational toys and Head Start up through the universities. This system is manned by the biggest horde of monks since the time of Henry VIII. It is the biggest industry in the country. It is mostly hocus-pocus. And the Abbots of this system are the chiefs of Science — e.g., the National Science Foundation — who talk about reform but work to expand the school budgets, step up the curriculum, inspire the endless catechism of tests, and increase the requirements for mandarin credentials.

These abuses are international, as the faith is. For instance, there is no essential difference between the military-industrial systems, or the school systems, of the Soviet Union and the United States. There are important differences in way of life and standard excessive urbanization, destruction of the biosphere, weaponry, disastrous foreign aid. Our protesters naturally single out our own country, and the United States is the most powerful country, but the corruption we are speaking of is not specifically American nor capitalist; it a disease of modern times.

But the analogy is to the Reformation; it is not to primitive Christianity or some other primitivism, the abandonment of technological civilization. There is indeed much talk about the doom of Western civilization, young people cast horoscopes, and a few Adamites actually do retire into the hills. but for the great mass of mankind, that's not where it's at. Despite all the movements for National Liberation, there is not the slightest interruption to the universalizing of Western civilization, including most of its delusions, into the so-called Third World.

Needless to say, the prospect of a new Reformation is a terrifying one. Given the intransigence and duplicity of established Power on the one hand, and the fanaticism of the protesters on the other, we may be headed for a Thirty Years' War.

Freedom and Autonomy

Many anarchist philosophers start from a lust for freedom. Where freedom is a metaphysical concept or a moral imperative, it leaves me cold — I cannot think in abstractions. But most often the freedom of anarchists is a deep animal cry or a religious plea like the hymn of the prisoners in *Fidelio*. They feel themselves imprisoned, existentially by the nature of things or by God; or because they have seen or suffered too much economic slavery; or they have been deprived of their liberties; or internally colonized by imperialists. To become human they must shake off restraint.

Since, by and large, my experience is roomy enough for me, I do not lust for freedom, any more than I want to "expand consciousness." I might feel differently, however, if I were subjected to literary censorship, like Solzhenitzen. My usual gripe has been not that I am imprisoned but that I am in exile or was born on the wrong planet; recently that I am bedridden. My real trouble is that the world is impractical for me, and I understand that my stupidity and cowardice make it even less practical than it could be.

To be sure, there are outrages that take me by the throat, like anybody else, and I lust to be free of them. Insults to humanity and the beauty of the world that keep me indignant. An atmosphere of lies, triviality, and vulgarity that suddenly makes me sick. The powers-that-be do not know the meaning of magnanimity, and often they are simply officious and spiteful; as Malatesta used to say, you just try to do your thing and they prevent you, and then you are to blame for the fight that ensues. Worst of all, the earth-destroying actions of power are demented; and as in ancient tragedies and histories we read how arrogant men committed sacrilege and brought down doom on themselves and those associated with them, so I sometimes am superstitiously afraid to belong to the same tribe and walk the same ground as our statesmen.

But no. Men have a right to be crazy, stupid, and arrogant. It's our special thing. Our mistake is to arm anybody with collective power. Anarchy is the only *safe* polity.

It is a common misconception that anarchists believe that "human nature is good" and so men can be trusted to rule themselves. In fact we tend to take the pessimistic view; people are not be trusted, so prevent the concentration of power. Men in authority are especially likely to be stupid because they are out of touch with concrete finite experience and instead keep interfering with other people's initiative and making them stupid and anxious. And imagine being deified like Mao-Tse-Tung or Kim Il Sung, what that must do to a man's character. Or habitually thinking about the unthinkable, like the masters of the Pentagon.

To me, the chief principle of anarchism is not freedom but autonomy. Since to initiate, and do it my way, and be an artist with concrete matter, is the kind of experience I like, I am restive about being given orders by external authorities, who don't concretely know the problem or the available means. Mostly, behavior is more graceful, forceful, and discriminating without the intervention of top-down authorities, whether State, collective, democracy, corporate bureaucracy, prison wardens, deans, pre-arranged curricula, or central planning. These may be necessary in certain emergencies, but it is at a cost to vitality. This is an empirical proposition in social psychology and I think the evidence is heavily in its favor. By and large, the use of power to do a job is inefficient in the fairly short run. Extrinsic power inhibits intrinsic function. As Aristotle said, "Soul is self-moving."

In his recent book *Beyond Freedom and Dignity*, B.F. Skinner holds that these are defensive prejudices that interfere with the operant conditioning of people toward their desired goals of happiness and harmony. (It is odd these days to read a cracker-barrel restatement of Bentham's utilitarianism.) He misses the point.

What is objectionable about operant conditioning is not that it violates freedom but that the consequent behavior is graceless and low-grade as well as labile — it is not assimilated as second nature. He is so impressed by the fact that an animal's behavior can be shaped at all to perform according to the trainer's goal, that he does not compare the performance with the inventive, flexible and maturing behavior of the animal initiating and responding in its natural field. And incidentally, dignity is not a specifically human prejudice, as he thinks, but the ordinary bearing of any animal, angrily defended when organic integrity or own space is insulted.

To lust for freedom is certainly a motive of political change stronger than autonomy. (I doubt that it is as stubborn, however. People who do their job their own way can usually find other means than revolt to keep doing it, including plenty of passive resistance to interference.) To make an anarchist revolution, Bakunin wanted, in his early period, to rely precisely on the outcast, delinquents, prostitutes, convicts, displaced peasants, lumpen proletarians, those who had nothing to lose, not even their chains, but who felt oppressed. There were enough troops of this kind in the grim heyday of industrialism and urbanization. But naturally, people who have nothing are hard to organize and consolidate for a long effort, and they are easily seduced by a fascist who can offer guns, revenge, and a moment's flush of power.

The pathos of oppressed people lusting for freedom is that, if they break free, they don't know what to do. Not having been autonomous, they do not know how to go about it, and before they learn it is usually too late. New managers have taken over, who may or may not be benevolent and imbued with the revolution, but who have never been in a hurry to abdicate.

The oppressed hope for too much from the New Society, instead of being stubbornly vigilant to do their own things. The only achieved liberation movement that I can think of was the American revolution, made largely by artisans, farmers, merchants, and professionals who had going concerns to begin with, wanted to get rid of interference, and afterwards enjoyed a prosperous quasi-anarchy for nearly thirty years — nobody cared much about the new government. They were protected by three thousand miles of ocean. The Catalonian revolution during the Spanish Civil War could have gone well, for the same reasons, but the fascists and communists did them in.

Anarchy requires competence and self-confidence, the sentiment that the world is *for* one. It does not thrive among the exploited, oppressed, and colonized. Thus, unfortunately, it lacks a powerful drive toward revolutionary change. Yet in the affluent liberal societies of Europe and America there is a hopeful possibility of the following kind: Fairly autonomous people, among the middle class, the young, craftsmen, and professionals, cannot help but see that they cannot continue so in the present institutions. They cannot do honest and useful work or practise a profession nobly; arts and sciences are corrupted; modest enterprise must be blown out of all proportion to survive; the young cannot find vocations; it is hard to raise children; talent is strangled by credentials; the natural environment is being destroyed; health is imperilled; community life is inane; neighborhoods are ugly and unsafe; public services do not work; taxes are squandered on war, schoolteachers, and politicians.

Then they may make changes, to extend the areas of freedom from encroachment. Such changes might be piecemeal and not dramatic, but they must be fundamental; for many of the present institutions cannot be recast and the tendency of the system as a whole is disastrous. I like the Marxist term "withering away of the State," but it must begin now, not afterwards; and the goal is not a New Society, but a tolerable society in which life can go on.

Education

Children's Rights

Children are an awkward subject for politics. Essays "toward the liberation of the child," the subtitle of the well-rounded collection on *Children's Rights,* always take contradictory tacks. Children should have "rights as full human beings," no different from those of adults: they should be able to vote, make contracts, and presumably commit felonies, just as adults do. On the contrary, runs another argument, they should have very special rights and immunities because they are children; their rights should fit their "stage of growth." Some say that the oppressive society of adults has so damaged the children that we must now provide them with remedial attention; on the contrary, say others, the best things we adults can do is to get off their backs.

Even under good conditions, this confusion is deeply rooted in the nature of things. Human beings do pass through distinctive and well-marked stages of life — childhood and adolescence, middle age, old age — and yet we all, at every age, interact, must use and enjoy one another, and are likely to abuse and injure one another. This situation is not something to cope with polemically or to understand in terms of "freedom," "democracy," "rights," and "power," like bringing lawyers into a family quarrel. It has to be solved by wise traditions in organic communities with considerable stability, with equity instead of law, and with love and compassion more than either. But in modern times there are no such traditions, communities, or stability and there are injustice, unnecessary suffering, and worst of all, plain waste of young life. So there has to be polemical politics.

There are problems of modern times that are really new, puzzling, and interesting. For example, what is an adequate substitute for the nuclear family? In a high technology, what is productive activity for adolescents and old people? Yet we have to think about such things when we are stupefied and politicized by the absurd conditions of modern times. (As an anarchist, I do not believe that power politics is the way to wisdom.) It is useful, however, to recognize that most people are honourably confused and badly blundering rather than to say that they are made of plastic or suffering from an emotional plague, that teachers are sadists, or that parents who love their children and are anxious for their futures are really treating them as property.

It has become common in liberation literature to say that childhood is an invention of the past few hundred years in Western

Europe, a means of rationalizing, controlling, and exploiting children. In more "normal" societies, it is claimed, children are just people, with the usual rights, immunities, and privileges, who take part in the community work according to their capacities. ("Adolescence" is an even more recent invention, a definition extended because of the trend toward earlier sexual maturation and longer exclusion from employment.) There is some truth in this thesis, but some liberators at once draw the polemical conclusion that children are identical to adults, must set up their own governments, and must have power to protect their interests.

A recent publication of the radical caucus of the American Summerhill Society quotes Huey Newton of the Black Panthers: "An unarmed people are slaves," and goes on to say, "We are asking for a 'human standard' to arm kids with, within which we as adults can deal with our own problems and uptightness while kids are free to determine their own lives." That is, adults give power to the kids by disarming themselves.

This is not a very authentic proposition. As an adult I am not at all willing to inhibit myself from doing my thing, I hope with temperance, justice, and compassion. The natural power that children have over me is not something I give them but stems from how they are and how I am. Nan Berger, in *Children's Rights*, complains that legislation in England does not recognize the rights of children as persons but merely protects them from "ill treatment, neglect, abandonment, and exposure." Although legislation (possibly) might deter battery and abandonment of children, I wonder whether it is indeed a possible way to recognize the dignity and initiative of persons.

Historically, treating children like little adults meant bringing a six-year-old to court for petty theft and hanging him, and having nine-year-olds pick straw in the factory, not because their labor was useful, but "to teach them good work habits." Presumably these children knew all about property rights and could contract their labor. Since the liberators of children do not mean this, they must think that in some respects children are special cases and must be protected from doing themselves harm.

But even excellent progressive educators have fallen into the same equal rights rhetoric. When Maria Montessori provided little chairs and tables in her classroom, she deprived the child of childhood, which more properly uses chairs and tables to crawl under and drape for tents. When A.S. Neill's kids are encourage to "govern" themselves, one man one vote, in their court and parliament, he is taking the social contract and political democracy much too seriously;

he is imposing adult ideas. This is not the form in which kids spontaneously choose up sides in a game, settle their disputes, and change the rules. Kids are far too shrewd to be democratic. They have more respect for strength, skill, and experience at the same time as they protect one another from being stepped on, humiliated, or left out. (They can also be as callous as the devil.)

In his detailed criticism of the English schools in *Children's Rights,* Michael Duane violates the rich and cloudy facts of human psychology in another way. He says there must be no religious instruction, that persons must be allowed to choose, when they reach the age of reason. This is a venerable and respectable sectarian position — Petrobrusian, adult baptism — but it is sectarian; it is not the obvious relation of faith and reason, which is *credere ut intellegere:* you commit yourself and then you understand. Would Duane make the same argument about his own faith in democracy and the need to protect children from that faith? Again, he opposes having assemblies, unless the children come together for their own deliberate purposes. But though most assemblies are certainly lousy, does he really think that this analysis is adequate to what ritual means to children?

Nevertheless, it is touching that the English can still talk about such profound issues at all. In our American schools we are constitutionally protected from religion. Assemblies, in our huge establishments, do not pretend to have any meaning of collective loyalty — or any meaning at all. We don't need to debate corporal punishment, because we can drug "hyperactives" or send them to special schools for the "emotionally disturbed."

There is an opposite interpretation of the concept of childhood. It is a fairly recent idea, but it can be regarded as a discovery of gradually refining civilization rather than a device of malevolent exploitation, just as Greek tragedy, romantic love, and Nature also sprang from definite historical socio-economic conditions but thereafter became permanent parts of how man has fashioned himself. This view makes children into a special class, not to control or mold them but to conserve them as natural resource or natural wonder. The key terms are not children's "rights" or "democracy" but their spontaneity, fantasy, animality, creativity, innocence. The British and North Americans especially have developed this notion in a vast juvenile literature that is sometimes cloying and whimsical, but often beautiful. It was, of course, a chief theme of Wordsworth: the child trails clouds of glory and his experience abounds in intimations of immortality, until the shades of the prison house begin to close about the growing boy, and girl.

Needless to say, the idea of childhood can be stifling, sentimental, and used to keep children out of practical life, so that they are ignorant and retarded. It has been used as a basis for emotional exploitation of children, to serve the fantasies of regressed adults — perhaps even especially by way-out educators who run "free" schools. And there is always plain hypocrisy — with sentimentality goes cruelty — just as our quite genuine advance in humanitarianism goes nicely with napalm. Nevertheless, childhood is a special stage. Neoteny is an important factor in human biology. Psychoanalytically, we assign the highest importance to maintaining as a distinct process the living through of child life, so that we may draw on child powers without inhibition.

And, in the climate of modern times, overurbanized, overtechnologized, too tightly organized, the chief present purpose of primary schooling — the only valid purpose, in my opinion — is to delay the socialization of children, to give their wildness a chance to express itself; for, at home, in the street, and in front of the TV set, children are swamped by social signals. As I have put it elsewhere, when the Irish monks invented academic schooling in the sixth century, there was some point to licking a few likely wild shepherds into social shape in order to take on the culture of Rome; now, when everything is too cultured, it is necessary to protect the wildness of the shepherds. I think that it is by implicitly performing this function that Summerhill is relevant in our generation. Neill's explicit purpose of making emotionally balanced individuals and co-operative citizens is far less important.

Values like neoteny, animality, fantasy, and wildness are incommensurable with political criteria like rights and justice. They are biological, psychological, aesthetic. I am not impressed with the argument that John Dewey relied on so heavily and that is repeated in *Children's Rights:* that liberating and reforming the education of children will make for a better society tomorrow; schools have never been that effective against the influence of either the going society or the youth peer group. But we must foster childhood, because it is good for ourselves, good for human culture, and perhaps good for the species.

A gloomier version of our situation is that what we owe to children is therapy. A good school is best regarded as a halfway house for recuperation, rescuing the children from the insane homes and cities in which they have already been socialized and deranged. Summerhill, as described, usually sounds like a therapeutic community: the wounded child can brood "by himself" in a secure and loving setting that imposes on him no pressure or compulsion, while nature heals.

When he was principal of a Harlem school, Elliott Shapiro tried out a curriculum consisting mostly of expressing hostility — the children gave talks, wrote compositions, and acted out why and how they hated their parents, their siblings, the police, the neighborhood, the school, the school's principal. The procedure raised their IQs, for stupidity is a character defence of turned-in hostility. There were also fewer windows broken from outside. Obviously, this technique is Frantz Fanon's prescription for colonized peoples; they must turn to hate and violence against the imperialist, in order to recover their own identities.

In my opinion, the only justification for high schools is as therapeutic halfway houses for the deranged. Normal adolescents can find themselves and grow further only by coping with the jobs, sex and chances of the real world — it is useless to feed them curricular imitations. I would simply abolish the high schools, replace them with apprenticeships and other substitutes, and protect the young from gross exploitation by putting the school money directly in their pockets. The very few who have authentic scholarly interests will gravitate to their own libraries, teachers, and academies, as they always did in the past, when they could afford it. In organic communities, adolescents cluster together in their own youth houses, for their fun and games and loud music, without bothering sober folk. I see no reason whatsoever for adults to set up or direct such nests or to be there at all unless invited.

Yet it is certainly the case at present that very many adolescents are so befuddled and discouraged that they cannot be thrown into society to cope, either to adjust or to be constructively revolutionary. They need free schools in order to get their heads together. The danger of such schools is that they take themselves too seriously, as counterculture rather than as hospitals. But the youth subculture is an obstacle to growing up. The young are right to cling to it, for it is theirs; but there is no excuse for adults to pander to it. In the best cases, free high schools are convenient administrative gimmicks to get around the compulsory education law — and officials do well to encourage them and save on the expense of truant officers. For the young, they provide a safe home base to return to when they are anxious or in need of medical or legal aid.

Philosophically, the right relationship among children, adolescents, and adults — groups that are so unlike and yet like and that make up one community — is a pluralism: in some areas they should leave one another severely alone; in other areas they need, use, and enjoy one another, can make demands, and have obligations. The really interesting facts of life have to do with the opportunities, dangers and limits of how grown-ups and children can get something from one another. Yet it is rare that this prima facie and commonsense point of view is taken by our present liberators and school reformers. In *Children's Rights,* only the psychiatrist Paul Adams gives a hint that parents and other adults might get some use, satisfaction, and even pleasure from children and adolescents instead of merely being obligated to them — and the obligation being mostly negative. The usual tone is that we are such bastards that we don't deserve any better.

When A.S. Neill says that his pupils don't know his religion, drug attitudes, or politics, I am simply baffled. He can't be taking his pupils very seriously, or he can't be taking his religion very seriously. If the young don't hear opinions about such things from a knowledgeable and trusted adult, from whom should they hear them? I too don't believe in "teaching" children unless they reach out and ask; it is folly to moralize or to try to coerce them into "learning" something. But why should children be protected from *my* reality? My religion, art, animality, and politics *are* my reality. I once had an argument in print with John Holt about Neill's proposition that at Summerhill rock and roll is equivalent to Bach, Beethoven, and Debussy. But it is *not* equivalent. More *happens* in two bars of the great music than in two minutes of the rock band, and this can be shown objectively — as John knows, for he is a cellist and a fanatical discophile. There is potentially more musical experience in better music, and my behavior will say this. Naturally kids can listen to what they like without lectures from me — unless, as sometimes happens, a kid bugs me with his nonsense about his music; and then I may take him by the scruff of the neck and make him listen to my music, plus an analysis of it.

It's a tough problem. I don't know any academic means of passing on the humanities; the schools do more harm than good, for they turn the young off. If the humanities do seem to survive, poorly, it is by contagion; some of us take them with surprising earnestness, some young people catch on.

Writers in *Children's Rights* mention Homer Lane, the inspired educator who did a good service by giving unruly delinquents a chance for responsibility and self-regulation. They point out, too, that his school was closed because of his alleged sexual misbehavior with some of the girls; but they make no further comment on this. I have found the same embarrassment and reticence when speaking to free school people in this country. They are rightly insistent on sexual freedom among the young, but they will not mention sexual relations between the young and adults, which are usually initiated by the young. Do such things not exist? Ought they not to? I understand that most of those who will read *Children's Rights* are probably even more squeamish, but let's face it: there are dangers, and there is also the possibility of more joy in the world. One of the chief attractions that the young have for adults is their youth, and the attraction is often sexual. Generous kids have models and heroes and crushes on them, and these too are often sexual. Yet there is not a trace of any of this in the recent literature. But the effect of silence and standoffishness is not neutral but repressive.

Many, perhaps most, craftsmen, professionals, scholars, and savants, need young apprentices, to see the tasks afresh through young eyes, to pass on the art as it was earlier passed on to them. But, in the relation of master and apprentice, the key is certainly not the freedom and rights of the young, nor the therapy of the young, but the often harsh discipline of the craft and the objective nature of things. It is these that give identity and dignity and finally, freedom. Yet from the talk of most free school people, one would not guess that there are crafts, professions, and a nature of things; rather, one would think that the world consists only of interpersonal relations and put-downs by irrational authority.

I don't know what to make of the claim that "student power" should determine the content and method of courses. Why would I agree to teach what is not important and not relevant in my eyes? And how would I know what to teach in such a case? Of course, the students are free to stay away from my classes — I give them their As anyway.

So there are areas of mutual need, demand, and giving. On the other hand, in many areas of experience it is best if children, adolescents, and adults have little to do with one another at all. There are entirely too many schoolteachers around who are eager to teach everything, including freedom and democracy and interpersonal relations. One of the beautiful experiments of the Peckham Health Center showed that when small children were permitted to freely use the apparatus of a fully equipped gymnasium (1) if there were older children present, there were many accidents, probably because of showing off and emulation; (2) if there was an adult teacher present, there were fewer accidents, but some children did not participate and some did not learn the apparatus; and (3) if the small children were left to themselves, all learned and there were no accidents.

It is interesting that, in her introductory essay to *Children's Rights,* on the history of the free school movement, Leila Berg's conclusions agree with those of Holt, Dennison, Huberman, and myself; all of us have come to hanker after deschooling society altogether, except perhaps for socially deprived or psychologically disturbed children. America has gone further down the school road than England, and we have had it.

A sign of the confusion of modern times is that we all pay too much attention to children, either depriving them of rights and freedom or trying to give them rights and freedom. This includes books of mine and this book on children's rights. I would suggest, as a program for the coming decade, that the best thing we adults could do for children and adolescents would be to renovate our own institutions and give the young a livable world to grow up in.

The Present Moment in Education

1

In every society, the education of the children is of the first importance. But in all societies, both primitive and highly civilized, until quite recently most education occurred incidentally. Adults did their work and other social tasks. The children were not excluded. The children were paid attention to and learned to be included; they were not "taught."

In most institutions and in most societies *incidental education* has been taken for granted. Incidental education takes place in community labor, master-apprentice arrangements, games, plays, sexual initiations, and religious rites.

Generally speaking, this incidental process suits the nature of learning better than direct teaching. The young experience cause and effect rather than pedagogic exercise. Reality is often complex, but every young person can take that reality in his own way, at his own time, according to his own interests and own initiative. Most importantly, he can imitate, identify, be approved, be disapproved, cooperate, or compete without suffering anxiety through being the center of attention.

The archetype of successful incidental education is that of an infant learning to speak, a formidable intellectual achievement that is universally accomplished. We do not know how it is done, but the main condition seems to be what we have been describing: Activity is going on involving speaking. The infant participates; he is attended to and spoken to; he plays freely with his speech sounds; it is advantageous to him to make himself understood.

Along with incidental education, most societies also maintain institutions specifically devoted to teaching the young, such as identity rites, catechisms, nurses, pedagogues, youth houses, and formal schooling. I think there is a peculiar aspect to what is learned through such means, rather than what is picked up incidentally.

Let me emphasize that it is only in the last century that a majority of the children in industrialized countries have gotten much direct teaching. Only in the past few decades has formal schooling been generally extended into adolescence and further. For example, in the United States in 1900, only 6 percent of the youngsters went through high school, and only one quarter of 1 percent went through college. Yet now, formal schooling has taken over, well or badly, very much of the more natural incidental education of most other institutions.

This state of affairs may or may not be necessary, but it has had consequences. These institutions, and the adults who run them, have correspondingly lost touch with the young; and on the other hand, the young do not know the adults who are involved in their chief activities.

Like jails and insane asylums, schools isolate society from its problems, whether in preventing crime, or in curing mental disease, or in bringing up the young. To a remarkable degree, the vital functions of growing up have become hermetically redefined in school terms. Community service means doing homework. Apprenticeship means passing tests for a job in the distant future. Sexual initiation is high school dating. Rites of passage consist in getting a diploma. Crime is breaking the school windows. Rebellion is sitting in on the Dean. In the absence of adult culture, the youth develop a subculture.

Usually, there has been a rough distinction between the content of what is learned in incidental education and what is learned in direct pedagogy. Teaching, whether directed by elders, priests, or academics, deals with what is not evident in ordinary affairs; pedagogy aims to teach what is abstract, intangible, or mysterious. As the center of attention, the learner is under pressure. All education socializes, but pedagogy socializes deliberately, instilling the morals and habits which are the social bonds.

There are two opposite interpretations of why pedagogy seeks to indoctrinate. In my opinion, both interpretations are correct. On the one hand, elders instill an ideology which will support their system of exploitation and the domination of the old over the young, and they, the elders, make a special effort to confuse and mystify because their system does not recommend itself to common sense.

On the other hand, there is a vague but important wisdom that must be passed on, a wisdom which does not appear on the surface and which requires special pointing out and cloistered reflection. The champions of the liberal arts colleges maintain that, one way or another, the young will pick up contemporary know-how and mores, but that the greatness of Mankind — Hippocrates, Beethoven, Enlightenment, Civil Liberties, the Sense of the Tragic — all will lapse without a trace unless scholars work at perpetuating these values. I sympathize with the problem as they state it; but, in fact, I have not heard of any method whatever, scholastic or otherwise, of teaching the humanities without killing them. I remember how at age twelve, browsing in the library, I read *Macbeth* with excitement; yet in class I could not understand a word of *Julius Caesar*, and I hated it. I'm pretty sure this is a common pattern. The survival of the humanities would seem to depend on random miracles which are becoming less frequent.

Unlike incidental learning which is natural and inevitable, formal schooling is deliberate intervention and must justify itself. We must ask not only whether such schooling is well done, but is it *worth* doing? *Can* it be done? Is teaching possible at all?

There is a line of critics from Lao-tse and Socrates to Carl Rogers who assert that there is no such thing as teaching either science or virtue; and there is strong evidence that schooling has little effect on either vocational ability or on citizenship. Donald Hoyt, in *American College Testing Reports* (1965), found that in any profession, college grades have had no correlation with life achievement.

At the other extreme, Dr. Skinner and the operant-conditioners claim that they can "instruct" for every kind of performance, and that they can control and shape human behavior much as they can the behavior of animals who have been sealed off from their ordinary environment. But it is disputable whether children are good subjects for such instruction in any society we might envisage.

The main line of educators from Confucius and Aristotle to John Dewey hold that one can teach the child good habits in morals, arts, and sciences through practice. The art is to provide the right tacks at the right moments; and Froebel, Herbert, Steiner, Piaget, etc., have different theories about this. But sociologists like Comte and Marx hold that social institutions overwhelmingly determine what is learned — so much so, that it is not worthwhile to be concerned with pedagogy. My bias is that "teaching" is largely a delusion.

In every advanced country, the school system has taken over a vast part of the educational functions of society. The educationists design toys for age two, train for every occupation, train for citizenship, train for sexuality, and explain and promote the humanities.

With trivial exceptions, what we mean by *school* — curriculum, texts, lessons, scheduled periods marked by bells, teachers, examinations, and graded promotion to the next step — was the invention of some Irish monks of the seventh century who thought to bring a bit of Rome to wild shepherds. It has been an amazing success story, probably more important than the Industrial Revolution.

No doubt it was a good thing, at first, for wild shepherds to have to sit still for a couple of hours and pay strict attention to penmanship and spelling. The imposed curriculum was entirely exotic and could only be learned by rote anyway. Mostly, of course, it was only aspiring clerics who were schooled.

By an historical accident, the same academic method later became the way of teaching the bookish part of some of the learned professions. There is no essential reason why law and medicine are not better learned through apprenticeship, but the bookish method was clerical, and therefore scholastic. Perhaps any special education based on abstract principles was part of a system of mysteries, and therefore clerical, and therefore scholastic.

The monkish rule of scheduled hours, texts, and lessons is also not an implausible method for giving a quick briefing to large numbers of students, who then embark on their real business. Jefferson insisted on universal compulsory schooling for short terms in predominantly rural communities, in order that children might be able to read the newspapers and catechized in libertarian political history. During the following century, in compulsory urban schools, the children of immigrants were socialized and taught standard English. The curriculum was the penmanship, the spelling, and the arithmetic needed for the business world.

At present, however, the context of schooling is quite different. The old monkish invention of formal schooling is now used as universal social engineering. Society is conceived as a controlled system of personnel and transactions, with various national goals depending on the particular nation. And the schools are the teaching machines for all personnel.

There is no other way of entry for the young. Teaching aims at psychological preparation in depth. Schooling for one's role, in graded steps, takes up to 20 years and more; it is the chief activity of growing up; any other interest may be interrupted — but not schooling. The motivation for a five-year-old's behavior is thus geared 15 years in the future.

In highly productive technologies like ours which do not need manpower, the function of long schooling is to keep the useless and obstreperous young *away* from the delicate social machine. The function of the school is to baby-sit the young and police them.

Yet the schools are not good playgrounds or reservations either. The texture of school experience is similar to adult experience. There is little break between playing with educational toys and watching educational TV, or between being in high school and dating, or between being in college and being drafted, or between being personnel of a corporation and watching NBC.

Since the trend has been to eliminate incidental education and deliberately to prepare the young for every aspect of ordinary life through schooling, we would expect pedagogy to have become functional. Yet radical students complain that today's schooling is ideological through and through. The simplest, and not altogether superficial, explanation of this paradox is that scholastic mystery has transformed adult business. It is society that has become mandarin.

None of this works. Contemporary schooling does not prepare for jobs and professions. For example, evidence compiled by Ivan Berg of Columbia shows that on the job dropouts do as well as high school graduates.

Nor has today's education made for peaceful baby-sitting and policing. Instead of an efficient gearing between the teaching machine and the rest of the social machine, the schools seem to run for their own sake. There IS a generation gap. Many youngsters fail; many drop out; others picket.

Predictably, the response of school administrators has been to refine the process; to make the curriculum more relevant, to start schooling earlier, to employ new technologies in teaching, to eliminate friction by admitting students to administrative functions.

But the chief objection to engineering in education is that it is inefficient. It tries to program too much, to pre-structure syllabi and lesson-plans. But human behavior is strong, graceful, and discriminating only to the extent that, in concrete situations, it creates its own structures as it goes along. Things can be learned securely, quickly, and naturally only through coping. As John Holt has pointed out, the teacher wants the child to learn the lesson according to the teaching plan; but the child quickly learns how to con the teacher, for getting a passing grade is the child's real problem of the moment.

It has frequently been said that human beings use only a small part — "just 2 percent" — of their abilities. Some educators therefore propose that much more demanding and intellectual tasks be set at a much earlier age. There is no doubt that most children can think and learn far more than they are challenged to. Yet it is likely that by far the greatest waste of ability occurs because a playful, hunting, sexy, dreamy, combative, passionate, artistic, manipulative, destructive, jealous, magnanimous, selfish and disinterested animal is continually thwarted by social organization — and perhaps especially by schooling.

If so, the main purpose of pedagogy should be to counteract and delay socialization as long as possible. For our situation is the opposite of the situation in the seventh century. Since the world has become overly scholastic, we must protect the wild shepherds.

Current high thought among schoolmen, for instance those of the National Science Foundation and those of the Harvard School of Education, is that the contemporary syllabus is indeed wasteful and depressing. But they would expand the schools and render the programming more psychological. Since the frontiers of knowledge are changing so rapidly, there is no use in burdening children with data that will be outdated in ten years, or with skills that will soon be better performed by machines; rather children must learn *to learn:* their cognitive faculties must be developed; they must be taught the big Ideas, concepts like the conservation of energy. This is exactly what Robert Hutchins was saying forty years ago.

Or more daringly, the children must not be *taught,* but be allowed to *discover.* They must be encouraged to guess and to brainstorm rather than be tested on the right answers.

In my opinion, in an academic setting, these proposals are never bona fide. As Gregory Bateson has noted with dolphins and trainers, and as John Holt has noticed in middle class schools, learning to learn means picking up the structure of behavior of the teachers, becoming expert in the academic process. In actual practice, the young discoverers are bound to discover what will get them past the College Board examinations. Guessers and dreamers are not free to balk and drop out for a semester to brood and let their theories germinate in the dark, as proper geniuses do.

It is a crucial question whether "cognitive faculties" does not mean the syntax of school performance. There is an eccentric passage in an early work of Piaget where he says that children in the playground seem to be using intellectual concepts, e.g. causality, a couple of years earlier than they are "developed" in the classroom, but he sticks to the classroom situation because it allows for his "scientific" observation. Yet this might mean that the formal routine of the classroom has hindered the spontaneous use of the intellect, and that the "concept" which is developed in the classroom is not an act of intellect grasping the world at all, but is a method of adjustment to the classroom, the constricted seats, the schedule, the teacher's expectation, the boring subject-matter to which one must pay attention.

2

Progressive education is best defined as a series of reactions to a school system that has become rigid. Progressive education aims to include what has been repressed; it aims to right the balance.

Moreover progressive education is a political movement; progressive education emerges when the social problem is breaking out. To put it more positively, an old regime is not adequate to cope with new conditions; new energy is needed. The form that progressive education takes in each era is prophetic of the next social revolution.

Rousseau reacted to the artificiality and insincerity of the royal court, and the parasitism, the callous formalism, and the pervasive superstition of the courtiers. The establishment of his day had simply become incompetent to govern. A generation later, it abdicated.

John Dewey reacted to a genteel culture that was irrelevant in an industrialized society. Dewey reacted to rococo decoration, to puritanism that denied animal nature, to censorship, and to rote performance imposed on children. Again, after a generation (by the end of the New Deal) Dewey's moral vision had largely come to be. In his lifetime, most of the program of the Populists and the Labor Movement had become law; education and culture (among whites) had become utilitarian and fairly classless; the revolution of Freud and Spock was well advanced; censorship was on its way out; and there was no more appliqué decoration.

A.S. Neill's Summerhill School, a recent form of progressive education, was likewise a reaction against social-engineering. Neill reacted against the trend to 1984 as Orwell came to call it, against obedience, authoritarian rules, organizational role-playing instead of being, the destruction wrought by competition and grade-getting. Since going to class is for children in the immutable nature of things, Neill's making of attendance a matter of choice was a transformation of reality; and to the extent that there was authentic self-government at Summerhill and to the extent that small children were indeed given power, the charisma of all institutions was challenged.

Progressive education has been criticized as a middle-class gimmick. The black community, especially, resents being used for "experiments." Poor children, it is claimed, need to learn the conventional wisdom so they can compete for power in the established system. Black parents demand "equality education" and expect their children to wear ties.

In my opinion, this criticism is wrongheaded. The scholastic evidence shows that the more experimental the high school, the more successfully its graduates compete in conventional colleges.

Black communities should run their own schools, and they should run them on the model of Summerhill. This has indeed been the case with the sporadic Freedom schools which have been influenced, directly or indirectly, by Neill.

I don't agree with the theory of *Head Start* that disadvantaged children require special training to prepare them for learning. I find nothing wrong with the development of their intellectual faculties; they have learned to speak, and they can make practical syllogisms very nicely, if they need to. If they have not learned the patterns by which they can succeed in school, the plausible move is to change the school. But, as Elliott Shapiro has suggested, the trouble might be that these children have been pushed too early to take responsibility for themselves and for their little brothers and sisters as well. The trouble is that their real problems have been all too insoluble. It's not that these children can't reason; the fact is that pure reason is of no use to them in their coping with their all too real difficulties.

What these kids need is freedom from pressure to perform. And, of course, they need better food, more quiet, and a less impoverished environment to grow up in — AT THEIR OWN PACE. These things are what the First Street School on the Lower East Side in New York, which was somewhat modeled on Summerhill, tried to provide.

Nevertheless, we must say that progressive education has been almost a total failure. The societies that have emerged after fulfilling their programs, were not what the visionaries had hoped for. French or American democracy was not what Rousseau had in mind. Dewey's social conceptions have ended up as technocracy, labor bureaucracy, and suburban conformity. The likelihood is that A.S. Neill's hope, too, will be badly realized. It is not hard to envisage a society in the near future in which self-reliant and happy people will be attendants of a technological infrastructure over which they have no control whatever, and whose purposes do not seem to them to be any of their business. Indeed, Neill describes with near satisfaction such success-stories among his own graduates. Alternately, it is conceivable that an affluent society will support its hippies like Indians on a reservation.

How to prevent these outcomes? Perhaps Neill protects his community a few years too long, both from the oppressive mechanistic world and from adolescent solitude — it is hard to be alone in Summerhill. Moreover, it seems to me that there is something inauthentic in Neill's latitudinarian lack of standards. For example, Beethoven and Rock 'n Roll are considered equivalent (though Neill himself prefers Beethoven). We are not only free organisms but parts of a mankind that historically has made strides with great inspirations and through terrible conflicts. We cannot slough off that accumulation of cultures, however burdensome, without becoming trivial. It seems to me that the noisy youth subculture of today is not grown-up — which is to the good — but also that it can *never* become grown-up.

Generally, the young of today have strong feelings for honesty, frankness, loyalty, fairness, affection, freedom and the other virtues of generous natures. They quickly resent the hypocrisy of politicians and administrators, and parents who mouth big abstractions, but who act badly. But the young themselves — like most politicians and administrators and many parents — seem to have forgotten the concrete reality of ideals like magnanimity, compassion, honor, consistency, civil liberty, integrity and justice — ideals which maintain and which re-create Mankind. Naturally, without these ideals and the conflicts they engender, there is no tragedy. Most young persons seem to disbelieve that tragedy exists, they always interpret impasse as timidity, and casuistry as finking out. I may be harsh, but though I am often astonished by their physical courage, I am not often impressed by their moral courage.

3

My own thinking is that:

(1) Incidental education (taking part in the ongoing activities of society) should be the chief means of learning.

(2) Most high schools should be eliminated. Other kinds of youth communities should take over the social functions of the high school.

(3) College training, generally, should follow — not precede — entry into the professions.

(4) The chief task of educators should be to see that the activities of society provide incidental education. If necessary, government and society should invent new useful activities offering new educational opportunities.

(5) The purpose of elementary pedagogy through age twelve should be to protect and nourish a child's free growth, since both the community and family pressure are too much for a child to withstand.

4

Let me review the arguments for this program:

We must drastically cut back schooling because our extended tutelage is against nature and actually arrests growth.

The effort to channel growing up according to a preconceived curriculum discourages the young and wastes many of the best of our powers to learn and cope.

Schooling does not prepare for real performance; it is largely carried on for its own sake. Only the academically talented, only 10 to 15 percent according to Conant, thrive in this useless activity without being bored, and without being harmed.

Our system of education, isolating as it does the young from the older generation, alienates the young.

Yet it makes no sense for many of the brightest and most sensitive of our young to simply drop out or to confront society with hostility. This state of affairs does not lead to social reconstruction. The complicated and confusing conditions of our times require fresh thinking, and therefore, what we need is participation, particularly by the young.

Young radicals seem to believe that political change will solve our chief problem. Or that our problems will solve themselves after political change. This is a delusion. Our novel problems of urbanization, technology, and ecology have not heretofore been faced by any political faith. The fact is that the educational systems of other advanced countries are no better than ours.

It has been my Calvinistic and Aristotelian experience that most people cannot organize their lives without productive activity. Of course, this does not necessarily mean paid activity. The professions, the services, industries, arts and sciences are the arenas. Radical politics and doing one's thing are careers for only a very few.

As things are, American society either excludes the young, or corrupts the young, or exploits the young. I believe we must make the rules of licensing and hiring more realistic, and we must get rid of mandarin requirements. We must design apprenticeships that are not exploitative.

Society desperately needs much work, both intellectual and manual, in urban renewal, in ecology, in communications, and in the arts. All these spheres could make use of young people. Many such enterprises are best organized by young people themselves, like the community development and the community action of "Vocations for Social Change." There are also excellent apprenticeships open for the brainy at the think-tanks like the Oceanic Institute at Makapuu Point, or in the Institute for Policy Studies in Washington, both of which are careless about checking diplomas. Our aim should be to multiply the paths of growing up. There should be ample opportunity for a young boy or girl to begin his career again, to cross over from one career to another, to take a moratorium, to travel, or to work on his own. To insure freedom of option, and to insure that the young can maintain and express their critical attitude, adolescents should be guaranteed a living. Giving a young person the present cost of a high school education would provide enough money for a young person to live on.

The advantage of making education less academic has, of course, occurred to many people. There are a myriad of programs to open the school to the world by: (1) recruiting professionals, artists, gurus, mothers, and dropouts as teachers' aides; and (2) granting academic credit for work-study, for community action, for the writing of novels, for service in mental hospitals, for spending one's junior year abroad, and for other kinds of released time.

Naturally, I am enthusiastic for this development, and I only want it to go the small further step of abolishing the present school establishment, instead of aggrandizing it.

There is also a movement in the United States, as there is in Cuba and China, for adolescent years to be devoted to public service. This is fine if the service is not compulsory nor regimenting.

It *is* possible for everyone's education to be tailor-made according to his own particular developing interest. Choices along the way will often be ill-conceived and wasteful, but such choices will nevertheless express desire, and will therefore immediately coincide with reality. Such choices will, therefore, converge to find the right vocation for a young person more quickly than through any other method. One's vocation is what one is good at and can do. Vocation is what employs a reasonable amount of one's powers. The use of the full power of a majority of the people would make for a stable society which would be far more efficient than our own. In such a set-up, those who have peculiar excellences are more likely to find their way when they have entry by doing something they can do well, and then proceeding to their more particular interests, and by being accepted for *what* they can do.

Academic schooling, of course, could be chosen by those with academic talents. Obviously, schools would be better off if unencumbered by sullen uninterested bodies. But the main use of academic teaching should be for those already busy in the sciences and the professions, who need academic courses along the way to acquire further knowledge. Cooper Union in New York City used to fulfill this function very well.

Of course, in such a set-up, employers would themselves provide ancillary academic training. In my opinion, this ancillary schooling would do more than any other single thing to give blacks, rurals, and other culturally deprived youth a fairer entry and a chance for advancement. As we have seen, there is no correlation *on the job* between competence and prior schooling.

This leads to another problem. Educationally, schooling on the job is usually superior to academic schooling, but the political and moral consequences of such a system are ambiguous. At present, a youth is hired because of his *credentials,* rather than for his actual skill. This system allows a measure of free-market democracy. However, if he is to be schooled on the job, he must be hired essentially for his promise. Such a system can lead to company paternalism like Japanese capitalism. On the other hand, if the young have options and they are allowed to organize and criticize, on-the-job education is the quickest way to workers' management which, in my opinion, is the only effective democracy.

University education — liberal arts and the principles of the professions — should be reserved only for adults who already know something, and who have something about which to philosophize. Otherwise, as Plato pointed out, such "education" is just mere verbalizing.

To provide a protective and life-nourishing environment for children through age twelve, Summerhill is an adequate model. I think Summerhill can be easily adapted to urban conditions. Probably, an even better model would be the Athenian pedagogue touring the city with his charges; but for this to work out, the streets and the working-places of the city will have to be made safe and more available than it is likely they will be. The prerequisite of city-planning is that children be able to *use* the city; for no city is governable if it does not grow citizens who feel that the city is theirs.

The goal of elementary pedagogy is a very modest one: a small child should be able, under his own steam, to poke interestedly into whatever goes on; and he should be able, through observation, through questions, and through practical imitation, to get something out of such poking around. In our society this is what happens at home pretty well up to age four; but after that, such random poking around becomes forbiddingly difficult.

5

I have often spelled out this program of incidental education, and I have found no takers. Curiously, I get the most respectful if wistful attention at teachers' colleges, even though what I propose is quite impossible under present administration. Teachers *know* how much they are wasting the children's time, and teachers understand that my proposals are fairly conservative.

However, in a general audience the response is incredulity. Against all evidence, people are convinced that what we are now doing must make sense or we wouldn't be doing it. It does not help if I point out that in dollars and cents it might be cheaper — and it would certainly be more productive — to eliminate most schools and have the community itself provide more of the education. Yet the majority in a general audience are willing to admit that they themselves got very little out of their school years. Occasionally, an old reactionary businessman agrees with me enthusiastically that book- learning isn't worth a penny.

Among radical students, my proposals are met by a sullen silence. They want Student Power, and for the most part, they are unwilling to answer whether they are authentically students at all. I think they're brainwashed. Naturally, it makes no difference to them if they demand "University Reform," or if the University is shut down altogether.

Instead of Student Power, what they should be demanding is (a) a more open entry into society, and (b) that education money should be spent more usefully, and (c) that licensing and hiring should be handled without consideration of irrelevant diplomas; and so forth. Youth Power can make the authentic demand for the right to take part in initiating and deciding the functions of society that concern them, as well as the right to govern their own lives — which are nobody else's business. Bear in mind that I am speaking of youths between age 17 and 25. At all other times in man's history, these individuals would already have found their places in the real world.

The Unteachables

This is a hard generation to teach what I think ought to be taught in colleges. This is not because the students are disrespectful or especially lazy; in my experience, they respect us more than we usually deserve and they work earnestly on much too heavy schedules. Of course, many of the students, probably the majority, ought not to be in academic settings at all (they ought to be getting their education in a variety of other ways) causing overcrowding, dilution, and standardization. But there are some other difficulties within the very essence of higher education which I want to discuss in what follows: (1) the culture we want to pass on is no longer a culture for these young; (2) the young are not serious with themselves; (3) and the auspices, methods, and aims of many of the colleges are irrelevant to the actual unprecedented present or the foreseeable future.

The culture I want to teach (I am myself trapped in it and cannot think or strive apart from it) is our Western tradition: the values which come from Greece, the Bible, Christianity, chivalry, the Free City of the twelfth century, the Renaissance, the heroic age of science, early nineteenth century utilitarianism and late nineteenth century naturalism. To indicate what I mean, here is a single typical proposition about each of these: The Greeks aspired to a civic excellence in which mere individual success would be shameful. The Bible teaches a created world and history in which we move as creatures. Christians have a spirit of crazy hope because we are always in the last times. Chivalry demands, in love and war, a personal loyalty, upon which honor depends. The Free Cities invented for us the juridical rights of social corporations. The Renaissance affirmed the imperious right of gifted individuals to seek immortality. Scientists carry on their disinterested dialogue with Nature, regardless of dogma or consequences. The Enlightenment decided once and for all that there is a common sensibility of all mankind. The Revolution showed that equality and fraternity are necessary for liberty. The economists assert that labor and enterprise must yield tangible satisfactions, not merely busy-work, profits, and power. The naturalists urge us to an honest ethic, intrinsic in our human condition.

Of course, these familiar crashing ideals are often in practical, and even theoretical, contradiction with one another, but that conflict itself is part of the Western tradition. And certainly they are only ideals — they never existed on land or sea — but they are inventions of the holy spirit and the human spirit that constitute the University, which is also an ideal.

As a teacher, naturally, I rarely mention such things. I take them for granted as assumed by everybody. But I am rudely disillusioned, for both the students and my younger colleagues take quite different things for granted. For instance, I have heard that the excellence of Socrates was a snobbish luxury that students nowadays cannot afford; that we know the created world only through "communications" like TV; that personal loyalty is appropriate only to juvenile gangs; that law is power; that fame is prestige and sales; that science is mastering Nature: that there is no such thing as humanity, only different patterns of culture; that education and ethics are programs for conditioning reflexes; and that the purpose of political economy is to increase the Gross National Product.

I do not mean to belittle these views, though I describe them somewhat bitterly. They make a lot of theoretical sense and they are realistic. It is better to believe them than hypocritically to assert ideals for which you do not strive. The bother with these views, however, is that they do not structure either enough life or a worthwhile life; that is, *as ideals* they are false. I think this is felt by most of the students and it is explicitly said by many young teachers. They regard me, nostalgically, as not really out of my mind but just "out of joint" — indeed, as a little enviable, because, although my values are delusions, one is justified by them if one believes and tries to act upon them. The current views do not seem to offer justification, and it is grim to live on without justification.

There is no mystery about how the thread of relevance snapped. Our history has been too disillusioning. Consider just the recent decades, overlooking the hundreds of years of hypocrisy. During the first World War, Western culture disgraced itself irremediably (read Freud's profound expression of dismay). The Russian revolution soon lost its Utopian élan, and the Moscow Trials of the 1930s were a terrible blow to many of the best youth. The Spanish Civil War was perhaps the watershed — one can almost say that 1938 was the year in which Western culture became irrelevant. The gas chambers and the atom bomb exposed what we were capable of doing. Since the second war, our American standard of living has sunk into affluence and nobody praises the "American Way of Life." Throughout the world, initiative and citizenship have vanished into personnel in the Organization. Rural life has suddenly crowded into urban sprawl, without forethought for community or the culture of cities. And the Cold War — deterrence of mutual overkill — is normal politics.

In this context, it is hard to talk with a straight face about identity, creation, Jeffersonian democracy, or the humanities.

But, of course, since young people cannot be merely regimented, they find their own pathetic, amiable, and desperate ideals. The sense of creatureliness reappears in their efforts, to make a "normal" adjustment and a "normal" marriage. The spirit of apocalypse is sought for in hallucinogenic drugs. Pride is physical toughness and self-aggrandizement. Social justice recurs as helping marginal groups. Science recurs as superstitious scruples about "method." Art regains a certain purity by restricting itself to art-action. Pragmatic utility somehow gets confused with engineering. Personal integrity is reaffirmed by "existential commitment," even though without rhyme or reason. None of this, nor all of it together, adds up to much; nobody's heart leaps up.

Perhaps my difficulty in teaching students now comes down to one hard nugget; I cannot get them to realize that the classical work was *about* something; it is not just part of the history of literature; it does not merely have an interesting symbolic structure. When Milton or Keats wrote, he was *for real* — he meant what he said and expected it to make a difference. The students do not grasp that any of that past excellence was for real and still is — for some of us. Their present goes back to about 1950. Naturally they do not have very impressive model heroes.

Since there are few self-justifying ideas or impressive models for them to grow up on, young people do not have much confidence nor take themselves very earnestly — except for private conceits which many of them take very seriously indeed.

In fact, adults actively discourage earnestness. As James Coleman of Johns Hopkins has pointed out, the "serious" activity of youth is going to school and getting at least passing grades; all the rest — music, driving, teenage commodities (more than $10 billion annually), dating, friendships, reading, hobbies, need for one's own money — all this is treated by the adults as frivolous. The quality of meaning of it makes little difference. Of course, many of these "frivolous" activities are those in which a child would normally find his identity and his vocation, explore his feelings, and learn to be responsible. It is a desperately superficial society if the art and music that form tastes are considered unimportant. Nevertheless, if any of these — whether a "hobby" that interferes with homework or "dating" that makes a youth want to be independent and to work through his feelings responsibly — threatens to interfere with the serious business of school, it is unhesitatingly interrupted, sometimes with threats and sanctions. And astoundingly, for the majority of the middle class, this kind of tutelage now continues for sixteen years, during which the young sit facing front and doing preassigned lessons. At twenty-one however, the young are responsibly supposed to get jobs, marry, vote for Presidents and bring up their own children.

The schedule and the tutelage are resisted; teenagers counter with their own subculture; there are all kinds of youth problems. But by and large the process succeeds, by *force majeure.* But it is not a generation notable for self-confidence, determination, initiative, pure taste or ingenuous idealism.

The favored literature expresses, as it should, the true situation. (It is really the last straw when the adults, who have created the situation for the young, try to censor their literature out of existence.) There are various moments of the hang-up. There are the stories that "make the scene" — where making the scene means visiting a social region where the experiences do not add up to become one's own, with friends who do not make any difference. These stories, naturally, do not dwell on the tragic part, what is missed by making the scene. As an alternative, there are picaresque, hipster, adventure-stories, whose heroes exploit the institutions of society, which are not their institutions, and win triumphs for themselves alone. Then there are novels of sensibility, of very early disillusionment with a powerful world that does not suit and to which one cannot belong, and the subsequent suffering or wry and plaintive adjustment. Finally, there is the more independent Beat poetry of willed withdrawal from the unsatisfactory institutions and the making of a world — often apocalyptic — out of one's own guts, with the help of Japanese sages, hallucinations, and introspective physiology; this genre, when genuine, does create a threadbare community; but of course it suits very few.

In order to have something of their own, in a situation where they are rendered powerless and irresponsible, many of the young maintain a fixed self-concept through thick and thin, as if living out autobiographies of a predetermined life. And it is this they nourish in the heroes of their literature. They defend the conceit with pride or self-reproach; it comes to the same thing, whether one says "I'm the greatest" or "I'm the greatest goof-off." They absorbingly meditate on this fiction and, if vocal, boringly retell it. In this action of affirming their self-concepts, they are, as I have said, very earnest, but it is an action that prevents awareness of anything or anybody else.

Such tutelage and conceit are not a climate in which to learn any objective subject matter. They are also a poor climate for love or any satisfactory sexual behavior. In my opinion, the violence of the sexual problems of teenagers is largely caused by the adult structure of control itself, and the consequent irresponsibility and conceit. (Of course this is hardly a new thing.) If students could regulate themselves according to their own institutions and impulses, there would soon be far more realism, responsibility, and seriousness, resulting in consideration for the other, responsibility for social consequences, and sincerity and courage regarding one's own feelings. For example, a major part of attractiveness between two people normally is fitness of character — sweetness, strength, candor, attentiveness — and this tends to produce security and realism. Instead, we find that they choose in conformity to movie-images, or to rouse the envy of peers, or because of fantastic ideas of brutality or sexuality. In courting, they lie to one another, instead of expressing their need; they conceal embarrassment instead of displaying it; and so they prevent any deepening of feeling. Normally, mutual enjoyment leads to mutual liking, closer knowledge, caring for. Instead, sexual activity is used as a means of conquest and epic boasting, or of being popular. Soon, if only in sheer self-protection, it is an axiom *not* to care for or become emotionally involved. Even worse, they do not follow actual desire, which has in it a lot of fine discrimination and organic prudence; but instead they do what they think they ought to desire, or they act for kicks or for experiment. There is fantastic, excessive expectation, and inevitable disappointment or disgust. Much of the sexual behavior is not sexual at all, but is conformity to gang behavior because one has no identity, or proving because one has no other proofs, or looking for apocalyptic experience to pierce the dullness.

In brief, adults do not take adolescents seriously, as if they really *had* those needs and feeling; and so, finally, the adolescents cannot make sense of their own needs and feelings.

The chief obstacle to college teaching however resides neither in the break with tradition nor in the lack of confidence and seriousness of the students, but in the methods and aims of the colleges themselves. My book, *The Community of Scholars,* is a modern retelling of Veblen's account in *The Higher Learning in America* of the cash-accounting mentality prevalent in administrators, professors, and the students themselves, the mania for credits and grades, the tight scheduling, the excessive load, the false economy of huge classes, the lack of contact between teacher and teacher, teacher and student; the lust for rank, buildings and grounds, grants, and endowments; the mobility for advancement and salary hikes; and the overestimation of the "tangible evidence" of publication. All this adds up to no educational community at all.

It is impossible to look candidly at the present vast expansion and tight interlocking of the entire school system — from the graduate schools to the grade schools — without judging that it has three main functions: apprentice-training for the government and a few giant corporations, baby-sitting of the young during a period of rising unemployment in which most youth are economically superfluous, and the aggrandizement of the school system itself which is forming a monkish class greater than any since the sixteenth century. It is this unlucky combination of power-drive, commercial greed, public and parental guilt, and humanitarianism that explains the billions of federal, corporation, and foundation money financing the expansion. Inevitably, the functions are sometimes in contradiction: e.g. the apprentice-training of technicians requires speed-up, advanced placement, an emphasis on mathematics and sciences, and incredible amounts of testing and competition for weeding out. But the unemployment requires the campaign against drop-outs, and the Secretary of Labor has just asked that the compulsory schooling age be raised to eighteen — even though in some high schools they now station policemen to keep order.

These motives appear on the surface to be hard-headed and realistic but they are disastrously irrelevant to the education of our young for even the next four or five years. For example — with regard to the apprentice-training — Robert Theobald, the economist, quotes a Rand estimate that, with the maturity of automation only 2 percent of the population will be required to provide the present hardware and routine services and the college-trained, middle-management position especially will be unnecessary. At present, for the average semiskilled job in an automated plant, no prior education whatever is required. And my hunch is that throughout the economy, the majority of employees are "over-hired," that is, they have more schooling than they will ever use on the job. The employers ask for high school and college diplomas simply because these are to be had for the asking.

Nevertheless we live in a highly technical and scientific environment and there is a crucial need for scientific education for the majority. But this is necessary not in order to run or devise the machinery — which a tiny fraction of the highly talented will do anyway — but in order to know how to live in the scientific environment. Thus, the educational emphasis ought to be on the intrinsic interests of the sciences as humanities, and on the ethics of the scientific way of life, on practical acquaintance with machines (in order to repair and feel at home with them), and on the sociology, economics, and politics of science (in order that citizens may not be entirely ignorant in the major area of policy). These purposes are very like the program that progressive education set for itself at the beginning at this century. But these purposes are radically different from present scientific schooling which is narrow and directed toward passing tests in order to select the few who will be technical scientists.

Unexpectedly, this pressure and narrow specialization are having another baneful effect: they put a premium on immaturity of emotional development and age. Students who have done nothing but lessons all their lives (and perhaps especially those who get good grades) are simply too childish to study social sciences, psychology, politics, or literature. It is possible to teach mathematics and physics to them, for the subjects suit their alert and schematizing minds, but it is difficult to teach them subjects that require life-experience and independence. (I have suggested elsewhere that prestigious liberal arts colleges should lead the way by requiring two years of post high school experience in some maturing activity such as making a living, community service or travel before college entrance.)

But undoubtedly the worst consequence of the subservience of the colleges and universities to the extramural aims of apprenticeship and baby-sitting is that the colleges become just the same as the world; the corporations, the colleges and the grade schools have become alike. Higher education loses its special place as critic, dissenter, stubborn guardian of standards, *sub specie aeternitatis* — which means, in effect, looking to the day *after* tomorrow. The students have no way of learning that the intellect has a function, that it swings a weight of its own. Professors rarely stand out — crotchety — against the consensus. The "important" men are more likely to be smooth articles and grant getters. The young seldom find impressive model heroes in the colleges.

What then? In spite of all this, we obviously cannot contemplate a future in which the bulk of our youth will be "useless." This very way of phrasing it is absurd, for the use and worth of society is measured by its human beings, not by its production of goods and services. It is this generation's great good fortune that it may see these goods and services produced with astonishing ease and abundance, but we must get rid of the notion that the automatic techniques appropriate for producing hardware, for logistics, or for chains of command have any relation whatever to education or to any other personal humane, or creative action.

What ought education to be for, at present? The foreseeable future (I am not thinking of a distant Utopia) *must* provide us a world in which we will go on making an effort from inner necessity, with honor or shame depending on it, because these goals of the continuing human adventure are worthwhile — community culture, community service, high culture, citizenly initiative, serious leisure, and peace. Education toward such a world is the only kind that is realistic. When students and teachers break out of lock step and insist on such education, the colleges will become themselves again.

Science and Technology

The Human Uses of Science

The contrast between [the consequences and] the expectations of the men who a generation or two ago strove, against great odds, to secure a place for science in education, is painful.

John Dewey, 1916

In the century-old debate between Science and the Humanities, the humanities are now a weak opponent. They are not sure of what they are and they do not seem to have much of use to offer; whereas science looms in the fullness of success, it has made new advances in theory, and its technological applications have transformed the modern world. Yet sadly, perhaps just because our humanities are so weak, we have been losing the basic humane values of science itself. Having lost our firm credulity about what man "is" and what society is "for," we have become confused about what is relevant, useful, or efficient. Thomas Huxley or Thorstein Veblen were thinking of a "scientific society" where people were critical and modest, accurate and objective; where they shared in an international community of inquiry; where they lived "naturally," without superstitions or taboos; and they hoped to make this come to be for every child. Is anybody saying anything like this? With us, the idea of a "scientific society" seems to have degenerated to applying the latest findings of professional experts to solve problems for an ignorant mass, problems often created by the ignorance of the mass, including the scientists. This is neither very noble nor very practical. To give the tone of it (at its worst), let me quote from the pitch of an International Business Machines demonstrator: "The demands that will be placed on us [to sell our machines] can be met, for one must never forget that we are the masters. We alone have that great instrument called the human mind. It weighs 2 pounds. It takes only this much space. It can store 15 billion bits of information. It can be fed on less than 1/2 an apple a day. If man were to build this mighty instrument, it would take all of the power supplied to the City of Rome and require a space as large as Palazzo dei Congressi. All of us have such a machine. We are the masters and not the servants. We can keep pace. Yes, and ahead of the pace if we wish!"

When I ask, "What is a scientific society?" I am not raising an academic question. In this essay I want to analyze two kinds of confusion that the scientific camp suffers from. There is a confusion between science and technology — this is glaringly displayed by such a spokesman as Sir Charles Snow in his recent book on "The Two Cultures." And there exists in both the popular and the scientific mind — though of course differently — a confusion between science and what has to be called magic and superstition. These confusions are socially disastrous. They cost us billions in social wealth, they damage backward peoples and retard their progress from poverty, they jeopardize our safety, and they distort the education of the next generation.

1. Science and Technology

There has always been an intimate and mutually productive relation between science and technology. Let me give only spectacular modern examples. It was a problem of navigation that first led to the momentous measurement of the speed of light. The study of thermodynamics, by Carnot, Joule, Kelvin, grew from experience with steam engines, was advanced by working on practical problems of steam engines, and led to discoveries in refrigeration. Darwin's proof of evolution through natural selection relied heavily on experience of breeding livestock, while Mendel's studies in genetics have led to endless uses in agriculture. At present the very word "technology" is used not so much to refer to practical arts as to the application of fairly up-to-date scientific concepts to the mass production of goods and services. It would be awkward to call carpentry "technology," and it would be wrong to call medicine "technology," but wallboard, canned foods, ship radar, and the manufacture — and prescription? — of penicillin are parts of our technology. Marxist philosophers have insisted on an indissoluble relation, if not formal identity, between science and technology; and *in a background sense*, this is, in my opinion, true. Especially experimental science would not much exist among peoples who lack elaborate industrial arts; they would not have the data, they would not have the techniques, and they would not consider it important. (Yet such peoples might be excellent naturalists and mathematicians, like the Greeks. And in social psychology, with its techniques of rhetoric and pedagogy, all peoples, of course, have plenty of experimental evidence of behavior — a point that is often overlooked.)

A dangerous confusion occurs, however, when contemporary science and the current style of technology come to exist in people's minds as one block, to be necessarily taken as a single whole. The effect of this is that political arguments for some kind or complex of technology, which indeed has been made possible by modern science, are illogically strengthened by the science itself. Contrariwise, if anybody opposes the mass production, the export to underdeveloped countries, or the widespread domestic use of certain machines, technical complexes, or therapies, he is sure to be "refuted" as an obscurantist, an irrationalist or aesthete, a pessimist or a Luddite. (Sir Charles Snow is liberal with this kind of logic.) Because the adventure of modern science must be pursued, it is concluded that there are no choices in the adoption of scientific technology. This is an error in reasoning, but unfortunately there are powerful vested interests in business and politics throughout the world, on both sides of the Iron Curtain, that want to reinforce this error and probably believe it.

The criteria for the practice of science and the practice of technology are distinct. One may affirm that the most absolute freedom and encouragement — including a blank check — should be given to the pursuit of scientific knowledge, and yet that the mass application of this knowledge to industrial arts, communications, pedagogy, medicine, etc., should be highly selective and discriminating, and even, at present, rather grudging in some departments and regions. I want to affirm both propositions and go on to suggest some political, moral, and psychological criteria for choosing technologies. (What an odd sound such a reasonable proposal has today!)

My reasons for praising science are, of course, the classical ones, but let me spell them out for the pleasure of it. The pursuit of natural truth is a transcending good that justifies itself, like compassion, social justice, fine art, or romantic love. No superior standard exists by which to limit such pursuits, even though the sky falls. The life of research and theory is one of the forms of human happiness. The submission of the intellect to nature is a kind of humble prayer. Scientific habits are positive virtues, and, negatively, science is the chief antidote to illusion, prejudice, and superstition. The adventure of discovery is itself romantic and delights the animal spirits; conversely, any restriction of curiosity and inquiry very soon proves to be psychologically depressing and morally disastrous, leading to trickery and lies. Sometimes (certainly at present) we may fear that the discovery of truth is dangerous or inopportune; nevertheless, we must risk it.

I have not mentioned the final proposition in the classical eulogy of science: that science is useful, it finds out all kinds of things for the general welfare. Precisely in our times, thoughtful scientists might, on reflection, deny this. "The invention of flight, for example, is probably, on balance, a curse." (John Ullmann.) From Hiroshima on, many scientists, for instance those associated with the *Bulletin of Atomic Scientists*, have shouldered responsibility for the spectacularly bad consequences of their work. This certainly does not mean that they give up studying nuclear physics; it does mean that they try to select and control the technical applications.

When we turn to technical applications we are in the realm of prudence and choice, we weigh and balance values, take account of consequences, and realize that consequences are often incalculable. But — apart from the recent cases of the bombs and fall-out, some smoke control, and the traditional cautiousness of medical men — there have been almost no criteria in this field beyond cost and marketability (and legality). On the contrary, the policy in advanced countries has been "as much as possible of all the latest," and the policy in backward countries is now "all of it, as quickly as possible." Yet this technology determines our ways of life. Ideally we should pay the most serious attention to selecting each particular innovation for mass adoption, and to continually reviewing the technology we have. At least we should be ruthless in halting the further proliferation of those machines and their complexes that have demonstrably become ruinous, like the cars and roads.

2. Some Criteria for Selecting Technology

Start with the criterion of Utility. And consider the limiting case of Afro-Asian regions of dire poverty and drudgery, populous and industrially backward. What capital and technicians are useful?

The demand of the Western-trained leaders in these regions (it is hard to know what the people would choose) is to industrialize totally on advanced Western models as quickly as possible, and attain something like the American standard of living. The policy to accomplish this may be to concentrate at once on heavy industry, steel mills, machine tools; or, less radically, to devote part of the production to native goods for export, to build up a balance of trade. Either way, the policy means hard work without immediate rewards, curtailment of consumption, a stringent and likely totalitarian dictatorship both for work-discipline and for very long-range planning, a corresponding increase of the bureaucracy, the enforcing of new work habits, the disruption of the age-old community forms, occasional famines, sometimes the need to repress tribal revolts. Further, there are bound to be immense mistakes; nor is it surprising if, at the end of the process, much has been created that is already outmoded, and even more that does not, after all, suit the native conditions, materials, and uses. Such things could be documented again and again from the history of the industrialization of Russia, India, Israel, China, the Congo, etc., etc.

This policy is understandable as a reaction of despair to economic and political colonialism, leading people to produce bombers and bombs before anything else. Importantly, however, it is an illusion sprung from a superstitious notion of what it means to be modern and scientific. As such, it is abetted by foreign promoters who are interested in exporting pipe lines, mining machinery, and paved roads. But also governments and international agencies, claiming to have only benevolent aims, willingly go along with it. Yet if there were no wish to make profits or wield political influence, it would certainly be more useful to restrict the import of technology, specifically to give each region as soon as possible a self-supporting livelihood: the industries and techniques directly necessary for the maximum mass production of basic subsistence, food, shelter, medicine, and clothing where it is essential. And otherwise hands off! (It is dismaying to see photographs proving American benevolence by showing Africans in a school learning business methods and typing, and dressed in collars and ties. Is any of this package useful? Is even literacy according to our methods so indispensable for these people?)

To make people quickly self-supporting would be a far cheaper gift and in the long run a safer investment. People would be better off almost at once and could then think up the advantages that come marginally next in order. They could make their own community adjustments to the new conditions. In the production of subsistence goods there cannot be great mistakes, for people know the values involved. Less prior training is required. Less is wasted on politicians and policemen; it is more difficult for grafters to take their toll. People come to a higher standard according to their own style and choice, and therefore can develop a living culture out of what they have, instead of suffering a profound alienation. And the relation of means and ends is fairly direct, so that people are not mystified.

For such a policy, the primary technicians required are geographers and physicians, to ascertain the health and resources of each region; then engineers and anthropologically trained craftsmen-teachers and agronomists. There is not so much need for geologists, metallurgists, etc., nor for economists and urbanists. And no need at all for geopoliticians, promoters, and commissars.

If we turn, next, to our own, the most advanced country, the need for selection is equally obvious, though less drastic. It is now generally conceded that much of our production for consumption is humanly useless, of poor quality, wasteful and demoralizing. (Meantime, economically, 30 percent of our people live in hardship, there is a critical shortage of housing, and so forth.) But in discussing the Affluent Society, let us by-pass utility as a familiar topic, and develop other criteria.

Efficiency, among us, tends to be measured solely in terms of a particular machine — e.g., gasoline per mile — or in terms of a particular complex of industrial operations — e.g., using the by-products. But if we look at our production more philosophically, in larger wholes and more remote effects, we see that some of our most cherished technical assumptions lead to inefficiency. We centralize as if the prime mover were still a huge steam engine that had to keep hot. For instance, it can be demonstrated that, except in highly automated factories where labor cost is small compared to fixed capital, or in heavy mining attached to its site, for the most part large industrial plants and concentrations of industry are less efficient than smaller ones that assemble parts machined in small shops; it is cheaper to transport the parts than the workers, a worker wastes more than an hour a day going to work and parking, etc. (No doubt an important reason for the concentration of big plants has nothing to do with technical efficiency, but with managerial control. I would strongly urge the unions to ask for some of that travel time to be paid, as the mine workers asked for portal-to-portal pay. Maybe that would lead to more efficient planning. As it is, however — for a reason that quite escapes me — a workman cannot count his carfare or fuel as a business expense against his income tax!) Certainly in the layout of cities, almost any kind of neighborhood plan and community-centered production would be far more efficient than our suburbs.

Similarly, by the evident principle that as the unit cost of production falls, the unit cost of distribution rises, it is likely that much of the vast technology of food processing and transportation is inefficient. Back in the thirties, when times were harder, Ralph Borsodi showed experimentally that, using domestic electrical apparatus, it was cheaper in hours and minutes of effort to grow and can one's own tomatoes than to buy the national brands — not to speak of the quality; other items, e.g., wheat and bread, were cheaper not on an individual but on a small co-operative basis; and still other items were cheaper maximum-mass-produced and nationally distributed. (I don't think anybody has ever tried to proved that our actual system of price-controlling semimonopolies is good for anything at all.) My conclusion is not that we ought to produce every item in the most efficient way — we have a surplus and it is not necessary to be all that efficient — but rather that, since our economists do not habitually survey alternate possibilities and make an accounting, our national housekeeping has become slovenly. Because of our slovenliness, we fall in bondage to the supermarket, we cannot get going a co-operative movement, our goods are poor in quality.

A more human-scaled production has obvious political and cultural advantages; it allows for more flexible planning, it is more conducive to scientific education and invention. We complain of the deadening centralism and conformity, and we put up with them because they are "efficient." But they are inefficient.

We hear rhetoric on the theme of learning to master the machine lest the machine master us. Let us consider a couple of criteria for the selection of technology and the users of technology, that directly address this problem. If possible, the operation of a machine should be Transparent and Comprehensible to its users. This can be aided by the design and casing of the machine, and by the education of the users. An important corollary is that a machine ought to be *repairable* by its *user.* Our present plight is that, in the use of cars, telephones, electricity and gas systems, radio equipment, refrigeration, etc., etc., the mass of people are in bondage to a system of service men for even trivial repairs. The service men notoriously take advantage, but much worse is the tendency of the manufacturers to build obsolescence and nonrepairability *into* the machinery. (This is a negative criterion indeed! But it is inevitable that a caste possessing mysterious knowledge will shear the sheep.) What is the consequence? Psychologically, we have developed an anxious climate in which we don't know how to buy because we can't judge quality. It would be very different if we began to introduce the convention that a consumer must learn to take apart a machine and know how it works before he is encouraged to buy it — much as some of us still frown on an adolescent who cannot fix his broken bicycle. To make an analogy: considering the quantity of cars and mileage, there are remarkably few automobile accidents, but this is because the Americans have been tested and know how to drive.

Fifty years ago, the twin ideas of Progressive Education (learning by doing) and Functionalism in planning and design were matured to meet just this problem of making people more adequate to their new technological means, and of molding the new means into a shape and style more able to be grasped. Both movements, and also the related

pragmatic philosophy, were criticized as antihumanistic, as abandon-
ing classical education and traditional canons of beauty. But their
principle was precisely humanistic, to reintegrate the new scientific
specialism with the common intellectual and moral life. We can see
that this is an American hope, to have the industrial revolution *and* a
broad fundamental democracy; it still haunts us in our philosophiz-
ing about the high schools. (In Europe, similar ideas were almost always far more social-revolutionary, whether we think of Rousseau or
Fourier, Kropotkin or the original Bauhaus.)

The British biologist Patrick Geddes, when he championed these
ideas fifty years ago, however, saw that we must also select among the
technologies. He was in the moral tradition of Ruskin, Morris, and the
Garden City planners; they had experienced the profound
dehumanization of the coal towns. But Geddes imagined that history
was on his side, for the "neotechnology" of electricity had come to
replace the "paleo technology" of coal and steam. Electricity satisfied
the criterion of cleanliness (Amenity); and its easy transmission allowed
ubiquitous sources of power, therefore we could plan more freely, e.g.,
for the culture of cities (the phrase is Lewis Mumford's, a disciple of
Geddes). Some of what Geddes hoped for has come about; but on the
whole the "forces of history" have not helped us much, in the absence
of positive political and moral selection. And by a melancholy irony —
history is good at creating melancholy irony — most of us followers of
Geddes wryly praise the hideous old slums over the neotechnological
slums, for they had more human scale and pullulation of life!

Finally, let us turn to some uncritical applications of science in
biology and psychology. The most obvious illustration is the craze for
antibiotic drugs. These have been mass produced and promoted —
with a simply fascinating lack of corresponding reduction in price —
with a now conceded disregard of the organism as a whole. A powerful therapy, indicated for emergencies (e.g., for a dangerous mas-
toiditis), is used for a quick cure of minor or really systemic infections.
Similarly, central-system sedatives and tranquilizers are administered
with disregard to malnutrition, bad living habits, and bad environment. Meantime, the scientific "untechnological" tradition of
medicine, from Hippocrates on — diet, exercise, natural living, airs,
and places — is neglected; and the crucial factor of resistance to disease, the profoundest secret in medicine (just as prevention is its
glory), is not studied. Mass immunity to a host of particular symptoms
seems to be the sought-for goal, rather than the optimum possible
health of each particular organism. But the aim of medicine is not, as
such, to increase the average life span of a population — a person can

be kept alive as a vegetable for years — but to foster the quality of life. If we want a single word for the criterion of selection that is here being abused, it is perhaps Relevance to the thing being treated.

The irrelevant application of technology to psychology is too rich to cope with; it would carry us away. Let us just mention the usual typical items. Dr. Skinner of Harvard has invented a machine that is useful for reinforcing appropriate responses, so it is now to be mass produced as a teaching machine, though it is irrelevant to the chief factors in either teaching or learning. (The purpose is to save money on teachers and have even bigger classes.) A new computer is installed in Iowa that can score millions of standard tests in very little time, so my boy's class is interrupted to take these tests, and the curriculum will surely be modified for the convenience of a mechanical scorer. In a town in Maine a well-financed research project, involving seventeen variables and plenty of work for the rented computer, discovers that boys tend to elect shop and girls tend to elect cooking; the author of the report comments "We used to think that this was so, now we know." What criterion is being violated here?

Perhaps it is Modesty: to have as few machines, methods, products (and research projects, as possible. Space is limited; people are multiplying; but the machines have multiplied most, with overpowering effect. The bridges and roads are more impressive than the rivers they span and the places they connect. Most immodest of all are the techniques of communication that have cluttered up the void and silence with images and words. It is now the rule that books are written to keep presses running, and the more radio channels we tap, the more drivel will be invented to broadcast.

Thus I have touched on half a dozen criteria for the humane selection of technologies: utility, efficiency, comprehensibility, repairability, ease and flexibility of use, amenity, and modesty. These values are esteemed by scientists and engineers; they are common ground between science and the humanities; they do not entail any conflict. Why are they not generally evident in our "scientific" society? I have purposely chosen only large and economically, rather than culturally, important examples: the type of foreign aid, the planning and distribution of cities, the organization of production, the American standard of living and public health, the methods of education.

3

Return now to the thread of our argument, the confusion of science and technology and the rhetoric of lumping them together.

Let a group that is pushing a particular technology be opposed, and this rhetoric is immediately called on. Thus the big drug companies, being investigated for their outrageous pricing and monopolistic stifling of small competitors, have righteously exclaimed that without their methods of mass production, promotion, and pricing, scientific research comes to an end — there will be no more Listers and Pasteurs. Equally far-fetched is the uncriticized assumption of all the large suppliers of scientific technology that they alone are the right sponsors and entrepreneurs of scientific thought and research: this gives them the licence to raid the universities for talent, to fill the public schools with their brochures, to influence the appropriation of school funds, to get tax exemptions for "scientific" foundations that are really parts of the firm, and even to dictate the lines of further research and sometimes actively to discourage "unprofitable" lines of research. In foreign aid and the export of capital, firms that have equipment to sell, and materials and fuels to buy, are wonderfully persuasive about helping backward societies to become modern scientific societies. The Pentagon also is an enthusiastic advocate and underwriter of pure research — though not especially on the genetic effects of radioactive fall-out.

For a couple of hundred years, our proliferating technologies have been selected on the criteria of marketability and profitability, and by and large the market has furthered usefulness and efficiency. (But not invariably. Moral economists like Ned Ludd and Coleridge, Ruskin and Ebenezer Howard have been critical for the same two centuries.) In the past fifty years, however, new conditions have developed that are unambiguously baneful. There has been systematic corruption of the public notion of what *is* useful. (An early typical example was the campaign that put across bleached flour as tastier and more "refined," since it spoiled less in the grain elevators.) The growing public ineptitude and ignorance, and a growing mystique of technical experts, have made rational restraint difficult. And finally, by an inevitable reflex, the stream of science itself is channelled and hampered by the too abundant technology that it has created.

This, I submit, is the context of the current debate about what should be taught and how it should be taught. Then it is dismaying to read arguments, like Sir Charles Snow's, from the "scientific point of view," that completely disregard it. Sir Charles is so puffed up with the importance of science in its technical applications that he fails to ask any scientific questions, or to have any qualms of scientific conscience. Apparently some scientists feel so grand about being on the governing board that they are stone-blind to the evident fact that they are not the makers of policy. Do they choose as scientists to have scientific knowledge kept secret? Are they satisfied as scientists that space exploration has so speedily become a means of spying that Russians and Americans cannot co-operate? (It is said that at present our instruments for gathering information are superior, but the Russian rockets can carry more payload: now, what would be logical? who is proposing it?) "The sciences," wrote Jenner — to Paris in 1803! — "are never at war." This follows from the essence of science as a consensus of observers.

But perhaps this is the kind of wisdom to be got from the humanities.

The fact that just now scientific technology is controlling, abusing, and threatening to devastate mankind is neither here nor there as an argument for how we should educate our youth to make a better world. There were long periods when priests had power, other periods when soldiers had it, and even periods when literary mandarins had it. All of them did useful things and all of them made a mess. So I would propose that scientists think twice about what kind of power they have, what they are co-operating with, and with whom, and try a little harder to know themselves. There is a well-known humanistic technique for this chastening enterprise, the method of Socrates. (Psychotherapy is one of its modern branches.) A little history, too, should be a required course.

4

Before proceeding to a deeper consideration, allow me to explain that I myself have never been able to distinguish between "science" and the "humanities" — perhaps this is *my* blind spot. The reasons for the absolute autonomy and indeed pre-eminence of science that I listed above are all humanistic reasons, they are what belong to a whole, free, risky human existence. The moral criteria for selecting and refining an industrial society that were listed above are common to scientists and humanists, they are philosophic. If scientists do not think in these terms about technology, it is that they have lost touch with common sense; if humanists do not think about technology at all, it is that they have become withdrawn and therefore stupid. But further — and this is a point that scientists and many modern literary critics are singularly unaware of — the chief content of literature is itself scientific, it is the worldly wisdom and "criticism of life" of good observers who, *in the field of human relations,* had plenty of empirical

experience and some pretty hard experiment. If the classics of literature do not much state summary propositions like those in sociology
and psychology, but rather have the complex density of poems and
plays, it is because the subject matter of human conduct requires this
density of statement; it is notoriously missed and distorted by less
concrete and moving language. The interpretation of literary statements is the job of humanists, using the tools of historical criticism,
linguistics, poetics. Certainly it is a subtle, difficult, and often vague
business; but I don't suppose that anybody in his right mind ever
thought that the science of man would be less complex than physics
or biology. Just consider how the idiomatic use of a language, so
judged by the consensus of millions of users of the language, must
give us far more experiential evidence for what is the human case
than could possibly be gathered by the trivial sampling of sociologists
and psychologists. I take it that this was the great rediscovery made
by Wittgenstein in his old age, and since developed by the new school
of linguistic philosophy.

5

A hundred years ago, when Matthew Arnold was debating with
T.H. Huxley about the merits of literature and science, there was a different cultural climate. Not only had scientific technology not yet
spread so triumphantly over the globe, but England was still somewhat a "Christian country." Arnold could rely heavily on tradition
and sentiment and arguments about conduct and character. In our
times, it is "Science" that has become the dominant belief, replacing
Christianity and many other faiths. It is now the scientists who rely
on assumptions of tradition, sentiment, and right conduct. I think it is
necessary to explore this profound change in order to explain the
present uncritical acceptance of the technical fruits of science. Radically new ways of behavior require profound changes in popular
belief. A system of thinking spreads unlimitedly when it no longer
meets serious opponents.

In my opinion, science has become a superstition for both the
mass of the people and scientists themselves. For the mass it has the
power of magic. For the scientists it has the exclusive virtue of an or-
thodox theology.

Roughly defined, magic is the power of affecting material nature,
including men's souls and bodies, by occult means known to a caste
of specialists. Let us recall that from deep in the Middle Ages, and earlier, the practice of experimental science was popularly linked with

magic rather than with the philosophic quest for truth or the immediate utility of industrial arts. The typical figure is Roger Bacon. For the savant or contemplative natural philosopher, gazing at the stars, people have always had a rational respect, sometimes good-humored; but experimental science is dangerous in its nature. If the systematic observation and manipulation can elicit truth, the discovered truth can be used to manipulate matter. And indeed, the early experimentalists were afraid of themselves. For instance, the great alchemists did not fail to insist that pure motives and religious life were essential to the work; and, in the same moral climate, there was a history and literature of charlatans, sorcerers' apprentices, and mad scientists.

We have poor memories and perhaps no longer keep in mind that Christianity, at least, once thrived greatly by its sacramental magic, its relics, and its miracle workers; and its present lapse is owing to the brute fact that, over several centuries, it has been defeated by experimental science in a frank and fair contest of miracles and wonders. Science has worked better against plagues and it has proved to be immensely better at flying and distant communication. As late as the Russian Revolution, a means of defeating Christianity was to take a moujik up in an airplane and prove to him that God wasn't in the sky after all. On the other hand, Christianity still does have something to say about conversion and peace and mind, for here it has a few fumbling techniques, like revivalism and prayer. Western science knows nothing about such matters and resists learning anything. But the Eastern technologists have invented brain washing.

Our hope was, during the Enlightenment, to dissolve all such magical fears. Tyrannies and castes were undermined; religion was refuted; progressive education began to be invented; and the claims of science, too, became modest (I think that this was the chief contribution of Hume). The climax of this effort against superstition was the amazing synthesis of Kant, who managed to combine Hume and Rousseau with his own background of astronomer and pietist. But the history has turned out otherwise. For political, economic, and technological reasons, magical fears have not been dissolved. The specialist caste of wonder workers has grown more specialist (and recently less modest), and the rest of the people more out of touch and inept. And inevitably, given the actual disasters that scientific technology has produced, superstitious respect for the wizards has become tinged with a lust to tear them limb from limb. Calling this antiscientific bent Luddite, machine-breaking, is to miss the public tone, which is rather a murderousness toward the scientists as persons, more like anti-Semitism. Wiser scientists, like Huxley or Helmholtz or Einstein, have been sensitive to the danger of scientific estrangement, but their efforts of a hundred years to enlighten the people have not succeeded.

In one respect the popular superstition of science is more desperate than the medieval superstition of the Church. In the past, as counterevidence to what the priest said, there was the tradition of scientific experience and natural philosophy, and especially every man's experience in industry and agriculture; but now it is just this kind of counterevidence that is preempted by the specialists. For instance, our learned physicians are much better than the ancients, but when they happen to be off on a wrong tangent, a patient cannot escape to his common prudence, veterinary wisdom, or old-wives' folklore. If a man does not trust in Science, in what shall he trust? It was to address just this problem that Kant, again, insisted that in the university the faculty of philosophy must stand apart as a critical "loyal opposition from the left" (the phrase is Kant's), in order to purge of superstition and extravagant claims the other faculties: of theology, law and medicine — and he would now surely have included engineering.

6

The majority of our modern scientists are certainly not magically afraid of their own powerful experiments, whose operations they understand better, and which they have the illusion of controlling. Indeed, the religious benevolence anxiously demanded of the experimenter by a Paracelsus is neglected even beyond the limits of prudence and common morals. First-rate scientists are today working, apparently indifferently, on fantastically harmful projects that ordinary mortals would shy away from; and, with no signs of extraordinary moral suffering, skilled mathematicians estimate that fifty million sudden American corpses would not set back the "economy" more than ten years. This is an odd frame of mind for natural philosophers to have arrived at. (I assume that we must take their "indifference" and lack of a position as a profound unconscious dissociation: they are warding off feelings of involvement, whether of fear, guilt, or power.)

To understand our scientists, let us contrast what might be called their "official" modern scientific ethics with a more traditional scientific attitude that has come down from the heroic age of the seventeenth century, and which many also hold.

The official modern position is that *scientists are dedicated to science.* Let us spell this out. (1) Science is a self-contained, infinitely self-accumulating and self-improving system of consensus, corrigible only by further science. Scientists are committed to this system and get their satisfaction in its service. (2) They do not get their satisfaction from the truth of nature, but from fitting the truth into the system of science. As such, nature is valueless (neutral); they do not love nature. (3) Truths of nature can, however, be usefully applied to human desires, but scientists do not properly have these either; so it is not the scientists who care about the applications of scientific discoveries. (4) Scientists are not responsible for the use made of their work. They may have sentimental biases, but these do not exert much force on them. The important thing is the chance to work, and all problems provide the chance for equally excellent service. (This does not, of course, preclude feelings of pride when use is made of one's work.)

What shall we make of this astonishing theological position, maintained with considerable dogmatism, that began to flower, I guess, in the German universities of the nineteenth century? It establishes a caste serving an abstract entity, the self-developing system of scientific consensus. The form of service is adherence to the "scientific method" and it is strict, sometimes obsessionally so, as when, in a particular case, no matter how results are attained, e.g., by luck, insight, or philosophical appraisal, they do not enter into Science until they are ritually checked and put in proper form. The method is the only sure way. With this goes a detachment from any other immediately human or divine commitments.

The dogmatism is pretty absolute. The fact that certain areas of experience have proved stubbornly *un*fruitful for the scientific method as we practise it, is not taken as problematic. Rather, sometimes such areas are slighted as absurd or nonexistent. (This is when, as C.D. Broad said on psychical phenomena, "The editor of *Nature* seems to think he is the Author of nature.") Sometimes, as with morals, fine arts, and letters, the areas are compartmentalized off as "subjective" and "emotional," although quite important — on this view, the emotions are denied any value as a means of knowledge (a view, by the way, that is biologically absurd on Darwinian grounds). And very often, as in social studies, problems are piously swamped with busy-work scientific approaches that yield little, but, being in proper form, preserve the seamless robe of science. It is frankly puzzling to me that the historians and philosophers of science do not systematically and empirically explore the failures of scientific method and the blank areas recalcitrant to scientific method. Finally, with regard to the applications of science, it is confidently promised that the fruits of scientific methods will produce happiness. Evidences to the contrary are not given much weight, and anyway they will be nullified by the further advance of science. For instance, "sin" is now experienced, by laymen and scientists both, as physical and mental disease, corrigible only by further modern science. Understand, my point is not that these prejudices and claims of modern science are necessarily false, but that we are obviously dealing with a rigid orthodoxy and plenty of superstition.

In ideal structure, the self-improving objective system of science that one serves is simply a theodicy, the working out of a gradually revealed plan; but it is a theodicy of a rather low grade, compared, say, with Augustine's, for it is too caste and obsessional and does not allow for personal and historical storm and stress. How, for instance, does our scientific theory account for the present facts of warring scientists? Is that part of the self-improving system? If so, how? If not, why do we not hear charges of lack of dedication?

Contrast with all this the more traditional view of science as natural philosophy, which goes back to the Renaissance and is still the abiding strength of many scientists. There is no doubt that from the beginning, and still today, the natural philosophers have regarded themselves as in rebellion against ecclesiastical dogma and popular prejudice and (as is common with banded rebels) they conceive themselves as devoted to a kind of personified Nature, from whom they get primary satisfactions. They would not say that "nature is neutral," though of course "she" is beyond men's petty concerns. They love nature, or are curious, or surprised, or awe-struck at finding Cosmos in Chaos. Sometimes they are fearful, like Job confronted with Warhorse and Leviathan, for nature is "red in tooth and claw." Correspondingly, nature provides principles, and often goals, of ethics. This is different from the excitement of a "modern scientist" in his confrontation of nature, which is rather that of solving a hard puzzle and getting on with the work of the self-contained system of science.

The contrast I am trying to draw can be expressed formally in terms of linguistic philosophy. The "modern scientist" has as a program a Unified Language of Science — the movement pushed by Neurath, Carnap, and other logical positivists and operationalists; because the unity of science is the communication and consensus of the scientists, and there is only one method. Natural philosophers, however, seem content to let language and method follow the various subject matters as they always have, with the faith that there will always prove to be coherence and mutual understanding, since Nature coheres. Historically, the movement for a Unified Language was premature; each separate science has continued to use its own vocabulary. But perhaps the present craze to program everything for computers will produce a unified language.

"Objectivity" can mean different things. For a natural philosopher it is nonattachment, keeping oneself out of it, in order not to disturb or contaminate the object of absorbed attention — though the philosopher may experimentally intervene to put the object in the proper frame. The fruition of this absorbed reflection is an insight or theory that unites him with the object. (The type is Darwin gazing long hours at the bee and the flower.) To the "modern scientist," objectivity is the detachment, necessary for accuracy, of the good reporter or scout, whose satisfaction comes from bringing home the true account to headquarters. Essentially it is the experiment that is reported and not the "object," for the natural object is what is indifferently whirled and banged.

Mostly, of course, there is no such sharp classification among our scientists as I have been describing; but I have been trying to make precise certain "modern" characteristics of the scientific attitude, as they seem to me, because they explain something important about "applied science" and "scientific technology."

7

"Applied science" is a peculiar notion, and I think a recent one, though it already seems commonplace. Normally we would conceive of a man's scientific thinking as a worth-while action in itself and as, besides, operating in the whole of life in either of two ways: His curiosity and experimenting might find out something exciting or practical, a new phenomenon, a new force, and he would then repeat the experience and regularize it for his own and other people's use. Thus he might give us a way to boil water or see great distances through a telescope. Or conversely, a man might have an important life problem, a virus or an enemy to destroy, or a great wish to fly; then he would concentrate his resources, including his science, to destroy the enemy, or to get off the ground. These are the familiar classical senses in which science is useful (of course mistakes may occur and a produced force get out of hand). In this context we would not come to say that "scientific knowledge may be well or badly used," for the scientist is precisely concerned in the product and consequences, either adding something of his own style to the world, or solving problems meaningful to mankind. The only danger would be the one feared by the alchemists, that the experimenter himself might be a devil.

But the case is very different when scientific knowledge is "applied," or when the scientist works, for money, etc., to solve the problems that do not concern him or that may even be trivial or distasteful to him. Now, an immense amount of our technology is of this kind, and this affects the quality of products and their consequences. For, instead of the human environment being illuminated and probably simplified by scientific intellect — made comprehensible, efficient, elegant, modest, etc. — it is rather flooded by technological products of science that have the following characteristics: they have been worked up in a spirit that is detached from ordinary uses, and yet they mix into ordinary uses; they are used in a way irrelevant to the scientist's human concern and often contrary to his concerns; they embody knowledge increasingly far removed from ordinary experience; and therefore they are imposed on society and compel people to move and work in ways increasingly strange to them. The machines that people use, are, effectually, canned rituals. The structure of a scientific world is a simple one: inquiry and intellect coping with problems. This has a lovely style, a kind of paradisal style, for the character of Paradise is to be practical. But the world we have is not a simple one. It consists of an isolated system of scientific knowledge with an esoteric style, a vast system of technological "applications" with venal and faddish purposes and style, a confused populace, and no direct approach to glaring problems.

Perhaps it is necessary for most scientists to continue to regard themselves as unconcerned priests of the system of science, supported and exploited by various dictators and brigands; but if so, their detachment and their puzzle solving will continue to saddle society with life-complicating, indirect, obsessional, and essentially irrelevant and boring products. Naturally, human beings are adaptable and malleable; and they manage fairly well to go through the song and dance of our industrial and other technological systems. But this is undesirable. People can be socialized to scientific technology, but they are not at present adequate to it. (If the present arrangements continue, they will become less so — it is estimated that only 15 percent of the youth is academically talented enough to study the sciences; and many of the 15 percent are merely test-passers and symbol-manipulators, without feeling for the causes of things; they are not scientists.) Therefore people are conformist and superstitious. And much of the technology is worthless anyway! If *this* is what is meant by a scientific society, the world of "the new scientific revolution," as Sir Charles Snow calls it, I cannot see the advantage of it, either for mankind or for science.

Prudent Technology

1

Whether or not it draws on new scientific research, technology is a branch of moral philosophy, not of science. It aims at prudent goods for the commonweal, to provide efficient means for these goods. At present, however, "scientific technology" occupies a bastard position, in the universities, in funding, and in the public mind. It is half tied to the theoretical sciences and half treated as mere know-how for political and commercial purposes. It has no principles of its own. To remedy this — so Karl Jaspers in Europe and Robert Hutchins in America have urged — technology must have its proper place on the faculty as a learned profession important in modern society, along with medicine, law, the humanities, and natural philosophy, learning from them and having something to teach them. As a moral philosopher, a technician should be able to criticize the programs given him to implement. As a professional in a community of learned professionals, a technologist must have a different kind of training and develop a different character from what we see at present among technicians and engineers. He should know something of the social sciences, law, the fine arts, and medicine, as well as relevant natural sciences.

Prudence is foresight, caution, utility. Thus it is up to the technologists, not merely to regulatory agencies of the government, to provide for safety and to think about remote effects. This is what Ralph Nadar sometimes says and Rachel Carson used to ask. An important aspect of caution is flexibility, to avoid the pyramiding catastrophe that occurs when something goes wrong in interlocking technologies, as in urban power failures. Naturally, to take responsibility often requires standing up to the front office, urban politicians, and the Pentagon, and technologists must organize themselves in order to have power to do it.

Often it is pretty clear that a technology has been oversold, like the cars. Then even though the public, seduced by advertising, wants more, technologists must balk, as any professional does when his client wants what isn't good for him. We are now repeating the same self-defeating congestion with the planes and airports: the more the technology is oversold, the less immediate utility it provides, the greater the costs, and the more damaging the remote effects. As this becomes evident, it is time for technologists to confer with sociologists and economists and ask deeper questions. Is so much travel necessary? Are there ways to diminish it? Instead, the recent history of technology has consisted largely of desperate efforts to remedy situations caused by previous overapplications of technology.

Technologists should certainly have a say about simple waste, for even in an affluent society there are priorities — consider the supersonic transport, which has little to recommend it. But the Moon shot has presented the more usual dilemma of authentic conflicting claims. I myself believe that space exploration is a great human adventure, with immense aesthetic and moral benefits, whatever the scientific or utilitarian uses. It must be pursued. Yet the context and auspices have been such that perhaps it would be better if it were not pursued.

These days, perhaps the chief moral criterion of a philosophic technology is modesty, having a sense of the whole and not obtruding more than a particular function warrants. Immodesty is always a danger of free enterprise, but when the same disposition to market is financed by big corporations, technologists rush into production with solutions that swamp the environment. This applies to the packaging and garbage, freeways that bulldoze neighborhoods, high rises that destroy landscape, wiping out species for a passing fashion, strip mining, scrapping an expensive machine rather than making a minor repair, draining a watershed for irrigation because (as in southern California) the cultivable land has been covered by asphalt. Given this disposition, it is not surprising that we defoliate a forest in order to expose a guerrilla and spray tear gas from a helicopter on a crowded campus.

Since we are technologically overcommitted, a good general maxim in advanced countries at present is to innovate in order to simplify, but otherwise to innovate as sparingly as possible. Every advanced country is overtechnologized; past a certain point, the quality of life diminishes with new "improvements." Yet no country is rightly technologized, making efficient use of available techniques. There are ingenious devices for unimportant functions, stressful mazes for essential functions, and drastic dislocation when anything goes wrong, which happens with increasing frequency. To add to the complexity, the mass of people tend to become incompetent, and dependent on repairmen. Indeed, unrepairability except by experts has become a desideratum of industrial design.

When I speak of slowing down or cutting back, the issue is not whether research and making working models should be encouraged or not. They should be, in every direction, and given a blank check. The point is to resist the temptation to apply every new device without a second thought. But the big corporate organization of research and development makes prudence and modesty very difficult; it is necessary to get big contracts and rush into production in order to pay the salaries of the big team, and to keep the team from dispersing. Like bureaucracies, technological organizations are finally run to maintain themselves in being, as a team, but they are more dangerous because in capitalist countries they are in a competitive arena and must stir up business.

It used to be the classical socialist objection to capitalism that it curtailed innovation and production in order to make the most out of existing capital. This objection still holds, of course — a serious example is the foot-dragging about producing an electric or steam car which, according to Ford, will take thirty years, though models adequate for urban use are ready for production at present. But by and large, the present menace of free enterprise is proving to be the same as its past glory, its fantastic productivity, its technological explosion. And this is not the classic overproduction that creates a glut on the market; it is overproduction that burdens life and the environment.

I mean the maxim of simplification quite strictly, to simplify the *technical* system. I am unimpressed by the argument that what is technically more complicated is really economically or politically simpler, for example, by complicating the packaging we improve the supermarkets; by throwing away the machine rather than repairing it we give cheaper and faster service all around; or even, by expanding the economy with trivial innovations, we increase employment, allay discontent, save on welfare. Such ideas may be profitable for private companies or political parties, but for society they have created an accelerating rat race. The technical structure of the environment is too important to be a political or economic pawn; the effect on the quality of life is too disastrous. The hidden social costs are not calculated: the auto graveyards, the torn-up streets, the longer miles of commuting, the advertising, the inflation, etc. As I pointed out in *People or Personnel*, a country with a fourth of our per capita income, such as Ireland, is not less well off; in some respects it is much richer, in some respects a little poorer. If possible, it is better to solve political problems by political means. For instance, if teaching machines and audio-visual aids are indeed educative, well and good; but if school boards hope to use them just to save money on teachers, then they are not good at all — nor do they save money.

Of course, the goals of right technology must come to terms with other values of society. I am not a technocrat. But the advantage of raising technology to be a responsible learned profession with its own principles is that it can have a voice in the debate and argue for *its* proper contribution to the community. Consider the important case of modular sizes in building, or prefabrication of a unit bathroom: these conflict with the short-run interest of manufacturers and craft unions, yet to deny them is technically an abomination. The usual recourse is for a government agency to set standards; such agencies accommodate to interests that have a strong voice; and at present technologists have no voice.

The crucial need for technological simplification, however, is not in the advanced countries — which can afford their clutter and probably deserve it — but in underdeveloped countries which must rapidly innovate in order to diminish disease, drudgery, and starvation. They cannot afford to make mistakes. It is now widely conceded that the technological aid we have given to such areas according to our own high style — a style often demanded by the native ruling groups — has done more harm than good. Even when, frequently if not usually, aid has been benevolent, without strings attached — and not military, and not dumping — it has nevertheless disrupted ways of life, fomented tribal wars, accelerated urbanization, decreased the food supply, gone to waste for lack of skills to use it, developed a do-nothing elite.

By contrast, a group of international scientists called Intermediate Technology argue that what is needed is techniques that use only native labor, resources, traditional customs, and teachable know-how, with the simple aim of remedying drudgery, disease, and hunger, so that people can then develop further in their own style. This avoids cultural imperialism. Such intermediate techniques may be quite primitive, on a level unknown among us for a couple of centuries, and yet they may pose extremely subtle problems, requiring exquisite scientific research and political and human understanding, to devise a very simple technology. Here is a reported case (by E.F. Schumacher, which I trust I remember accurately). In Botswana, a very poor country, pasture was overgrazed, but the economy could be salvaged if the land was fenced. There was not local material for fencing, and imported fencing was prohibitively expensive. The solution was to find a formula and technique to make posts out of mud, and a pedagogic method to teach people how to do it.

In *The Two Cultures,* C.P. Snow berated the humanists for their irrelevance when two-thirds of mankind are starving and what is needed is science and technology. The humanities have perhaps been irrelevant; but unless technology is itself more humanistic and philosophical, it too is of no use. There is only one culture.

And, let me make a remark about amenity as a technical criterion. It is discouraging to see the concern about beautifying a highway and banning billboards, and about the cosmetic appearance of cars, when there is no regard for the ugliness of bumper-to-bumper traffic and the suffering of the drivers. Or the concern for preserving a historical landmark while the neighborhood is torn up and the city has no shape. Without moral philosophy, people have nothing but sentiments.

2

The complement to prudent technology is the ecological approach in science. To simplify the technical system and modestly pinpoint our artificial intervention in the environment is to make it possible for the environment to survive in its complexity, evolved for a billion years, whereas the overwhelming instant intervention of tightly interlocked and bulldozing technology has already disrupted many of the delicate sequences and balances. The calculable consequences are already frightening, but of course we don't know enough, and won't in the foreseeable future, to predict the remote effects of much of what we have done.

Cyberneticists come to the same cautious thinking. The use of computers has enabled us to carry out inept programs on the basis of willful analyses; but we have also become increasingly alert to the fact that things respond, systematically, continually, cumulatively; they cannot simply be manipulated or pushed around. Whether bacteria, weeds, bugs, the technologically unemployed, or unpleasant thoughts, we cannot simply eliminate and forget them; repressed, they return in new forms. A complicated system works most efficiently if its parts readjust themselves decentrally, with a minimum of central intervention or control, except in cases of breakdown. Usually there is an advantage in a central clearing house of information about the gross total situation, but technical decision and execution require more minute local information. The fantastically rehearsed Moon landing hung on a last-second correction on the spot. To make decisions in headquarters means to rely on information from the field that is cumulatively abstract and may be irrelevant, and to execute by chain-of-command is to use standards that cumulatively do not fit the abilities of real individuals in concrete situations. By and large it is better, given a sense of the whole picture, for those in the field to decide what to do and to do it. But with organisms too, this has long been the bias of psychosomatic medicine, the Wisdom of the Body, as Cannon called it. To cite a classic experiment of Ralph Hefferline of Columbia: A subject is wired to suffer an annoying regular buzz, which can be delayed and finally eliminated if he makes a precise but unlikely gesture, say, by twisting his ankle in a certain way; then it is found that he adjusts more quickly if he is *not* told the method and it is left to his spontaneous twitching than if he is told and tries deliberately to help himself — he adjusts better without conscious control, either the experimenter's or his own.

Technological modesty, fittingness, is not negative. It is the ecological wisdom of co-operating with Nature rather than trying to master her. (The personification of "Nature" is linguistic wisdom.) A well-known example is the long-run superiority of partial pest control in farming by using biological rather than chemical deterrents. The living defenders work harder, at the right moment, and with more pinpointed targets. But let me give another example because it is so lovely (I have forgotten the name of my informant): A tribe in Yucatan educates its children to identify and pull up all weeds in the region; then what is left is a garden of useful plants that have chosen to be there and that now thrive.

In the life sciences there are at present two opposite trends in methodology. The rule is still to increase experimental intervention; but there is also a considerable revival of old-fashioned naturalism, mainly watching and thinking, with very modest intervention. Thus, in medicine, there is new diagnostic machinery, new drugs, spectacular surgery; but there is also a new respect for family practice with a psychosomatic background, and a strong push, among young doctors and students, for a social-psychological and sociological approach, aimed at prevention and building up resistance. In psychology, the operant conditioners multiply and refine their machinery to give maximum control of the organism and the environment (I have not heard of any dramatic discoveries, but likely I don't understand); on the other hand, the most interesting psychology in recent years has certainly come from animal naturalists: studies of the pecking order, territoriality, learning to control aggression, language of the bees, overcrowding among rats, communication of dolphins.

On a fair judgment, both contrasting approaches give positive results. The logical scientific problem that arises is, What is there in the nature of things that makes a certain method, or even moral attitude, work well or poorly in a given case? This question is not much studied. Every scientist seems to know what *the* scientific method is.

"In the pure glow of molecular biology," says Barry Commoner, "studying the biology of sewage is a dull and distasteful exercise hardly worth the attention of a modern biologist. [But] the systems which are at risk in the environment are natural and because they are natural, complex. For this reason they are not readily approached by the atomistic methodology which is so characteristic of much of modern biological research. Any new basic knowledge which is expected to elucidate environmental biology, and guide our efforts to cope with the balance of nature, must be relevant to the natural biological systems which are the arena in which these problems exist."

Another contrast of style, extremely relevant at present, is that between Big Science and old-fashioned shoestring science. There is plenty of research, with corresponding technology, that can be done only by Big Science; yet much, and perhaps most, of science will always be shoestring science, for which it is absurd to use the fancy and expensive equipment that has gotten to be the fashion.

Consider urban medicine. The problem, given a shortage of doctors and facilities, is how to improve the level of mass health, the vital statistics, and yet to practise medicine which aims at the maximum possible health for each person. Perhaps the most efficient use of Big Science technology for the general health would be to have compulsory biennial checkups, as we inspect cars, for early diagnosis and to forestall chronic conditions and their accumulating costs. But up to now, Dr. Michael Halberstam cautions me, mass diagnosis has not paid off as much as hoped. For this an excellent machine would be a total diagnostic bus that would visit the neighborhoods — as we do chest X-rays. It could be designed by Bell Lab, for instance. On the other hand, for actual treatment and especially for convalescence, the evidence seems to be that small personalized hospitals are best. And to revive family practice, maybe the right idea is to offer a doctor a splendid suite in a public housing project. Here, big corporations might best keep out of it.

It is fantastically expensive to provide and run a hospital bed; yet very many of the beds (up to a third?) are occupied by cases, e.g. tonsillectomies, that could better be dealt with at home if conditions are good, or in tiny infirmaries on each street.

Our contemporary practice makes little sense. We have expensive technology stored in specialists' offices and big hospitals which is unavailable for mass use in the neighborhoods; yet every individual, even if he is quite rich, finds it almost impossible to get attention for himself as an individual whole organism in his setting. He is sent from specialist to specialist and exists as a bag of symptoms and a file of test scores.

In automating, there is an analogous dilemma of how to cope with masses of people and get economies of scale without losing the individual at great consequent human and economic cost. A question of immense importance for the immediate future is, Which functions should be automated or organized to use business machines, and which should not? This question also is not getting asked, and the present disposition is that the sky is the limit for extraction, refining, manufacturing, processing, packaging, transportation, clerical work, ticketing, transactions, information retrieval, recruitment, middle management, evaluation, diagnosis, instruction, and even research and invention. Whether the machines can do all these kinds of jobs and more is partly an empirical question, but it also partly depends on what is meant by doing a job. Very often, for example in college admissions, machines are acquired for putative economies (which do not eventuate), but the true reason is that an overgrown and over-centralized organization cannot be administered without them. The technology conceals the essential trouble, perhaps that there is no community of the faculty and that students are treated like things. The function is badly performed, and finally the system breaks down anyway. I doubt that enterprises in which interpersonal relations are very important are suited to much programming.

But worse, what can happen is that the real function of an enterprise is subtly altered to make it suitable for the mechanical system. (For example, "information retrieval" is taken as an adequate replacement for critical scholarship.) Incommensurable factors, individual differences, local context, the weighing of evidence, are quietly overlooked, though they may be of the essence. The system, with its subtly transformed purposes, seems to run very smoothly, it is productive, and it is more and more out of line with the nature of things and the real problems. Meantime the system is geared in with other enterprises of society, and its products are taken at face value. Thus, major public policy may depend on welfare or unemployment statistics which, as they are tabulated, are not about anything real. In such a case, the particular system may not break down; the whole society may explode.

I need hardly point out that American society is peculiarly liable to the corruption of inauthenticity. Busily producing phoney products, it lives by public relations, abstract ideals, front politics, show-business communications, mandarin credentials. It is preeminently overtechnologized. And computer technologists especially suffer the euphoria of being in a new and rapidly expanding field. It is so astonishing that a robot can do the job at all, or seem to do it, that it is easy to blink at the fact that he is doing it badly or isn't really doing quite the job.

3

The current political assumption is that scientists and inventors, and even social scientists, are value-neutral, but that their discoveries are "applied" by those who make decisions for the nation. Counter to this, I have been insinuating into the reader's mind a kind of Jeffersonian democracy or guild socialism (I am really an anarchist), namely, that scientists and inventors and other workmen are responsible for the uses of the work they do, and they ought to be competent to judge these uses and have a say in deciding them. They usually are competent. To give a poignant example, Ford assembly-line workers, according to Harvey Swados who worked with them, are accurately critical of the glut of cars, but they have no way to vent their dissatisfaction with their useless occupation except to leave nuts and bolts to rattle in the body.

My bias is also pluralistic. Instead of the few national goals of a few decision-makers, I think that there are many goods in many activities of life, and many professions and other interest groups each with its own criteria and goals, that must be taken into account. It is better not to organize too tightly, or there is unnecessary trouble. A society that distributes power widely is superficially conflictory but fundamentally stable.

Research and development ought to be widely decentralized, the national fund for them being distributed through thousands of centers of initiative and decision. This would not be chaotic. We seem to have forgotten that for four hundred years, Western science majestically progressed with no central direction whatever, yet with exquisite international co-ordination, little duplication, almost nothing getting lost, in constant communication despite slow facilities. The reason was simply that all scientists wanted to get on with the same enterprise of testing the boundaries of knowledge, and they relied on one another.

And it is noteworthy that something similar holds also in invention and innovation, even in recent decades when there has been such a concentration of funding and apparent concentration of opportunity. The majority of big advances have still come from independents, partnerships, and tiny companies (evidence published by the Senate Subcommittee on Antitrust and Monopoly, May 1965). To name a few, jet engines, xerography, automatic transmission, cellophane, air conditioning, quick freeze, antibiotics, and tranquilizers. Big technological teams must have disadvantages that outweigh their advantages — such as lack of single-mindedness, poor communications, awkward scheduling, not to speak of enormous overhead and offices full of idle people or people doing busywork. Naturally, big corporations have taken over the innovations, but the Senate evidence is that 90 percent of the government subsidy has gone for last-stage development for production, which they ought to have paid for out of their own pockets.

In the exploding technology, a remarkable phenomenon has been that enterprising young fellows split off from big firms, form small companies of their own, and succeed mightily. A recent study of such cases along Route 128 shows that the salient characteristic of the independents is that their fathers were independents!

We now have a theory that we have learned to learn, and that we can program technical progress, directed by a central planning board. But this doesn't make it so. The essence of the new still seems to be that nobody has thought of it before, and the ones who get ideas are those in direct contact with the work. *Too precise* a preconception of what is wanted discourages creativity more than it channels it; and bureaucratic memoranda from distant directors don't help. This is especially true when, as at present, so much of the preconception of what is wanted comes from desperate political anxiety in emergencies. Solutions that emerge from such an attitude rarely strike out on new paths, but rather repeat traditional thinking with new gimmicks; they tend to compound the problem. A priceless advantage of widespread decentralization is that it engages more minds, and more mind, instead of a few panicky (or greedy) corporate minds.

A homespun advantage of small groups, according to the Senate testimony, is that co-workers can talk to one another, without schedules, reports, clock-watching, and face-saving.

An important hope in decentralizing science is to develop knowledgeable citizens, and provide not only a bigger pool of scientists and inventors but also a public better able to protect itself and know how to judge the enormous budgets asked for. The safety of the environment is too important to be left to scientists, even ecologists. During the last decades of the nineteenth century and the first decade of the twentieth, the heyday of public faith in the beneficent religion of science and invention, say, from Pasteur and Huxley to Edison and the Wright brothers, philosophers of science had a vision of a "scientific way of life," one in which people would be objective, respectful of evidence, accurate, free of superstition and taboo, immune to irrational authority, experimental. All would be well, is the impression one gets from Thomas Huxley, if everybody knew the splendid ninth edition of the *Encyclopedia Britannica* with its articles by Darwin and Clerk Maxwell. Veblen put his faith in the modesty and matter-of-factness of Engineers to govern. Louis Sullivan and Frank Lloyd Wright spoke for an austere functionalism and respect for the nature of materials and industrial processes. Patrick Geddes thought that new technology would finally get us out of the horrors of the Industrial Revolution and produce good communities. John Dewey devised a system of education to rear pragmatic and experimental citizens who would be at home in the new technological world, rather than estranged from it. Now fifty years later, we are in the swamp of a scientific and technological environment, and there are more scientists alive, etc., etc. But the mention of the "scientific way of life" seems like black humor.

Many of those who have grown up since 1945 and have never seen any other state of science and technology, assume that rationalism itself is totally evil and dehumanizing. It is probably more significant than we like to think that they go in for astrology and the Book of Changes, as well as inducing psychedelic dreams by technological means. Jacques Ellul, a more philosophic critic than the hippies, tries to show that technology is necessarily overcontrolling, standardizing, and voraciously inclusive, so that there is no place for freedom. But I doubt that any of this is intrinsic to science and technology. The crude history has been, rather, that they have fallen, willingly, under the dominion of money and power. Like Christianity or communism, the scientific way of life has never been tried. And, as in the other two cases, we have gotten the horrors of abusing a good idea, *corruptio optimi pessima*.

A Causerie at the Military-Industrial

The National Security Industrial Association (NSIA) was founded in 1944 by James Forrestal, to maintain and enhance the beautiful wartime communication between the armament industries and the government. At present it comprises 400 members, including of course all the giant aircraft, electronics, motors, oil, and chemical corporations, but also many one would not expect: not only General Dynamics, General Motors, and General Telephone and Electronics, but General Foods and General Learning; not only Sperry Rand, RCA, and Lockheed, but Servco and Otis Elevators. It is a wealthy club. The military budget is $84 billion.

At the recent biennial symposium, held on October 18 and 19 in the State Department auditorium, the theme was "Research and Development in the 1970s." To my not unalloyed pleasure, I was invited to participate as one of the seventeen speakers and assigned the topic "Planning for the Socio-Economic Environment." Naturally I could make the usual speculations about why I was thus "co-opted." I doubt that they expected to pick my brains for any profitable ideas. But it is useful for feeders at the public trough to present an image of wide-ranging discussion. It is comfortable to be able to say, "You see? these far-outniks are impractical." And business meetings are dull and I am notoriously stimulating. But the letter of invitation from Henri Busignies of ITT, the chairman of the symposium committee, said only, "Your accomplishments throughout your distinguished career eminently qualify you to speak with authority on the subject."

What is an intellectual man to do in such a case? I agree with the Gandhian principle, always co-operate, within the limits of honor, truth, and justice. But how to co-operate with the military-industrial club! during the Vietnam war 1967! It was certainly not the time to reason about basic premises, as is my usual approach, so I decided simply to confront them and soberly tell them off.

Fortunately it was the week of the demonstration at the Pentagon, when there would be thousands of my friends in Washington. So I tipped them off and thirty students from Cornell and Harpur drove down early to picket the auditorium, with a good leaflet about the evil environment for youth produced by the military corporations. When they came, the white helmets sprang up, plus the cameras and reporters. In the face of this dangerous invasion, the State Department of the United States was put under security, the doors were bolted, and the industrialists [and I] were not allowed to exit — on the 23rd Street side. Inside, I spoke as follows:

R&D for the Socio-Economic Environment of the 1970s

I am astonished that at a conference on planning for the future, you have not invited a single speaker under the age of thirty, the group that is going to live in that future. I am pleased that some of the young people have come to pound on the door anyway, but it is too bad that they aren't allowed to come in.

This is a bad forum for this topic. Your program mentions the "emerging national goals" of urban development, continuing education, and improving the quality of man's environment. I would add another essential goal, reviving American democracy; and at least two indispensable international goals, to rescue the majority of mankind from deepening poverty, and to insure the survival of mankind as a species. These goals indeed require research and experimentation of the highest sophistication, but not by you. You people are unfitted by your commitments, your experience, your customary methods, your recruitment, and your moral disposition. You are the military industrial of the United States, the most dangerous body of men at the present in the world, for you not only implement our disastrous policies but are an overwhelming lobby for them, and you expand and rigidify the wrong use of brains, resources, and labor so that change becomes difficult. Most likely the trends you represent will be interrupted by a shambles of riots, alienation, ecological catastrophes, wars, and revolutions, so that current long-range planning, including this conference, is irrelevant. But if we ask what *are* the technological needs and what ought to be researched in this coming period, in the six areas I have mentioned, the best service that you people could perform is rather rapidly to phase yourselves out, passing on your relevant knowledge to people better qualified, or reorganizing yourselves with entirely different sponsors and commitments, so that you learn to think and feel in a different way. Since you are most of the R&D that there is, we cannot do without you as people, but we cannot do with you as you are.

In aiding technically underdeveloped regions, the need in the foreseeable future is for an intermediate technology, scientifically sophisticated but tailored to their local skills, tribal or other local social organization, plentiful labor force, and available raw materials. The aim is to help them out of starvation, disease, and drudgery without involving them in an international cash nexus of an entirely different order of magnitude. Let them take off at their own pace and in their own style. For models of appropriate technical analyses, I recommend you to E.F. Schumacher, of the British Coal Board, and his associates. Instead, you people — and your counterparts in Europe and Russia — have been imposing your technology, seducing native elites mostly corrupted by Western education, arming them, indeed often using them as a dumping ground for obsolete weapons. As Dr. Busignies pointed out yesterday, your aim must be, while maintaining leadership, to allow very little technical gap, in order to do business. Thus, you have involved these people in a wildly inflationary economy, have driven them into instant urbanization, and increased the amount of disease and destitution. You have disrupted ancient social patterns, debauched their cultures, fomented tribal and other wars, and in Vietnam yourselves engaged in genocide. You have systematically entangled them in Great Power struggles. It is not in your interest, and you do not have the minds or the methods, to take these peoples seriously as people.

The survival of the human species, at least in a civilized State, demands radical disarmament, and there are several feasible political means to achieve this if we willed it. By the same token, we must drastically de-energize the archaic system of Nation-States, e.g. by internationalizing space exploration, expanding operations like the international Geophysical Year, de-nationalizing Peace Corps and aid programs, opening scientific information and travel. Instead, you — and your counterparts in Europe, Russia, and China — have rigidified and aggrandized the States with a Maginot-line kind of policy called Deterrence, which has continually escalated rather than stabilized. As Jerome Wiesner has demonstrated, past a certain point your operations have increased insecurity rather than diminished it. But this has been to your interest. Even in the present condition of national rivalry, it has been estimated, by Marc Raskin who sat in on the National Security Council, that the real needs of our defence should cost less than a fourth of the budget you have pork-barrelled. You have tried, unsuccessfully, to saddle us with the scientifically ludicrous Civil Defense program. You have sabotaged the technology of inspection for disarmament. Now you are saddling us with the anti-missile missiles and the multi-warhead missiles (MIRV). You have corrupted the human adventure of space with programs for armed platforms in orbit. Although we are the most heavily armed and the most naturally protected of the Great Powers, you have seen to it that we spend a vastly greater amount and perhaps a higher proportion of our wealth on armaments than any other nation.

This brings me to your effect on the climate of the economy. The wealth of a nation is to provide useful goods and services, with an emphasis first on necessities and broad-spread comforts, simply as a decent background for un-economic life and culture; an indefinitely expanding economy is a rat-race. There ought to be an even spread regionally, and no group must be allowed to fall outside of society. At present, thanks to the scientific ingenuity and hard work of previous generations, we could in America allow a modest livelihood to everyone as a constitutional right. And on the other hand, as the young have been saying by their style and actions, there is an imperative need to simplify the standard of living, since the affluent standard has become frivolous, tawdry, and distracting from life itself. But you people have distorted the structure of a rational economy. Since 1945, half of new investment has gone into your products, not subject to the market nor even to Congressional check. This year, 86 percent of money for research is for arms and rockets. You push through the colossally useless Super-Sonic Transport. At least 20 percent of the economy is directly dependent on your enterprises. The profits and salaries of these enterprises are not normally distributed but go heavily to certain groups while others are excluded to the point of being out-caste. Your system is a major factor in producing the riots in Newark. [*At this remark there were indignant protests.*]

Some regions of the country are heavily favored — especially Pasadena and Dallas — and others disadvantaged. Public goods have been neglected. A disproportionate share of brains has been drained from more useful invention and development. And worst of all, you have enthusiastically supported an essentially mercantilist economics that measures economic health in terms of abstract Gross National Product and rate of growth, instead of concrete human well-being. Both domestically and internationally, you have been the bellwether of meaningless expansion, and this has sharpened poverty in our own slums and rural regions and for the majority of mankind. It has been argued that military expenditure, precisely because it is isolated and wasteful, is a stabilizer of an economy, providing employment and investment opportunities when necessary; but your unbridled expansion has been the chief factor of social instability.

Dramatically intervening in education, you have again disrupted the normal structure. Great universities have come to be financed largely for your programs. Faculties have become unbalanced; your kind of people do not fit into the community of scholars. The wandering dialogue of science with the unknown is straitjacketed for petty military projects. You speak increasingly of the need for personal creativity, but this is not to listen to the Creator Spirit for ideas, but to harness it to your ideas. This is blasphemous. There has been secrecy, which is intolerable to true academics and scientists. The political, and morally dubious co-opting of science, engineering, and social science has disgusted and alienated many of the best students. Further, you have warped the method of education, beginning with the primary grades. Your need for narrowly expert personnel has led to processing the young to be test-passers, with a gross exaggeration of credits and grading. You have used the wealth of the public and parents to train apprentices for yourselves. Your electronics companies have gone into the "education industries" and tried to palm off teaching machines, audio-visual aids, and programmed lessons in excess of the evidence for their utility. But the educational requirements of our society in the foreseeable future demand a very different spirit and method. Rather than processing the young, the problem is how to help the young grow up free and inventive in a highly scientific and socially complicated world. We do not need professional personnel so much as autonomous professionals who can criticize the programs handed to them and be ethically responsible. Do you encourage criticism of your programs by either the subsidized professors or the students? [*At this, Mr Charles Herzfeld, the chairman of the meeting, shouted, "Yes!" and there was loud applause for the interruption, yet I doubt that there is much such encouragement.*] We need fewer lessons and tests, and there ought to be much less necessity and prestige attached to mandarin requirements.

Let us turn to urbanism. *Prima facie*, there are parts of urban planning — construction, depollution, the logistics of transportation — where your talents ought to be peculiarly useful. Unfortunately, it is your companies who have oversold the planes and the cars, polluted the air and water, and balked at even trivial remedies, so that I do not see how you can be morally trusted with the job. The chief present and future problems in this field, however, are of a different kind. They are two. The long-range problem is to diminish the urbanization and suburban sprawl altogether, for they are economically unviable and socially harmful. For this, the most direct means, and the one I favor, is to cut down rural emigration and encourage rural return, by means of rural reconstruction and regional cultural development. The aim should be a 20 percent rural ration instead of the present 5 percent. This is an aspect of using high technology for simplification, increasing real goods but probably diminishing the Gross National Product measured in cash. Such a program is not for you. Your thinking is never to simplify and retrench, but always to devise new equipment to alleviate the mess that you have helped to make with your previous equipment.

Secondly, the immediately urgent urban problem is how to diminish powerlessness, anomie, alienation, and mental disease. For this the best strategy is to decentralize urban administration, in policing, schooling, social welfare, neighborhood renewal, and in real-estate and business ownership. Such community development often requires heightening conflict and risking technical inefficiency for intangible gains of initiative and solidarity. This also is obviously not your style. You want to concentrate capital and power. Your systems analyses of social problems always tend toward standardization, centralization, and bureaucratic control, although these are not necessary in the method. You do not like to feed your computers indefinite factors and unknown parameters where spirit, spite, enthusiasm, revenge, invention, etc., will make the difference. To be frank, your programs are usually grounded in puerile theories of social psychology, political science, and moral philosophy. There is a great need for research and trying out in this field, but the likely cast of characters might be small farmers, Negro matriarchs, political activists, long-haired students, and assorted sages. Not you. Let's face it. You are essentially producers of exquisite hardware and good at the logistics of moving objects around, but mostly with the crude aim of destroying things rather than reconstructing or creating anything, which is a harder task. Yet you boldly enter into fields like penology, pedagogy, hospital management, domestic architecture, and planning the next decade — wherever there is a likely budget.

I will use the last heading, improving the quality of man's environment, as a catch-all for some general remarks. In a society that is cluttered, overcentralized, and overadministered, we should aim at simplification, decentralization, and decontrol. These require highly sophisticated research to determine where, how, and how much. Further, for the first time in history, the scale of the artificial and technological has dwarfed the natural landscape. In prudence, we must begin to think of a principled limitation on artifice and to cut back on some of our present gigantic impositions, if only to insure that we do not commit some terrible ecological blunder. But as Dr. Smelt of Lockheed explained to us yesterday, it is the genius of American technology to go very rapidly from R&D to application: in this context, he said, prudence is not a virtue. A particular case is automation: which human functions should be computerized or automated, which should not? This question — it is both an analytic and an empirical one — ought to be critical in the next decade, but I would not trust IBM salesmen to solve it. Another problem is how man can feel free and at home within the technological environment itself. For instance, comprehending a machine and being able to repair it is one thing; being a mere user and in bondage to service systems is another. Also, to feel free, a man must have a rather strong say in the close environment that he must deal with. But these requirements of a technology are not taken into account by you. Despite Dr. Smelt, technology *is* a branch of moral philosophy, subordinate to criteria like prudence, modesty, safety, amenity, flexibility, cheapness, easy comprehension, repairability, and so forth. If such moral criteria became paramount in the work of technologists, the quality of the environment would be more livable.

Still a further problem is how to raise the scientific and technical culture of the whole people, and here your imperialistic grab of the R&D money and of the system of education has done immeasurable damage. You have seen to it that the lion's share has gone to your few giant firms and a few giant universities, although in fact very many, perhaps more than half of, important innovations still come from independents and tiny firms. I was pleased that Dr. Dessauer of Xerox pointed this out this morning. If the money were distributed more widely, there would probably be more discovery and invention, and what is more important, there would be a larger pool of scientific and competent people. You make a fanfare about the spin-off of a few socially useful items, but your whole enterprise is notoriously wasteful — for instance, five billions go down the drain when after a couple of years you change the design of a submarine, sorry about that. When you talk about spin-off, you people remind me of the TV networks who, after twenty years of nothing, boast that they did broadcast the McCarthy hearings and the Kennedy funeral. [*This remark led to free and friendly laughter; I do not know whether at the other industry or at their own hoax.*] Finally, concentrating the grants, you narrow the field of discovery and innovation, creating an illusion of technological determinism, as if we *had* to develop in a certain style. But if we had put our brains and money into electric cars, we would now have electric cars; if we had concentrated on intensive agriculture, we would now find that this is the most efficient, and so forth. And in grabbing the funds, you are not even honest; 90 percent of the R&D money goes in fact to shaping up for production, which as entrepreneurs you should pay out of your own pockets.

No doubt some of these remarks have been unfair and ignorant. [*Frantic applause.*] By and large they are undeniable, and I have not been picking nits.

These remarks have certainly been harsh and moralistic. We are none of us saints, and ordinarily I would be ashamed to use such a tone. But you are the manufacturers of napalm, fragmentation bombs, the planes that destroy rice. Your weapons have killed hundreds of thousands in Vietnam and you will kill other hundreds of thousands in other Vietnams. I am sure that most of you would concede that much of what you do is ugly and harmful, at home and abroad. But you would say that it is necessary for the American way of life, at home and abroad, and therefore you cannot do otherwise. Since we believe, however, that that way of life itself is unnecessary, ugly, and un-American [*Shouts of "Who are we?"*] — we are I and those people outside — we cannot condone your present operations; they should be wiped off the slate.

Most of the 300 in the audience did not applaud these remarks, but there was quite strong applause from a couple of dozen. Afterward these sought me out singly and explained, "Thanks for having the courage" or more significantly, "Those kids outside are right. My son is doing the same thing in Boston — Ohio State — etc."

The chairman of the session, Charles Herzfeld of ITT, felt obliged to exclaim, "The remark about our committing genocide in Vietnam is obscene. He does not say what is really intolerable there, the Viet Cong single out college graduates for extermination."!!

More poignantly, the director of the symposium, a courteous and intelligent man, apologized to the gathering for having exposed them to me, which must have been a wrench for him to say. He had of course seen my text beforehand.

We went out by the exit onto the other avenue, and I was able to rejoin the more amiable company of the young people, who were now sitting with their backs pressed against the auditorium doors, still among the white helmets. I answered their questions about the proceedings and we dispersed.

Modern Culture in Crisis

Format and Colloquial Speech

Format and Empty Speech

By "format" I mean imposing on the literary process a style that is extrinsic to it. The dictionary tells the history very well:

> **Format.** — n. **1.** the shape and size of a book as determined by the number of times the original sheet has been folded to form the leaves. **2.** the general physical appearance of a book, magazine, or newspaper, such as the type face, binding, quality of paper, margins, etc. **3.** the organization, plan, style or type of something: *They tailored their script to a half-hour format. The format of the show allowed for topical controversial gags.* **4.** *Computer Technol.* the organization or disposition of symbols on a magnetic tape, punch card, or the like, in accordance with the input requirements of a computer, card-sort machine, etc. — *v.t.* **5.** *Computer Technol.* to adapt (the organization of disposition of coded information) on a magnetic tape, punch card, or the like, to conform to the input requirements of a computer, card-sort machine, etc.

Format has no literary power, and finally it destroys literary power. It is especially disastrous to the common standard style, because it co-opts it and takes the heart out of it.

Thus, an editor chops a sentence here and there, and also my last paragraph, because 3,000 words is the right length for the format of his magazine. An assistant editor rewrites me just to be busy and earn his keep. A daily column must appear though the columnist has nothing to say that day. An editor of *Harper's* asks me to simplify an argument because, he says, the readers of the magazine cannot digest more than two thoughts to one article. At another magazine they rewrite in *Time*-style. A young fellow writes his thesis in the style of professional competence of his department. Obviously, the effect of format is worse if the writer must adapt himself and write, rather than just having his writing mashed. Since writing is inherently spontaneous and original, a writer cannot produce what is not his own without a broken spirit.

American television is especially productive of format. The networks are a big investment of capital, so broadcasting time is cut up for sale to the fraction of a minute, and programs are tailored to the strips. A mass medium aims at a big audience, so the programs must be sensational enough to attract many and bland enough not to offend any. In the peculiar system of semi-monopolies, where a few baronial firms compete in such a way as to keep one another in business, if one network hits on a new show or newscast, the others at once program a close imitation. Legally the channels are public property, so the licensed stations must be politically impartial and present all sides of controversial issues; the most convenient way of handling this is to present no controversial issue. But there is another rule that a certain fraction of time must be devoted to public service, including political controversy; and a way of economically handling this is to have a panel of wildly divergent points of view debating an issue for the required twenty-six minutes. This sometimes produces heat, never light, usually nothing. It is a format. What is glaring in the whole enterprise is the almost entire lack of will to *say* anything, rather than just provide a frame for the ads.

Format is not like censorship that tries to obliterate speech, and so sometimes empowers it by making it important. And it is not like propaganda that simply tells lies. Rather, authority imposes format on speech because it need speech, but not autonomous speech. Format is speech colonized, broken-spirited. It is a use of speech as social cement, but it is not like the small talk of acquaintances of the street in their spontaneous style; it is a collective style for a mass. So in appearance it is often indistinguishable from the current literary standard. But in actual use it is evident from the first sentence that it does not tell anything.

Of course, empty style is nothing new. Diplomats, administrators of all kinds, and other public relators, who have to make remarks about what is none of our business, have always used a style to drain meaning from what they say. It can be a fine art — cf. Proust on the virtuosity of Norpois. But modern society has unique resources of technology and social organization to separate speech from living speakers. I do not think that any previous era has ever worked up a universal pedagogy and a general Theory of Communications to sidetrack human speech as such. In Newspeak, George Orwell was shooting at not quite the right target. He was thinking of *control* of speech by the lies and propaganda of crude totalitarian regimes; but I doubt that this is humanly feasible. (In the end the State is bound together by simple fright, not brainwashing.) The government of a complicated modern society cannot lie *much*. But by format, even without trying, it can kill feeling, memory, learning, observation, imagination, logic, grammar, or any other faculty of free writing.

The schools try hard to teach the empty style. There is frantic anxiety about the schools' failing to teach children to read and write; there have been riots on the street about it; the President of the United States has called the matter our top priority. But so far as I know, none of those who are frantic — parents rich and poor, nor the President — have pointed out that reading and writing spring from speaking, our human way of being in the world; that they are not tools but arts, and their content is imagination and truth. Occasionally a sensitive teacher pipes up that children might learn reading and writing if these were interesting and sprang from what the children wanted to know and had to say, if they were relevant to their personal lives and had some practical function. But mostly the remedies that are proposed are mechanical or administrative; there are debates between sounding out and word recognition and quarrels about who controls the schools.

The reason for anxiety is simply that if children do not learn the tools of reading and writing, they cannot advance through school, and if they don't get school diplomas, they won't get well-paying jobs in a mandarin society. Literacy is incidental, a kind of catalyst that drops out of the equation. To pass the tests really requires just the same verbal skills — nothing much else has been learned — and there is no correlation between having the diplomas and competence in any job or profession. School style exists for the schools. So some of us have suggested that if it and they did not exist, that too would be very well. (Rather, change the rules for licensing and hiring.)

In most urban and suburban communities, most children will pick up the printed code anyway, school or no school. (In ghetto and depressed rural communities, they might not.) It is likely that school-teaching destroys more genuine literacy than it produces. But it is hard to know if most people think that reading and writing have any value anyway, either in themselves or for their use, except that they are indispensable in how we go about things. Contrast the common respect for mathematics, which are taken to be *about* something and are powerful, productive, magical; yet there is no panic if people are mathematically illiterate.

Thus, during the long years of compulsory schooling, reading and writing are a kind of format, an imposed style with no intrinsic relation to good speech. And this must be characteristic of any mandarin society, even when, as in medieval China, the style of literacy

happens to be the standard literary classics. With us, as school reading and writing cease to have literary meaning, university study of
Literature ceases to be about human speech, speech in its great examples. (It is a nice question, what university English studies *are*
about.) And as fewer people read authentically, on-going literature
may well become one of the minor arts, for connoisseurs, like rose
gardening or weaving.

Naturally, when the imposing authority takes itself seriously as
right and good, as in the Soviet Union, mandarin literacy is affirmed
as excellent, the vehicle of all social and scientific progress, as well as
the way to get ahead. Consider the following of the Russian
pedagogue L.S. Vygotsky, which seems to say that it is necessary to
destroy natural style:

> In learning to write, the child must disengage himself
> from the sensory aspect of speech and replace words by
> images of words. It is the abstract quality of language
> that is the main stumbling block to learning to write,
> not the underdevelopment of small muscles .... Our
> studies show that a child has little motivation to learn
> writing when we begin to teach it. Written language
> demands conscious work .... The concrete totality of
> traits [must be] destroyed through abstraction; then
> the possibility of unifying traits on a different basis
> opens up. Only the mastery of abstraction enables the
> child to progress to the formation of genuine concepts.

This odd view of writing and teaching writing is the precise opposite
of a literary approach, e.g. Sylvia Ashton-Warner's, which tries to get
writing from the child's spontaneous native speech, with all its sen-
suality and animal need.

The use of words is already detachment from, control of, the
stream of experience; to go the further step of Vygotsky is to control
the speaker. It is a socially-induced aphasia.

In any case, the literature that is the fruit of this method of teaching writing is also taken very seriously, as the mandarin literacy is. It
is carefully regulated in style, and it is reproduced in millions of
copies. In Russia, writing that is more literary in a traditional sense
does *not* become a minor art for connoisseurs, but is circulated in
manuscript for a band of criminal conspirators.

The Resistance of Colloquial Speech

The forces of format, "to conform to the input requirements" of a social or technical system, can quickly debase public language and the standard literary style. Strong writers are less affected; society does not know how to produce them and it does not even know how to inhibit them, except by violence.

But colloquial speech is quite impervious to corruption by format. It has an irrepressible vitality to defy, ridicule, or appropriate. It gobbles up format like everything else. There are too many immediate occasions, face-to-face meetings, eye-witnessings, common sense problems, for common speech to be regimented. People who can talk can be oppressed but not brainwashed. Modern cities are depressing and unhealthy, but the people are not mechanical.

Once out of bounds, children do not talk like school. In America, adults talk like school less than they used, because (I like to think) the school style has so little literary value that it's not worth adopting. Children imitate the TV, but soon do it sarcastically. Adults imitate the ads less than they used because there has been overexposure. The young are in revolt against the ads, so the ads lamely have to imitate the young. In totalitarian countries, even after a generation of benevolent instruction by all the schools, mass media, labor unions, etc., young Czechs and Poles, who have never known any other dispensation, have not learned what is good for them; apparently, they have their ideas by conversation with one another. American voters almost never repeat the sentences of politicians; rather, they tell you their own lay political theories and that they can't stand the personalities of certain candidates.

By and large, adolescents are the most susceptible to empty format. They often seem to take TV images for reality. In serious moments they often sound like a textbook in social psychology: A girl has a "meaningful relationship with her boyfriend," people are "consumed by negative feelings toward someone in the group" — I am quoting from *WIN*, the best of the youth movement magazines. And it is amazing how the language of underground newspapers, identical by dozens, is actually spoken by teenagers. But this language is less format that it seems. It is filling the vacuum of adolescent speechlessness. The stereotypes serve as glue for ganging together, and the ganging is real though the language is spurious. A rock festival is usually a commercial hoax, but the pilgrimage to it is not.

More poignant is the speech of a highly articulate, but unread, militant *chicana* housewife, who declaims social worker Newspeak during a demonstration because she has no other public words. But her passion gives it life, if not sense.

The deep pathos of colloquial speech — with its indestructible good sense, eye-witnessing, communal vitality, and crotchetiness (including much private error and deep-rooted tribal prejudice) — is that in highly organized societies its field of operation is strictly limited. We can speak good colloquial where we have freedom to initiate and decide. When our actions are predetermined by institutional and political frameworks that are imposed on us, we necessarily become anxious, unconfident of ourselves, and we fall into institutional and ideological format and its mesmerized thoughts. Thus in our societies there is continually spoken a dual language: Intimately, people talk sense — about politics, the commodities, the schools, the police, etc. — yet they also talk format, and act on it. In totalitarian societies, where a strong effort is made to reform colloquial speech to official format, the effort cannot succeed, but people do begin to whisper and fall silent; finally, only a few brave writers, who have a very special obligation to honourable speech, continue to talk like human beings.

In America, our colloquial is certainly not much improved by respectable literary models. It is a loss, because people would express themselves more clearly and forcefully if they could express themselves a little more literarily yet without sounding like a book, and they could thereby also extend the boundaries of their human expression into more public domains — at least somewhat (there would be conflict). A few of us writers do the best we can. Some of the young pick up our language — and turn it into *their* format!

There is a kind of style to our speech. It is the style of urban confusion: a Yiddish that chews and can assimilate the ads, the sociological jargon, the political double-talk, the canned entertainment.

The Limits of Local Liberty

It is now a common fear that the cities are ungovernable, or, in other words, that this nation of cities is ungovernable. Certainly a major underlying cause of the trouble is our military imperialism, with its grotesque priorities, as part of the power structure of the world misdirecting our financial resources. But I think there are two chief problems specific to the cities themselves. (1) There are not enough *citizens* — people who feel that the city is theirs and care for it. (2) Urban areas may now be both too extensive and too dense to be technically and fiscally workable.

Gross results of the lack of citizenship are the flight to the suburbs and the insularity of the well-to-do, and, on the other hand, the anomie, vandalism and riots of the poor, especially the young. The lack of technical viability of urban areas shows up, after a certain extent and density, in the sudden disproportionate rise in costs for city services and the increase of congestion, pollution, noise and social complexity beyond tolerable levels.

These two kinds of trouble aggravate each other. The flight of the middle class diminishes the tax base as well as the number of those who have the levers of influence to make improvements. The anomie of the poor increases the costs for policing, welfare, remedial schooling, etc. Conversely, deteriorating environments and rising costs drive away those who can afford to leave, and further alienate and madden those who must stay.

The political remedy that has been, correctly, proposed for the lack of citizens is traditional Jeffersonianism: to "give," or gracefully surrender, power to the people themselves in their neighborhoods to initiate, decide and execute the affairs that concern them closely. (Let me recommend a fine restatement of the Jeffersonian idea in present urban conditions, *Neighborhood Government* by Milton Kotler.) The affairs that concern people closely are (1) local functions, like policing, housing, schooling, welfare, neighborhood services — primarily, the areas in which family life occurs; and (2) the jobs and professions in which people are engaged. There are also, of course, close national concerns, like the draft and the April 15 federal taxes, but it is local life and occupations that make up the city. And in these matters, according to the Jeffersonian theory, people know the score and are competent to govern themselves directly, or could soon become so with practice. In our system citizenship springs from liberty and so must start from local and occupational liberty.

The drive for local-territorial liberty is the strongest revolutionary political movement of our times, both in this country and internationally. It is a protest against galloping centralization, oligarchic representative government, political and cultural imperialism, bureaucracy, administration, establishment, illegitimate authority. It has used the slogans of decentralization, participatory democracy, community control, community development, black power, student power, national liberation, neighborhood city halls, maximum feasible participation. In all these, the essence is self-determination of people's own place.

By and large, however, in both theory and practice, the liberty of occupation and function has been neglected. There has been little mention of workers' management and the kind of education and apprenticeship of the young that are necessary for this. Professional and guild autonomy has been readily sacrificed for narrow economic advantage. Producers' and consumers' co-operatives are in eclipse. Few talk about rural reconstruction and rural culture. All over the world there are brave movements of national liberation, but these movements have been very unimpressive, in my opinion, in providing alternatives to the centralizing style in economic and industrial planning; technology, social engineering, mandarinism, regional planning and excessive urbanization.

Perhaps the neglect of occupational liberty has been inevitable. The movement for self-determination has been led by the colonized and alienated, the blacks, Spanish-speaking Americans and the young. (The groups that have been occupationally hurt, like the small farmers and the technologically unemployed whites in non-urban areas, seem to have been simply demoralized by the forces against them.) Stripped of economic power and even civil rights, and living in a culture of poverty, or a youth subculture, which is very similar, the alienated have no resources other than their mere political existence — protest, demonstrations, riots, physical fighting. On the other hand, professionals, small businessmen, industrial workers and middle-class citizens, who have other resources with which to assert power, have too much of a stake in money and status in the affluent system to mobilize for their fundamental liberties. (Movements like Wallace's are sentimental in regard to liberty, but repressive in regard to institutional structure.)

Led by the out-caste and the young, political action has consisted mainly of physical activism to attain power — and this process is also conceived as the source of political goals: the organization of demonstrations and confrontations leads to a structure of power that will then discover its uses. (There has been little functional direct action of the genre of Danilo Dolci, e.g., putting the unemployed to work on something that is socially needed but is not being done, and then demanding recognition and pay.) The activist theory, whether that of Saul Alinsky, black power militants or youthful organizers in universities and poor neighborhoods, stresses conflict and solidarity rather than program, utility or final satisfaction. The "issues" are whatever is convenient to radicalize people and to win. According to this theory, when people control the neighborhood or campus or the budget for schools and welfare, they will know what to do for their further advantage. I think this is probably true for policing, welfare, city services, parietal rules, improvement of housing and perhaps small business. At the very least it is a way of getting rid of intolerable abuses that prevent any functioning at all.

But I doubt that this kind of activism and power provides a sufficient basis for many other functions. For instance, primary education will not be greatly better unless the community itself surrenders power to the children and teachers in individual schools, but local neighborhoods are as unlikely to do this as central administrators. Student power in high schools and colleges is, in my opinion, irrelevant (except on extracurricular issues) because most of the "students" are not *bona fide*: they ought not to be in academic institutions; their proper enemy is the system of credentials (the unrealistic practices of hiring and licensing) and the draft that oppress them. The relevant model of the past — labor union activism — led to important gains, but not to workers' management.

Solutions to the problems of traffic, the glut of garbage, pollution, density, renewal, zoning, and the use of technology are crucial to make cities livable, but they require a different kind of professional thought and political action than activism. We cannot finally have good and free cities unless the out-caste groups, the professionals, the middle class and the industrial workers all have more liberty and begin to co-operate with each other. I don't know how to bring this about, but I'm sure the truculence and disdain of the New Left do not help.

Indeed, the chief obstacles in the way of radical decentralization and local liberty are not those that are always mentioned: the size of populations, the complexity of society and technology, putative economies of scale, the national economy. In my opinion, free citizens could cope with such problems by subdividing administration, simplifying where complexity has too many disadvantages, federating where that is worthwhile, and controlling necessary bureaucracies from below. And in many of the functions we are concerned with, enormous gains can be made in efficiency and reducing cost just by operating on a smaller scale. (I have tried to show this in *People or Personnel*.)

Rather, the difficulties are as follows: First, many of the young activists who are spearheading the movement for local power are so alienated in spirit that they are not really interested in program, function and final satisfaction. They seem to be more interested in seizing power, or at least in creating disruption, than in running their own lives in livable neighborhoods. The offspring of black immigrants from rural regions have endured a terribly uprooted adolescence in ugly ghettos, but why is it that many of the young white radicals from middle-class suburbs also seem unable to believe in such things as family, autonomous professions, honest business, useful jobs and civic responsibility? A good deal of the activism for power, liberation and democracy looks like a compound of resentment, one-upping and spiritual striving for meaning in a meaningless world rather than a struggle for the political freedom to function. But perhaps I just don't dig.

Secondly, the neglect of liberation of jobs and professions makes local liberty untenable. Centralized corporations today displace families at will, those of both retrained workingmen and junior executives from middle-class neighborhoods. The constant mobility that results is fatal to neighborhood government. On the other hand, if poor people were to politically entrench themselves on their turf, their neighborhoods could become mere enclaves, like Indian reservations, well or badly funded, but not free because they are not important.

The remedy for the other chief trouble of our cities — their unworkability because of sheer size and density — is obvious: some dispersal of the population. This issue is at present much less politically alive than neighborhood government; it will seem important only when a series of major technical catastrophes and fiscal bankruptcies have occurred. The thinking is still overwhelmingly in the other direction. All official planning is founded on horrendously increased estimates of urban population in the 1980s and 1990s. The planners extrapolate from recent and continuing trends as if these were laws of nature rather than patently the result of bad policy. For example, in the past thirty-five years, because of technological "improvements" that were profitable to a few corporations but entirely disregarded social costs, 1,100,000 blacks and 800,000 Puerto Ricans came to New York because they could not make a living where they were.

And this excessive urbanization is worldwide. It occurs most of all in the poor countries that desperately cannot afford to lose their rural population and food supply. (In the United States, indeed, the flight to the city has finally slowed down. A 5-percent rural population seems to be the minimum. We shall now see, as has been predicted, the chain grocers and their plantations milk the consumers without fear of reviving competition from small producers. Quality has already sharply deteriorated.)

I speak of "some dispersal" because even a modest thrust in this direction, especially combined with "some" rural reconstruction, would have great value for our overburdened cities. To begin with, the difference between tolerable and intolerable crowding in many city functions is often a matter of only a few percentage points, for instance in traffic, mass transit, hospital beds, class size in schools, availability of empty housing, drain on water and power, waiting in line for services. And to repeat, it is only after a certain point that it becomes disproportionately costly to add facilities to ease the situation. With many of our gravest problems, instead of looking for global panaceas, we would do better to rely on solutions consisting of 3 percent of this, 6 percent of that, and 2 percent of the other. A small percentage of dispersal would often be a great help.

More important, the use of the countryside to help solve urban problems gives a mind-stretching opportunity to poor people whose life in the city now provides no significant alternatives. There is strong evidence that many black and Spanish-speaking immigrants wish they had not come to the northern cities — a thousand Puerto Ricans a week leave New York to try again back home. But of course the children of these immigrants have no such psychological alternative. The majority of today's slum children reach the age of thirteen without having ventured outside their few square blocks.

Dispersal can be physically accomplished by building New Towns. This is the thinking of the planners, and a couple have actually been built. But I would argue for rural reconstruction as another important alternative, for the following traditional reasons. A livable city is the city of its region. City and country use each other precisely because of their differences. At present, while the cities swell and fester, beautiful rural regions are being depopulated. If, however, it were made financially possible thousands now on city welfare would choose to live in the country and get more for their money, perhaps also doing some subsistence farming. (This was, of course, tried during the Great Depression.) The country could provide a better life for many of the lonely aged, and for most of the harmless "insane" who are really just incompetent to cope with urban complexity. City children would profit immensely by spending a year or so in under-populated country schools, living with farmers. The old-fashioned vacation on the farm, instead of at the "resort," could be revived. In such ways, the city could spend its money to better advantage for it-self, and the country get needed cash as well as rejoin the mainstream of social utility. I think this concept of city-country interchange is a better basis for rural reconstruction than other aesthetic and philosophical motives that withdraw from the urban mainstream.

Instead of being symbiotic, present urbanization is destructive of city and country both. The in-growing urban area becomes socially and physically too complex and the costs mount. The countryside is stripped of purpose and people. The city invades the country with city-controlled resorts, superhighways, colleges, supermarkets and inflationary prices. Instead of profiting by providing useful services in its own style and with its own management, the country is further impoverished and colonized. Instead of diversity, simplicity and do-it-yourself, we get uniformity, complexity and staggering expense.

Racism, Spite, Guilt and Non-Violence

White Racism

The premise of the Kerner report on civil disorders is, "Race prejudice has shaped our history decisively .... White racism is essentially responsible for the explosive mixture which has been accumulating in our cities since the end of World War II." Both parts of this are not true. Since the end of World War II it was a rapacious policy of rural enclosure and, in Puerto Rico, a rapacious mercantilism that drove unprepared colored peoples north in unassimilable quantities, whether their reception would be racist or not; and add the whites disemployed out of Appalachia. To account for the explosive mixture, one does not need fancy new concepts like white racism; the old story of criminal neglect of social costs for private gain is more to the point. Further, historically, with notable exceptions, the northern whites have not been racially prejudiced — though they have been something else, perhaps more disastrous. It is best to get rid of these clichés and call each thing by its right name.

In classical psychology, race prejudice is a projection onto others of one's own unacceptable traits. It is a species of paranoia, the repressed traits returning as floating threats. It is characteristic of the authoritarian personality, brought up with severe inhibition of the child's initiative and animal nature; and the paranoia is excited by economic or other insecurity that makes the adult ego labile. Typically, a failing petty bourgeoisie with puritanic upbringing will have racial prejudices. The Germans were classically racist, with a full-blown ideology of Aryan supremacy that made them feel grand, whereas the Jews poisoned the bloodstream and were responsible for the Versailles treaty. Degraded by the Civil War, Southern whites developed the full-blown racism of the Ku Klux Klan; they had to be better than somebody, and niggers were inferior, apelike, a threat to Southern womanhood.

In this classical sense, the northern white middle class has hardly been racist at all. Their upbringing, though not free, has been unrestrictive by European standards. They certainly have not failed economically. Where there *is* more authoritarianism and insecurity, as among newly prosperous blue-collar workers — e.g., Poles, Italians,

Irish, or Appalachians in Chicago — there is more racial prejudice; the same holds for retired rentiers like the Californians threatened by inflation. But the usual majority objections to blacks that have caused the suburban flight have not been "prejudices" but a Gradgrind kind of facts, narrowly realistic. Blacks do downgrade the schools and make it hard for junior to compete for MIT; they make streets unsafe; they swell taxes by being on relief and not pulling their oar; they are not prepared for better jobs that have (irrelevant) mandarin requirements. By contrast, in the important area of discrimination in unionized semi-skilled jobs, there have been strong prejudices by blue-collar workers; and the most vehement opposition to open housing has come in rentier neighborhoods.

In many cities the police are recruited from just the most prejudiced classes, and this has been calamitous. And everywhere, of course, police are subject to the factual prejudices of their dangerous craft; poor suspects of any color have never gotten loving care from cops. (It happens that hippies and vocal pacifists are the worst treated of all, but this is an effect of paranoiac prejudice, since these pose an inner threat to the policeman's manly perfection.) Schoolteachers are a striking example of a kind of factual prejudice produced by narrow craft idiocy; probably most of them start out with fairly innocent attitudes, but when little black children do not learn to read *Dick and Jane*, the teacher's annoyance and anxiety, fearful of the supervisor, can come close to hatred.

Historically, there has been, and persists, a northern middle-class exclusiveness, provincial and conformist, that could reasonably be called "racist." But let us look at this, too, accurately, for the remedy depends on the diagnosis. Blacks have always been strange. There were few in the eastern and middle-western country and towns from which many of the whites came. Their mores were not necessarily inferior, ludicrous, or bad, but unknown. When blacks were hired as domestics, for instance by New York Jews, they were not looked down on but treated like articles of furniture. Not in business, they did not belong to clubs. Living in their own neighborhoods, they did not belong to white churches. But to be socially excluded has been the common fate of immigrant poor. Color is not the decisive factor: black Puerto Ricans, even with their culture of poverty, now make an easier adjustment. But Negroes have been continually recruited from an entirely inappropriate slave and depressed-rural background, and their exclusion has been fatally cumulative. Then, with the recent overwhelming influx of new immigrants, and their teeming offspring, the familiar atmosphere of the northern cities has changed drastically; strangeness has become menace; panic flight has ensued.

What picture of the white middle class emerges from this analysis? It is not so much racist as narrow, self-righteous, and busy. But of course. This is the same tribe that, north and south, displaced the Indians, had Negro slaves in the first place, needlessly bombed Hiroshima, and destroys Vietnamese. Whether one calls it brash enterprise or imperialist arrogance, to these people their victims are not quite persons. If the deviants shape up, fine, one does business with them — and even extraordinary efforts are made to help them to shape up. But if they persist in being themselves, they are exterminable. "Essentially," as the Kerner report puts it, busy self-centered people do not want to be thwarted or bothered. This bleakly explains more than "racism" does.

On the other hand, the Americans have the virtues of their defects, and these are more promising. Being busy, self-interested, independent, and successful, they have also been spectacularly extroverted, pragmatic, and generous. They will pay enormous sums to convert the heathen, wash the unwashed, and teach the mentally retarded to spell. And there has been an absolute contradiction in their racial attitudes. For instance, on the one hand there was the smug silence about the Indians and Negroes in classical New England literature; on the other hand there was the pan-humanism of Cooper and Walt Whitman. The framers of the Declaration of Independence obviously meant it when they said all men were created equal; yet some of the same authors allowed the organic charter, the Constitution, to speak of "three-fifths of a person." (This was exactly the kind of detail on which Gandhi would have fasted to the death.) The bother with the premise of the Kerner report is that, if it were true, nothing less would avail than psychiatry for epidemic paranoia, probably including shock treatment — and this is, of course, the proposition of the black terrorists. A more *prima facie* diagnosis allows us to appeal to the outgoingness, the pragmatism, the enlightened self-interest of Americans.

Unfortunately, in modern conditions, we must notice the *increasing* anxiety and privatism of the middle class. As businesses become more centralized and the standard of living more demanding and complicated, independence and enterprise are severely constricted. And more and more we see that American horse sense and generosity, which have been saving graces, give way to a desperate need to keep things under control. Self-righteousness can then become "efficient," a cold violence that has no inner check. There is a fanaticism of business as usual, called Preserving Law and Order, manner of Mayor Daley. If citizens fail to social-engineer the deviant into conformity, they quickly resort to mechanical measures, police, tanks, marines, bombers. When the threatened victims respond with desperate counter-measures, it is necessary to up the ante and there can be a massacre. Yet in modern conditions, it is again not necessary to speak of "white racism"; what is evident is a *general* drive to dispossess, control, and ignore human beings who are useless and bothersome, whether small farmers, displaced coal-miners, the aged, the alienated young, the vastly increasing number of "insane." And unassimilable racial minorities.

But modern conditions also have advantages. The very centralization and affluence that dehumanize allow also for pragmatic remedies on a grand scale; an 800 billion Gross National Product and the mass media can mount "crash programs." Second is the remarkable moral development of the young, sophisticated and free of economic pressure. In their own way they are as ignorant and self-righteous as the day is long, but they are not narrow, mechanical or privatist, and they disregard caste and color. Finally, there is evidence that there is still life in the American democratic process itself, that peculiar mixture of morality, civil liberties, self-interest, and sporadic violence, swelling to make institutional change. Led by the young, the blacks, and the increasingly impatient "new class" of intellectuals, there is a revival of populism. Even the mass media, which have done so much to brainwash us, now seem — sensationally and inaccurately — to be informing us, because the journalists are new intellectuals. It is an odd "System."

Black Racism

In the nature of the case, blacks in the United States are, by and large, racist, from Uncle Toms to Black Muslims. Whites can disregard blacks, but blacks can hardly disregard the power that owns and runs everything. Whiteness, as Fanon points out, inevitably invades the unconscious. Frustrated and deprived, blacks project onto the whites the put-down and hostility that they themselves feel. It would be too bitter to see truly the indifference that is usually really there.

(It is hardly necessary to discuss racial relations in order to make a catalogue of human sadness. But on the black side, lack of acquaintance, the mutual misunderstanding of manners and signals, must be especially devastating. For instance, willing to be friendly but being suspicious and vulnerable, he may start out with testing, either boring politeness or probing insult. But if the white is a simple person, he will be bored or annoyed, and shrug and sign off, and the world is so much worse than it was. This can quickly spiral downward to general mutual avoidance and fear. Yet, given ghetto conditions, it would be unusual for a black child *not* to grow up with suspicion, if the only whites he is exposed to are police, schoolteachers, and bill-collectors.)

The sophisticated ideology of Racism itself has been picked up by intelligent blacks from white paranoids; it is a fairly recent invention of Germans, Boers, and the Ku Klux Klan. (Until the nineteenth century, race was not much used as a projection-screen. Even anti-Semitism was mainly religious and could usually be alleviated by conversion.) And now we see that the artifact of a "racist society" is picked up from black militants by the Kerner report. Presumably the report's rhetorical purpose in this is to sting white guilt in order to get action, but, as we shall see, this is a slender reed to lean on.

At present, southern blacks are less racist than northern blacks. Being more acquainted with real white madmen, they themselves have less paranoia and more sense of plain injustice; whereas northern blacks have to cope with bland unconcern or downgrading by neutral rules, at the same time as they are suffering. A case in point is "Law and Order." A Jim Crow law is mad on the face of it; but to northern middle-class whites, due process is only reasonable, it provides a neutral forum for discussion and legislation. They cannot see that to dispossessed people due process is precisely the usual runaround that they have been getting. Besides, northern blacks are now a more failing class than southern. The excessive urbanization is fiscally and physically unworkable, and is unlivable. Religion and family are shattered. There is more anomie. The great bloc of immigrants and estranged youth may have a little more money but they are much worse off than they were in the rural areas from which they were driven.

A poignant example of the clash of black racism and white lack of empathy was the expulsion of white students from the Civil Rights and Black Power movements, e.g., from SNCC. Innocently righteous and confident in themselves, the white students took too much initiative and too much for granted. This made it hard for the blacks to run their own show, which was indispensable if they were to regain their own confidence. If the blacks had responded with fraternal, even if angry, competition, it might have cemented a deeper friendship. Instead they responded with jealousy, including sexual jealousy, and expulsion. The possibility of free co-operation has been foreclosed.

Yet, since the blacks still need help, for instance funds and facilities and to swell a demonstration, there now develops the ugly situation that sympathetic whites are manipulated, hustled, or lied to; and it must be a further humiliation for blacks to do this.

During the recent fracas at Columbia, the blacks invited their SDS allies out of a joint action because, a leader said, "They were shaky and would vacillate and panic and could not be depended on. With black kids the issue is clear, to fight racism." (One is struck by the testimonial to Socrates' definition of courage, to have an idea.) My guess is that the whites had a more complicated idea; but in fact the more structural issue of the action, to fight military infiltration of the university, did get lost in the shuffle, so the blacks were proved correct.

Generally speaking, it has been a mistake, in my opinion, for black militants to try to make "integration" and "black power" absolute and incompatible. The basic theory behind it is nonsense, to lay stress on the color of civilization as the Germans laid stress on its nationhood; and, practically, too much science and wisdom, as well as wealth, resides in the dominant community to try to dissociate from it without being continually phoney. It is stupid to regard Galileo or Faraday as "white" rather than as human — and to be saying it into a microphone. And negatively, it would be stupid to have a black and white committee against nuclear fallout or cancer. (By contrast, draft resistance warrants separate committees, since those with and those without student deferments have different problems.) I doubt that, outside the South, there are many middle-class whites who have any feelings at all about being "white" as such. To the extent that to belong to a racial or national group is indeed a cause of pride — frankly, as a child of the Enlightenment, I think this is thin gruel — the minority group will thrive best in a mixed society where it has influential soul-brothers or *Landsmänner*. And politically, the majority of blacks and the best of the whites in fact want "integration" and will insist on it.

Nevertheless, illogic has its place. *Le coeur a ses raisons que la raison ne connait point.* It is now thinkable that there *could* be a black committee against nuclear fallout, whereas ten years ago it was impossible to mount a protest in Harlem on this issue at all. People have to humanize themselves in their own way. It produces a curious dilemma. For example, at the Conference for New Politics, just the most energetic of the blacks insist on the official recognition of their caucus; whereas just those whites who are most thoughtful and most deeply committed to social justice are embarrassed and do not know what to do with this demand, because in fact the unity of mankind is the truth.

Spite

The actual situation, without fancy constructs, is that some are hurting and the others don't care. Starting from this obvious premise, for the oppressed a primitive method of coping is spite. Spite probably played a part in the expulsion from SNCC — "you aren't invited": it is the chief ingredient in the black theater of insult, genre of LeRoi Jones; and I think it has been an important factor in the riots — "burn, baby, burn." Spite is the vitality of the powerless; it is a way of not being resigned, of keeping a lost fight alive by preventing the dominator from enjoying his domination.

(Needless to say, let me say at once, there are other factors in the riots. In some cities there has been evidence of a political plan for insurrection, part of a plan for world insurrection. The looting speaks for itself as reasonable free appropriation by people who are hopelessly poor. Burning white businesses in the ghetto makes a rational, though desperate, political point. There is a spontaneous explosion of frustration. In any culture of poverty there is a carelessness about one's own possessions and life, just as the homicide rate is high. On the part of the intelligent and energetic young, who have played a big role, rioting is exactly equivalent to white youth uprising on campuses and streets around the world, in fascist, corporate liberal, and communist countries: it is an *acte gratuit* of freedom in the face of irrational authority; the youth component is more important than the racial or ideological component.)

Commentators seem to be unwilling to say the word spite; yet it is not an ugly or useless passion. It is a means of preserving or even finding identity. Saul Alinsky especially has often tried to use it for community development, e.g., by organizing dispossessed and fragmented people simply to take revenge on short-weight grocers. But the trouble with spite, of course, as Alinsky also knows, is that its victories do not add up, and the letdown can lead to worse despair.

Spite is often self-destructive, "biting off one's nose to spite one's face"; one burns down one's own neighborhood partly because one cannot burn down theirs, but also to make them feel bad. This purpose usually fails; to "natural calamities" the affluent Americans promptly respond with clothing and canned goods, and do not feel bad but good. To hit home, it is necessary to produce an apocalypse as when Malcolm X, during his fanatical period, prayed for an atom bomb to destroy New York, Allah's revenge. But I have heard, too, of a "political" purpose of self-destruction, to make precisely the unengaged blacks worse off and so swell the Cadres of revolt. This motive, if it exists, is evil.

Somewhat more practical is spitework as blackmail. It is possible that some riot areas, like Watts or Newark, have received a tangible pay-off, as well as sociology. C.V. Hamilton puts it formally when, in a recent essay, he speaks of a *quid pro quo*: "Blacks receive economic support and political power; whites receive a chance to live in a healthy, developing, equitable society." But the results have been meager, and, as a political proposition, shakedown must finally produce a devastating backlash. Nevertheless, the same substance can be put in a theoretical form that is quite acceptable political science and hopefully workable: "For the commonweal of a pluralistic society, it is necessary for every group to flourish, and every group has the duty to throw its weight around to get justice for itself and the whole." It is not newsy in American history that this might involve some violence; consider, for instance, the burned barns and derailed trains of 1885 agrarianism, or the defiance of court and police in the labor movement, with many killed. Hamilton has to use the language of blackmail because he cannot speak of commonweal; he seems to need the ideology of race war in order to organize a following.

In my opinion, we would be much further along if Black Power had long ago presented its concrete political program, e.g., local control of police, schools, and other services; the underwriting of local small businesses and co-operative housing. Such things are perfectly plausible and, if fought for, would by now have been won. (I have been plugging them for twenty years, but I have no troops.) If a decade ago, as we urged, the integrationists had asked for the guaranteed income for all Americans instead of welfare, would now have it; liberals get used to anything, once they hear the words. Five years ago, the March on Washington should have highlighted the Vietnam War, as some of us again urged. But moderate black leaders insisted that these things were too far out. And militant black leaders insisted on the spiteful recourse of sulking and putting on the whites the burden of guessing what is needed and coming across to prove their good will. Blacks shouted "Black Power!" and puzzled sympathetic whites asked, "What is Black Power?" A painful example has been James Baldwin's gambit: he forces the white interlocutor to ask, "But what do you want?" "You know what we want." "No, I really don't." "We want just what you want." Perhaps Baldwin says this ingenuously, but he is in error; for usually the white man does not think of himself as a "white man," but just as an individual in his own state of confusion and misery, in which being white does not help at all. Unless he is very empathetic, he does not see the disadvantage of being *not* white. If Baldwin would say, "We need thus and so to live better. How can *you* be of use in *our* getting it?" then the white man will either help according to his abilities or confess that he doesn't care enough to put himself out. Of course, a psychological use of the spiteful gambit is to avoid the risk of rejection.

But this is water under the bridge. Concrete programs for local control *are* emerging, there is certainly more acquaintance, and despite spectacular militant tactics there seems to be diminishing backlash. One has the impression that, in the white community, private groups small and large are far ahead of the political officials and Congress. These include, let me say wryly, big business corporations which have a natural self-interest in fire-prevention and will even make an extra buck out of racial harmony — you'll see.

But to account for the slow emergence of concrete demands, we must bear in mind, too, that dispossessed and dependent people are disoriented and do not themselves know what they want. If something positive is given, it is suspected as second-rate or a trap or a token never adequate to need. If something is taken or achieved by one's own effort, it thereby becomes degraded, or is a cause of envy among one's fellows and proves that one has been "co-opted." This is the neurosis of the victimized that Robert Jay Lifton has been studying.

Sensitive minds, like James Baldwin again, understand perfectly that just to get into the middle-class American mainstream is not humanly good enough; but then it is hard for him to explain to poor people what, these days, would be humanly good enough. Consider the current social imputation of many jobs as "menial." When I was young, driving a bus or trailer-truck was manly, difficult, and responsible; now when there are many black drivers, it is ordinary. Construction work used to be skilled; but a black or Spanish bricklayer or mason tends to be considered unskilled. White road-workers in Vermont have a decent job; black roadworkers with the same equipment have a menial job. Postman, a job requiring unusual tact and judgment, has always been a dignified occupation; now that, like other Federal employment, it is open to many blacks, my guess is that it will be considered drab. A German or Jewish waiter is a mentor or kibitzer, a black waiter has a servile job. This social imputation of worth is made, of course, by both whites and blacks. Whites, however, usually do not give it a second thought, as their young move into other jobs. The question is why the blacks go along with the same imputation. The dismaying thing is that objective criteria like the kind of work, the worth of the product or service, and often even the wages count for very little. In this frame of mind, it is impossible to be free and independent.

But this subjective evaluation by the standards of public relations is endemic in American society. Nothing is regarded as itself, on its own merits. Thus, in the present essay which ought to be on politics and ends and means, I find myself discussing emotions and unconscious emotions, like racism, spite, revenge, and guilt. I find this pretty sickening. Perhaps the chief hope in the young, with their flesh-and-blood interests, simplifications of the standard of living, casteless friendships, and direct action, is that they will bring us back to objective reality, however crude.

Guilt

A chief use of spite is to make the others feel guilty; this not only prevents their enjoying their domination but may result in tangible "amends." It is clear that with many middle-class whites, this ruse has disastrously succeeded. Disastrously, because no good has ever come from feeling guilty, neither intelligence, policy, nor compassion. The guilty do not pay attention to the object but only to themselves, and not even to their own interests, which might make sense, but to their anxieties.

Psychoanalytically, guilt is repressed resentment and this is latent dynamite. For a time the guilty may forbear retaliation for annoyance or insult and may pay token amends, but soon they turn a deaf ear and then resentfully get even.

The dilemma is that blacks are indeed victims, of a system of property relations and policing, but the present-day northern whites, as persons, are not consciously nor importantly victimizers. There is exploitation by black people in their own neighborhoods, which can be helped by phasing out of their neighborhoods; but such exploitation is trivial in the Gross National Product and is overwhelmingly outweighed by the general tax-cost in black social services, special services, special policing, etc. Since they are not economically necessary, blacks cannot get redress by striking and bargaining. Since most whites are not exploiting them, they cannot give them redress by stopping their exploitation. When there is disorder and the cops crack down, the whites feel that *they* were aggressed on, and this is technically true. The black demand "Just get off our backs," makes sense in asking whites to stop running the ghettos through the school bureaucracy, the welfare bureaucracy, the police, and slumlords; but it is a poor slogan since, in the inflationary urbanism and high technology, blacks simply must have white subsidy, professional help, and jobs in the only economy that there is.

Almost all whites now agree blacks ought to get preferential treatment and there are stirrings in this direction. But this cannot come to much if it is done by guilt, to make amends; it must be done for political motives, self-interest, decency, commonweal, and justice. Unhappily, the Americans, who neglect other public works, whose rivers stink, whose town are hideous, whose country-side is despoiled, and whose children are mis-educated, neglect this public good too. My guess is that, just beneath the surface, it is they who have the slogan, "Get off our backs."

Really to remedy our domestic colonialism (and our foreign colonialism) requires profound institutional changes and structural changes in the economy. We would have to divert the military technology to useful production; control the inflation that makes poor people poorer; reverse the policy of rural enclosures that swells the cities; manage the advertising, design, and pricing of consumer goods so that people can live decently without being in the rat race; get rid of the irrelevant mandarin diplomas for licensing and hiring. To stop being exclusive, American society would have to be about human beings rather than the Gross National Product, and the privatist competition for a cut. It would have to give up its delusion of social-engineering everybody, and tailor its help to local needs and local social organization. But all this amounts to a religious conversion and seems hopeless. It is possible that we cannot have such a conversion without convulsions; unfortunately I do not hear of any convulsions that would lead to the relevant conversion. The violent champions of Che or Lenin rarely say anything relevant to the real problems of a country like ours. It is understandable that blacks are hung up on their gut issues of being hemmed in and pushed around, but it is distressing that the Peace and Freedom Party or Students for a Democratic Society cannot get beyond gut issues. Radical liberals, like Harrington, Keyserling, or Rustin, propose New Dealish remedies like more public housing, schooling, and transit, that would recreate the same problems bigger and worse. Liberals feel guilty. "Conservatives" arm the police.

Non-Violence

Meantime we must live with the immediate problem: what to *do* when some are hurting and others, who have power, don't care? *How* to make narrow, busy, and self-righteous people understand that other people exist?

It was exactly for this problem that Gandhi, A.J. Muste, and Martin Luther King devised and experimented the strategy of active massive non-violent confrontation, both non-violent resistance and aggressive non-violence. In my opinion, this is the only strategy that addresses all aspects of the situation. It challenges unconcern. It attacks institutions and confronts people as well. It personalizes the conflict so that habitual and mechanical responses are not easy. It diminishes strangeness. It opens possibilities for the narrow to grow and come across, instead of shutting them out. It interrupts the downward spiral of the oppressed into despair, fanaticism, and brutality. Most important, it is the only realistic strategy, for it leads to, rather than prevents, the achievement of a future community among the combatants. We will have to live together in some community or other. How? In what community? We really do not know, but non-violent conflict is the way to discover and invent it.

Non-violence is aggressive. Since the injustices in society reside mainly in the institutional system, though the personal agents may be innocent or even quite sympathetic, it is necessary to prevent the unjust institutions from grinding on as usual. It is necessary not to shun conflict but to seek it out. So Gandhi, Muste, and King were continually inventing campaigns to foment apparent disorder where things apparently had been orderly.

Naturally, aggressive massive non-violence is not safe. (Gandhi lost thousands.) If only mathematically, when there is a big crowd, some will be hurt — sometimes because of one's own young hotheads, more usually because the police panic and try to enforce impossible Byzantine restrictions, Law and Order. On the other hand, actions of this kind are far less likely to lead to a shambles. In the present climate of cold violence armed with a lethal technology, this is a major concern.

I do not think that non-violence is incompatible with fringes of violence or flare-ups of violence, so long as its own course is steadily political, appealing to justice, self-interest, and commonweal, and if the political object of the campaign speaks for itself. Gandhi, of course, was a purist about avoiding violence, though he said that it was better to be violent against injustice than to do nothing; both Muste and King were willing to co-operate with violent groups, if they did not try to take over. Psychologically, indeed, it is probably an advantage for a non-violent movement to have a group like the Black Panthers in the wings, committed to violent self-defense, for this quiets down the more rabid opposition and makes a calmer zone for real political and economic confrontation. (Sometimes it doesn't work out so smoothly.)

Non-violence, and King's own campaigns, do not necessarily prejudge the issue between "integration" and "black power." Separatism is ruled out, however, since the point of confrontation is to come to mutual recognition and commonweal. It is not necessary to "love" one's enemies, but there must be a belief that common humanity is more basic than racial difference; and this belief must be *bona fide* or non-violence becomes a mere tactic and has no energy. Certainly King's followers took his universalist Christian rhetoric at face value. (So did I.) As I have said, it is the only realistic position; it is the tendency of history. In the world, we cannot continue to have "peaceful" co-existence, which is really cold war; we will come to community or perish. In this country, it is not the case that there could be two societies, as the Kerner report threatens. Either the dominant group will hem in the blacks in *apartheid* reservations, which is un-thinkably abhorrent, or there will be a democratic pluralism or general miscegenation, each of which has attractions.

In the northern cities, however — and this is a grim complication — there are two distinct problems which somehow have to be solved at the same time. The first is the one we have been discussing, how to get whites to pay attention to blacks as existing, and for this aggressive non-violence makes the most sense. But the second problem is that we have allowed, in the ghettos, the formation of what Oscar Lewis calls a Culture of Poverty, insulated, ingrown, dependent; and how can such a culture become free and independent? I don't know; but it is possible that rioting, burning, hurling insults, apparently stupid militancy, and an extravagant black racist ideology are indeed means of regaining confidence at this level of dispiritment. King, as he came to deal with northern problems, had begun to take this factor into account, though it clearly pained his heart and mind. And it is encouraging that whites, and white officials like Lindsay, may be finding the compassion that is here the only relevant thing we have to give.

The violent who are interested in insurrection and "revolutionary" overturn inevitably consider non-violence as "reformist." According to their theory, since it is piecemeal and does not aim to demolish the System and replace it (with what?), it cannot change anything. In my view, especially in complicated and highly organized societies, it is only by opening areas of freedom piecemeal that we will transform our lives. "Seizing power" in such societies is precisely counter-revolution and stops the social revolution short. But the human contact of aggressive non-violence is exquisitely relevant to the deepest danger of modern times, the mechanical violence of 1984. Because of it and the new spirit of the young, we will not have 1984.

Finally, it is said that non-violence might suit the Hindus but it is contrary to American spirit and tradition. Quite the contrary. It seems to me to be simply an extension of traditional American populism, the democratic process as conceived by Jefferson, that has always revived in times of great crisis: acting "illegally" and "petitioning," rousing the general will, protected by the Bill of Rights, with fringes of violence, and ending up with important institutional change. In every major country in the world, power is terribly deeply entrenched; but America is the most likely place for a non-violent movement toward freedom to succeed.

Since I have this occasion, let me say a word about the death of Martin King. He was a stubborn, reasonable man, and political without being a fink. I do not know any other national leader for whose death I would have wept.

In my opinion, the extraordinary general grief of the Americans was not, as has been charged, hypocritical or empty. The grief for death and sympathy for survivors is one of the few emotions that bring all people, even divided families, together. I think that whites now recognize blacks a little more as persons than they did before, and this should have consequences.

Civil Disobedience

Law and Legitimacy

During the early Thirties, students got a thorough extracurricular education in the political economy. They experienced the Depression, the labor movement, the New Deal, the subtle in-fighting of Left sects; and Marxian, Keynesian, managerial and technocratic theories provided adequate terms for discussion. Present-day students are hopelessly ill-informed, and uninterested, in these matters. But they have had other experiences. Sitting-in and being jailed, demonstrating, resisting the draft, defying authority in the schools and on the streets have confronted them with the fundamental problems of political science, the premises of allegiance and legitimacy by which political societies operate at all. For a teacher it is thrilling, if poignant, to see how real these abstractions have become.

But the theoretical framework for discussion has been astonishingly meager. Learning by doing, the young have rediscovered a kind of populism and "participatory democracy"; they have been seduced by theories of mountain guerrilla warfare and putschism, and some of them like to quote Chairman Mao that political power comes from the barrel of a gun. But I have heard little analysis of what Sovereignty and Law really are in modern industrial and urban societies, though it is about these that there is evidently a profound conflict in this period. In the vacuum of historical knowledge and philosophical criticism, the dissenters are too ready to concede (or boast) that they are lawless and civilly disobedient. And the powers that be, police, school administrators, and the Texan President, are able to sound off, and practise, clichés about Law and Order that are certainly not American political science. So it is useful to make some academic remarks about elementary topics. Alas, it is even necessary, to rehearse our case — I am writing in the spring of 1968, and some of us are under indictment.

Administrators talk about Law and Order and Respect for Authority as if these things had an absolute sanction: without them there can be no negotiation, whether the situation is a riot, a strike of municipal employees, a student protest against Dow Chemical, or burning draft cards. The tone is curiously theocratic, as if the government existed by divine right. Law and Order sounds like the doctrine of the authoritarian personality, where the Sovereign has been internalized from childhood and has a nonrational charisma. But although this psychology does exist, by and large the Americans are not conformist in this way. Indeed, they have become increasingly sceptical, or cynical, of their moral rigidity, at the same time as they resort more readily to violent suppression of deviation or infringement.

The "reasons," given in editorials, are that we must have safe streets; in a democracy, there is a due process for changing the laws; violation is contagious and we are tending toward "anarchy." But do safe streets depend on strictly enforcing the law? Every editorial *also* points out that sociologically the means of keeping the peace is to diminish tension, and economically and politically it is to give the disaffected a stake and a say. And in the history of American cities, of course, peace has often been best preserved by bribery, deals under the table, patronage of local bosses, blinking or negligent enforcement. In the complex circumstances of civil disorder, the extralegal is likely to give rough justice, whereas strict enforcement, for instance when the reform-minded *Daily News* makes the police close Eighth Avenue bars, is sure to cause unnecessary suffering.

Even when it is not substantively unjust, Law and Order is a cultural style of those who know the ropes, have access to lawyers, and are not habitually on the verge of animal despair; such a high style, however convenient for society, cannot be taught by tanks and mace. But what is most dismaying is that a well-intentioned group like the Commission on Civil Disorders regards Order and Due Process as a neutral platform to discuss substantive remedies; it cannot see that to an oppressed group just these things are the usual intolerable hang-up of White Power: theft, repression and run-around.

I do not think there is empirical evidence that all violation is contagious. The sociological probability, and what little evidence there is, is the other way: those who break the law for political reasons, articulate or inarticulate, are less likely to commit delinquencies or crimes, since there is less *anomie*; they have a stake and a say if only by being able to act at all. And Jefferson, of course, argued just the opposite of punctilious law: since laws are bound to be defied, he said, it is better to have as few as possible, rather than to try for stricter enforcement.

When a disaffected group indeed has power, nobody takes absolutism seriously. The organized teachers and garbage collectors of New York disregarded the Condon-Wadlin and Taylor laws against strikes by municipal employees, and got their way — nor did the Republic fall in ruins. Only the New York *Times*, not even Governor

Rockefeller or Mayor Lindsay, bothered to mention the threat to Law and Order.

I suppose the climax of divine-right theory in American history has been the law making draft-card burning a felony, punishable by five years in prison or $10,000 fine or both. Since draft-card burning does not help a youth avoid the draft, what is this felony? It is *lèse majesté*, injury to the sacred sovereignty of Law embodied in a piece of paper. Yet congress enacted this law almost unanimously.

Certainly the disobedient do not *feel* that the law is sacred. If it were, any deliberate infringement — whether by Dr. Spock, a Black Power agitator, a garbage collector or a driver risking a parking ticket — would involve a tragic conflict genre of Corneille: Love vs. Duty. Among infringers, I see a good deal of calculation of consequences, and on the part of Dr. Spock, Dr. King, etc., an admirable courage and patriotism, but I do not see the signs of inner tragic conflict.

The Authority of Law is Limited

If we turn, now, to the more tonic American conception that the sanction of law is the social compact of the sovereign people, we see that it is rarely necessary, in the kinds of cases we are concerned with, to speak of "civil disobedience" or "lawlessness." What social promises do people actually consider binding? There are drastic limitations. Let me list half a dozen that are relevant to present problems.

(Of course, few believe in the mythical hypothesis of compact, or in any other single explanation, to account for the real force of law. We must include custom, inertia, prerational community ties, good-natured mutual regard, fear of the police, a residue of infantile awe of the overwhelming, and the energy bound up in belonging to any institution whatever. Yet compact is not a mere fiction. Communities do come to such agreements. Immigrants sometimes choose one system of laws over another; and, negatively, there are times when men consciously ask themselves, "What have I bargained for? Do I want to live with these people in this arrangement?")

Since an underlying purpose of the compact is security of life and liberty, it is broken if the sovereign jails you or threatens your life; you have a (natural) duty to try to escape. In our society, this point of Hobbes' is important. There is a formidable number of persons in jail, or certified as insane, or in juvenile reformatories; and there is an increasing number of middle-class youth who have been "radicalized," returned to a state of nature, by incarceration. Likewise, the more brutal the police, the less the allegiance of the citizens.

In large areas of personal and animal life, as in the case of vices harmless to others, high-spirited persons have a definite under-standing that law is irrelevant and should be simply disregarded. Al-most all "moral" legislation — on gambling, sex, alcohol, drugs, obscenity — is increasingly likely to be nullified by massive non-publicized disobedience. Not that these areas are "private" or trivial, but one does not make a social contract about them. The medievals more realistically declared that they were subject to canon law, not to the king. For better or worse, we do not have courts of conscience, but it is a human disaster for their functions to be taken over by policemen and night magistrates.

The sovereign cannot intervene in professional prerogatives, as by a law against teaching evolution. Every teacher is duty-bound to defy it. A physician will not inform against a patient, a lawyer a client, a teacher a student, a journalist an informant. At present, there is bound to be a case where a scientist publishes his government-clas-sified or company-owned research, because scientists have an obliga-tion to publish. (By and large, however, for narrow economic reasons, professionals have been playing the dangerous game of giving more and more prerogative in licensing to the State. By deciding who prac-tises, the State will finally determine what is practised.)

By the Bill of Rights, speech, religion, and political acts like an as-sembly and petition are beyond the reach of the law. As I have argued elsewhere, it is a mistake to interpret these "rights" as a compact; rather they state areas of anarchy in which people cannot make con-tracts in a free society, any more than to sell themselves into slavery.

Obviously the compact is broken if the law goes berserk, for ex-ample if the government prepares for nuclear war. Therefore we refused the nuclear shelter drills.

The law cannot command what is immoral or dehumanizing, whether co-operation with the Vietnam War or paying rent where conditions are unlivable. In such cases, it is unnecessary to talk about allegiance to a "higher law" or about conflict with the judg-ments of Nuremberg (though these might be legally convenient in a court), for a man cannot be responsible for what demoralizes and degrades him from being a responsible agent altogether. And note that all these classes of cases have nothing to do with the usual question: "Is every individual supposed to decide what laws he will obey?" — for it is the social contract itself that is irrelevant or self-contradictory.

Finally the bindingness of promises is subject to essential change of circumstances. Due process, electing new representatives to make new laws, is supposed to meet this need and roughly does; but due process is itself part of the social agreement and in times of crises, of course, it is always a live question as to whether it is adequate or whether sovereignty reverts closer to the people, seeking the General Will by other means. The vague concept that sovereignty resides in the People is usually meaningless, but precisely at critical moments it begins to have a vague meaning. American political history consists spectacularly of illegal actions that become legal, belatedly confirmed by the lawmakers. Civil rights trespassers, unions defying injunctions, suffragettes and agrarians being violent, abolitionists aiding runaway slaves, and back to the Boston Tea Party — were these people practising "civil disobedience" or were they "insurrectionary"? I think neither. Rather, in urgent haste they were exercising their sovereignty, practising direct democracy, disregarding the apparent law and sure of the emerging law. And by the time many cases went through a long, often deliberately protracted, course of appeals, the lawbreakers were no longer guilty, for their acts were no longer crimes. Hopefully, the current Vietnam protest is following the same schedule. To be sure, this direct political process is not always benign; the Ku Klux Klan also created law by populist means.

Thus, if we stick to a literal social contract, asking what is it that men really mean to promise, the authority of law is limited indeed. It is often justifiable to break a law as unwarranted, and reasonable to test it as unconstitutional or outdated. By this analysis it is almost never necessary, except for cases of individual conscience, to invoke a fancy concept like "civil disobedience," which concedes the warrant of the law but must for extraordinary reasons defy it.

The Function of Law and Order

Clearly, law has more authority than this among the Americans. We are not nearly so rational and libertarian. We do not believe in divine right but we do not have a social contract either. What would be a more realistic theory, more approximate to the gross present facts? I am afraid that it is something like the following:

There is an immense social advantage in having any regular code that everybody abides by without question, even if it is quite unreasonable and sometimes outrageous. This confirms people's expectations and permits them to act out their social roles. If the code is violated, people become so anxious about their roles that they want government to exert brute force to maintain Law and Order — this is part of government's role in the division of labor. Law and Order in this sense does not need moral authority; it is equivalent to saying, "Shape up; don't bother us; we're busy."

The sanction is avoidance of anxiety. This explains the tone of absolutism, without the tradition, religion or moral and ritual imperatives that humanized ancient theocracies. Gripped by anxiety, people can commit enormities of injustice and stupidity just in order to keep things under control. For instance, we enact draconian penalties for drugs, though our reasoned opinion is increasingly permissive. Minority groups that do not or cannot shape up must be squelched and kept out of sight, though everybody now concedes that they have just grievances and that suppression doesn't work anyway. The polls vote for stepping up the Vietnam war just when information, in the press and on television, is that the war is more and more evil and also militarily dubious. Squeamishness and stubbornness can go as far as using nuclear weapons, a massacre on the streets, and concentration camps for dissenters.

Conversely, the strategy of those who protest — the "civil disobedients," the "guerrilla fighters," the "rioters" — ceases to be justice and reconstruction and becomes simply to prevent business as usual. Lively young people, distinguished scholars, and the most talented leaders of the poor spend their time thinking up ways to make trouble. Our ideal aim is certainly to get the politically degenerate Americans back to liberty, law and the business of the commonwealth, but sometimes the purpose gets lost in the shuffle.

The Regime Itself is Illegitimate

The rising tide of "civil disobedience" and "lawlessness" is not defiance of law and order; it is a challenge that the regime itself is illegitimate. Maybe it asks a question: Can the modern society we have described be a political society at all? In my opinion, even the rising rate of crime is due mainly to *anomie*, confusion about norms and therefore lack of allegiance, rather than to any increase in criminal types (though that probably also exists under modern urban conditions).

"Civil disobedience" especially is a misnomer. According to this concept the law expresses the social sovereignty that we have ourselves conceded, and therefore we logically accept the penalties if we disobey, though we may have to disobey nevertheless. But in the interesting and massive cases, the warrant of the law is *not* conceded and its penalties are *not* agreed to. Indeed, I doubt that people *en masse* ever disobey what they agree to be roughly fair and just, even if it violates conscience.

Thus, Gandhi's major campaigns were carried on under the slogan Swaraj, self-rule for the Indians; the British Raj who was disobeyed had no legitimate sovereignty at all. It was a war of national liberation. The reasons for the nonviolence, which was what the "civil disobedience" amounted to, were twofold: Materially, Gandhi thought, probably correctly, that such a tactic would be ultimately less destructive of the country and people. (The Vietcong have judged otherwise, probably incorrectly.) Spiritually, Gandhi knew that such a means — of disciplined personal confrontation — would elevate people rather than brutalize them, and ease the transition to a necessary future community with the British.

The campaigns led by Dr. King in the South illustrate the drive against illegitimacy even more clearly. Segregation and denial of civil rights are illegitimate on the face of them; no human being would freely enter into such a degrading contract. Besides, King was able to rely on the contradiction between the illegitimate laws and a larger legitimate tradition of Christianity, the Declaration of Independence and the federal Constitution. Once the blacks made the challenge, the white Southerners could not maintain their inner confusion, and the federal government, though late and gracelessly, has had to confirm the protest.

Now, in resistance to the draft, Dr. Spock and Dr. Coffin declare that they are committing "civil disobedience" and are "willing and ready" to go to jail if convicted. No doubt they have a theory of what they are doing. Most of the co-conspirators, however, including myself, regard the present regime as frighteningly illegitimate, especially in military and imperial affairs; and we are not "willing" to accept the penalties for our actions, though we may have to pay them willy-nilly. The regime is illegitimate because it is dominated by a subsidized military-industrial group that cannot be democratically changed. There is a "hidden government" of CIA and FBI. The regime has continually lied and withheld information to deceive the American people; and with a federal budget of $425 millions for public relations, democratic choice becomes almost impossible. Even so, the President deliberately violated the overwhelming electoral mandate of 1964; it transpires that he planned to violate it even while he was running. The regime presents us with *faits accomplis*; the Senate balks with talk but in fact rubber-stamps the *faits accomplis*; it has become an image like the Roman senate in the first century. Many have resigned from the government, but they then do not "come clean" but continue to behave as members of the oligarchy. Disregarding the protests of millions and defying the opinion of mankind, the regime escalates an unjust war, uses horrible means, is destroying a culture and a people. Pursuing this berserk adventure, it neglects our own national welfare. Etc., etc. Then we judge that the government is a usurper and the Republic is in danger. On our present course, we will soon end up like the Romans, or 1984, or not survive at all.

Naturally, if the government is illegitimate, then at a public trial we ought to win. If the Americans are still a political community, we will — but of course, that is the question.

Let me make another point. The methods of protest we are using are positively good in themselves, as well as for trying to stop the Vietnam war. They characterize the kind of America I want, one with much more direct democracy, decentralized decision-making, a system of checks and balances that works, less streamlined elections. Our system should condone civil disobedience vigilant of authority, crowds on the street and riot when the provocation is grave. I am a Jeffersonian because it seems to me that only a libertarian, populist and pluralist political structure can make citizens at all in the modern world. This brings me back to the main subject of this essay, the social, technological and psychological conditions that underlie the present crisis of sovereignty and law.

The Sense of Sovereignty Lost

In highly organized countries, each in its own way, most of the major social functions, the economy, technology, education, communications, welfare, warfare and government, form a centrally organized system directed by an oligarchy. I do not think this structure is necessary for industrialization or high technology; it is not even especially efficient, certainly not for many functions. But is has been inevitable because of the present drives to power, reinvestment, armament and national aggrandizement.

The effects on citizenship have been variously compelling. Where the tradition was authoritarian to begin with and the national ideology is centralizing, as in Fascist Germany or Communist Russia, citizens have given allegiance to the industrial sovereign not much differently than to older despotisms, but with less leeway for private life, local custom or religion. In Communist China, where the new ideology is centralizing but the tradition was radically decentralist, there is a turbulence and struggle of allegiances. But in the United States, where both ideology and tradition have been decentralist and democratic, in the new dispensation citizenship and allegiance have simply tended to lapse. Since they can no longer effectually make important decisions about their destiny, Americans lose the sense of sovereignty altogether and retreat to privatism. Politics becomes just another profession, unusually phoney, with its own professional personnel.

Our situation is a peculiar one. The Americans do not identify with the ruling oligarchy, which is foreign to their tradition; a major part of it — the military-industrial and the CIA and the FBI — is even a "hidden government." The politicians carefully cajole the people's sensibilities and respect their freedom, so long as these remain private. And we have hit on the following accommodation: in high matters of State, War and Empire, the oligarchy presents *faits accomplis*; in more local matters, people resent being pushed around. Budgets in the billions are not debated; small sums are debated.

The Constitution is what I described above: the social compact is acquiescence to the social machine, and citizenship consists in playing appropriate roles as producers, functionaries and consumers. The machine is productive; the roles, to such as have them, are rewarding. And human nature being what it is, there develops a new kind of allegiance, to the rich and streamlined style. This provides the norm of correct behavior for workmen, inspires the supermarkets, and emboldens soldiers at the front.

A typical and very important class is the new professionals. Being essential to tend the engine and steer, they are well paid in salary and prestige. An expensive system of education has been devised to prepare the young for these roles. At the same time, the professionals become mere personnel. There is no place for the autonomy, ethics, and guild spirit that used to characterized them as people and citizens. *Mutatis mutandis*, the same can be said of the working class.

On the other hand, large groups of the population are allowed to drop out as socially useless, for instance, farmers, racial minorities, the incompetent, the old, many of the young. These are then treated as objects of social engineering and are also lost as citizens.

In an unpolitical situation like this, it is hard for good observers to distinguish between riot and riotous protest, or between a juvenile delinquent, a rebel without a cause and an inarticulate guerrilla. On a poll, to say "I don't know," might mean one is judicious, a moron, or a cynic about the question or the options. Student protest may be political or adolescent crisis or alienation. Conversely, there is evidence that good behavior may be dangerous apathy or obsessional neurosis. According to a recent study, a selection by schoolteachers of well-rounded "all-American boys" proves to consist heavily of pre-psychotics.

With this background, we can understand "civil disobedience" and "lawlessness." What happens politically in the United States when the system steers a disastrous course? There is free speech and assembly and a strong tradition of democracy, but the traditional structures of remedy have fallen into desuetude or become phoney. Bourgeois reformers, critical professionals, organizations of farmers and workmen, political machines of the poor have mainly been co-opted. Inevitably protest reappears at a more primitive or inchoate level.

The "civil disobedients" are nostalgic patriots without available political means. The new "lawless" are the oppressed without political means. Instead of having a program or a party, the protesters try, as Mario Savio said, to "throw themselves on the gears and the levers to stop the machine." Students think up ways to stop traffic; professionals form groups simply to nullify the law; citizens mount continual demonstrations and jump up and down with signs; the physically oppressed burn down their own neighborhoods. I think few of these people regard themselves as subversive. They know, with varying degrees of consciousness, that they are legitimate, the regime is not.

A promising aspect of it is the revival of populism, sovereignty reverting to the people. One can sense it infallibly during the big rallies, the March on Washington in '63 or the peace rallies in New York and at the Pentagon in April and October '67. Except among a few Leninists, the mood is euphoric, the heady feeling of the sovereign people invincible — for a couple of hours. The draft-card burners are proud. The elders who abet them feel like Americans. The young who invest the Pentagon sing *The Star-Spangled Banner*. The children of Birmingham attacked by dogs look like Christians. Physicians who support Dr. Levy feel Hippocratic, and professors who protest classified research feel academic. On the other hand, the government with the mightiest military power in the history of the world does not alter its course because of so much sweetness and light. The police of the cities are preparing an arsenal of anti-riot weapons. Organized workmen beat up peace picketers. We look forward apprehensively to August in Chicago.

But I am oversimplifying. In this romantic picture of the American people rising to confront the usurper, we must notice that

Lyndon Johnson, the Pentagon and the majority of Americans are also Americans. And they and the new populists are equally trapped in modern times. Even if we survive our present troubles with safety and honor, can anything like the social contract exist again in contemporary managerial and technological conditions? Perhaps "sovereignty" and "law," in any American sense, are outmoded concepts .... This is the furthest I can take these reflections until we see more history.

Decentralizing Power

Some *Prima Facie* Objections to Decentralism

Throughout our society, a centralizing style of organizing has been pushed so far as to become ineffective and wasteful, humanly stultifying, and ruinous to democracy. It is so in industries, government, labor unions, schools and science, culture and agriculture. And the tight interlocking of these central organizations has created, in my opinion, a critical situation. Modest, direct, or independent action has become extremely difficult in almost every function of society. We need at present a strong admixture of decentralism; the problem is where, how much, and how to get it.

In a centralized system, the function to be performed is the goal of the organization rather than of any persons (except as they identify with the organization). The persons are personnel. Authority is top-down. Information is gathered from below in the field, is processed to be usable by those above. Decisions are made in headquarters, and policy, schedule, and standard procedure are transmitted downward by chain of command. The enterprise as a whole is divided into departments of operation to which personnel are assigned with distinct roles, to give standard performance. This is the system in Mr. Goldwater's department store, in the Federal government and in the State governments, in most elementary and higher education, in the CIO, in hospitals, in neighborhood renewal, in network broadcasting, and in the deals that chain grocers make with farmers. The system was designed for disciplining armies, for bureaucratic record-keeping and tax-collection, and for certain kinds of mass-production. It has now pervaded every field.

The principle of decentralism is that people are engaged in the function they perform; the organization is how they co-operate. Authority is delegated away from the top as much as possible and there are many centers of decision and policy-making. Information is conveyed and discussed in face-to-face contacts between field and headquarters. And each person becomes aware of the whole operation. He works at it in his own way according to his capacities. Groups arrange their own schedules. Historically, this system of voluntary association has yielded most of the values of civilization, but it is thought to be entirely unworkable under modern conditions and the very sound of it is strange.

Now if, lecturing at a college, I happen to mention that some function of society which is highly centralized could be much decentralized without loss of efficiency or perhaps with a gain in efficiency, at once the students want to talk about nothing else. This insistence of theirs used to surprise me, and I tested it experimentally by slipping in a decentralist remark during lectures on entirely different subjects. The students unerringly latched onto the remark. In their questions, for twenty minutes they might pursue the main theme — e.g. nuclear pacifism or even the sexual revolution — but they returned to decentralization for many hours, attacking me with scepticism, hot objections, or hard puzzlers.

From their tone, it is clear that something is at stake for their existence. They feel trapped in the present system of society that allows them so little say or initiative, and that indeed is like the schooling that they have been enduring for twelve to sixteen years. The querulousness and biting sarcasm mean that, if decentralization *is* possible, they have become needlessly resigned; they hotly defend the second best that they have opted for instead. But the seriousness and hard questions are asked with a tone of sceptical wistfulness that *I* will be able to resolve all difficulties. If I confess at some point that I don't know the answer, at once the students invent answers for me, to prove that decentralization *is* possible after all.

Naturally at each college we go over the same ground. The very sameness of the discussion is disheartening evidence that the centralist style exists as a mass-superstition, never before questioned in the students' minds. If I point to some commonplace defect of any centralized system, and that leaps to the eye in the organization of their own college, I am regarded as a daring sage. They have taken for granted that there can be no other method of organization.

So let me here discuss these usual preliminary objections.

Decentralization is not lack of order or planning, but a kind of co-ordination that relies on different motives for integration and cohesiveness than top-down direction, standard rules, and extrinsic rewards like salary and status. It is not "anarchy." (But of course most Anarchists, like the anarcho-syndicalists or the community-anarchists, have not been "anarchists" either, but decentralists.)

The Example of Science

As an example of decentralist co-ordination, the anarchist Prince Kropotkin, who was a geographer, used to point spectacularly to the history of Western science from the heroic age of Vesalius, Copernicus, and Galileo up to his own time of Pasteur, Curie, Kelvin, and J.J. Thomson. The progress of science, in all branches, was exquisitely co-ordinated. There were voluntary associations, publications, regional and international conferences. The PhD system guaranteed that new research would be speedily disseminated to several hundred university libraries. There was continual private correspondence, even across warring boundaries. Yet in this vast common enterprise, so amazingly productive, there was no central direction whatever.

The chief bond of cohesion, of course, was that all scientists had the common aim of exploring Nature, as well as their personal or clique rivalries. The delicate integration of effort occurred because they followed the new data or worked with the frontier theories. It was almost uniquely rare — so far as we know: the case of Mendel is famous — that important work dropped out of the dialogue.

Most other big objective values, like beauty or compassion, have also thrived by voluntary association and independent solitude (although the technique of theological salvation has tended to be centralist). Almost by definition, the progress of social justice has been by voluntary association, since the central authority is what is rebelled against. And of course, to preserve liberty, the American political system was deliberately designed as a polarity of centralist and decentralist organizations, limiting the power of the Sovereign and with in-built checks and balances at every level.

But we must also remember that in its early period, celebrated by Adam Smith, the free enterprise system of partnerships and vigilant joint stockholders was, in theory, a model of decentralized co-ordination, as opposed to the centralized system of mercantilism and royal patents and monopolies that it replaced. It placed an absolute reliance on the voluntary association and on the cohesive influence of natural forces: Economic Man and the Laws of the Market. Pretty soon, however, the stockholders stopped attending to business and became absentee investors or even gamblers on the Stock Exchange. And almost from the beginning in this country, notably in the bank and the tariff, there was a revival of State monopolies.

Some Criteria for Decentralization

A student asks, "But how can you decentralize air traffic control?" You can't. Many functions are central by their nature. Let me quickly enumerate some of the chief kinds. (The process and use of centralizing is in itself a fascinating subject, but this article is about the shortcomings of centralization, not its virtues.)

Central authority is necessary where there are no district limits and something positive must be done, as in epidemic control or smog control, or when an arbitrary decision is required and there is not time for reflection, or when we have to set arbitrary standards for a whole field, but the particular standards are indifferent, e.g. weights and measures or money.

Centralization is temporarily necessary when an emergency requires the concentration of all powers in a concerted effort. (Here the decentralist alternative would be to scatter or go underground.) But history has shown that emergency centralization can be fateful, for the centralized organization tends to outlive the emergency, and then its very existence creates a chronic emergency; people soon become helpless without its direction.

Central authority is convenient to perform routine or "merely" administrative functions when we have more important things to do. This is the Marxist theory of the withering away of the State to "mere" administration. But this too can be fateful, for administration soon encroaches on everything else. It is thus that the "executive secretary" of an organization ends up running the show.

Central organization is the most rational when the logistics of a situation outweighs consideration of the particulars involved. These are all the cases of ticketing and tax-collecting, where one person is like another; or the mass production and distribution of a standard item that is good enough and that everybody needs. Besides, there are monopolies that must be regulated and licensed by central authority (or nationalized). Some monopolies are natural or become so by circumstances, like urban water supply. Some enterprises become monopolistic because they are so heavily capitalized that competition is prohibitively risky or wasteful. They grow until they become the inevitable nature of things, and then must be so treated. For instance, the railroads of Europe were decentrally planned and constructed, with voluntary agreement on gauges and schedules; but eventually, as monopolies, they were nationalized and partly internationalized.

My bias is decentralist, yet in some functions I think we need more centralization than we have. For instance, there ought to be uniform modular standards in building materials and fixtures. Building is a typical example of how we do things backwards: where there ought to be decentralization, in the design which requires artistry, and in the decision of each neighborhood on how it wants to live, we get bureaucratic or routine design and the standards of absentee sociologists or the profits of a promoter; but where there could be important savings, in materials and the process of construction, e.g.

mass-producing a standard bathroom, we do not standardize. Similarly, there ought to be standardization of machine parts and design, especially for domestic machinery and cars, to make repairs easier. Again, it is certainly absurd for the expensive enterprise of space exploration to be internationally competitive, instead of centrally planning and departmentalizing the work, with crews and honors shared.

Finally, automatic and computer technology is by nature highly centralizing, in its style and in its applications, and this is a massive phenomenon of the present and immediate future. Where it is relevant, this technology should be maximized as quickly as possible and many such plants should be treated as monopolies. *But perhaps the profoundest problem that faces modern society is to decide in what functions the automatic and computer style is not relevant, and there sharply to curtail it or eliminate it.*

A Marxist student objects that blurring the division of labor, local option, face-to-face communication, and other decentralist positions are relics of a peasant ideology, provincial and illiberal.

In fact, there have always been two strands to decentralist thinking. Some authors, e.g. Lao-tse or Tolstoy, make a conservative peasant critique of centralized court and town as inorganic, verbal, and ritualistic. But other authors, e.g. Proudhon or Kropotkin, make a democratic-urban critique of centralized bureaucracy and power, including feudal-industrial power, as exploiting, inefficient and discouraging initiative. In our present era of State-socialism, corporate feudalism, regimented schooling, brainwashing mass communications, and urban anomie, both kinds of critique make sense. We need to revive both peasant self-reliance and the democratic power of professional and technical guilds.

Any decentralization that could occur at present would inevitably be post-urban and post-centralist; it could not be provincial. There is no American who has not been formed by national TV, and no region that has not been homogenized by the roads and chain stores. A model of present day decentralization is the Israeli *kibbutz*. Some would say that such a voluntary community is fanatical, but no one would deny that it is cosmopolitan and rationalistic; it is post-centralist and post-urban.

Decentralizing has its risks. Suppose that the school system of a Northern city were radically decentralized, given over to the parents and teachers of each school. Without doubt some of the schools would be Birchite and some would be badly neglected. Yet it is hard to imagine that many schools would be worse than the present least-

common-denominator. There would certainly be more experimentation. There would be meaningful other choices to move to, *and* it
could be arranged that all the schools would exist in a framework of
general standards that they would have to achieve or suffer the consequences.

"States Rights"

Invariably some student argues that without the intervention of
the Federal government the Negroes in the South will never get their
civil rights. This may or may not be so; but certainly most progress
toward civil rights has come from local action that has embarrassed
and put pressure on Washington. And the Negro organizations themselves have been decentrally co-ordinated; as Dr. King has pointed
out, the "leadership" is continually following the localities. But the
basic error of this student is to think that the "States Rights" of the
segregationists is decentralist (although an authentic regionalism
would be decentralist). If each locality indeed had its option, the
counties where the Negroes are in a majority would have very different rules! And again, there would be a meaningful choice for other
Negroes to move to.

The relation of decentralization to physical and social mobility is
an important topic; let us stay with it for another page. As the example of science has shown, it is possible to have decentralist community without territorial community. Yet decentralist philosophies
have prized stability, "rootedness," subtle awareness of environment,
as a means to the integration of the domestic, technical, economic,
political, and cultural functions of life, and to provide a physical community in which the young can grow up.

The Americans have always been quick to form voluntary associations — Tocqueville mentions the trait with admiration; yet
Americans have always been mobile, usually going *away*, individuals
and families leaving communities that did not offer enough opportunity, in order to try new territory known by hearsay. Historically,
the country was open at the margins, because of either the geographical frontier or new jobs that attracted immigrants. When people settled, they again formed voluntary associations. Thus, to a degree,
voluntary mobility favored decentralization. On the other hand, the
new ties and settlements tended to become more homogenous and
national.

At present, however, the country is closed at the margins, yet the
physical (and social) mobility is even greater. Negroes migrate north

because the sharecropping has failed and they are barred from the factories; Northern middle-class whites move to the suburbs to escape the Negroes; farm families have dwindled to 8 percent. Unfortunately, none of these groups is moving *to* anything. And much moving is ordered by the central organization itself; national corporations send their employees and families to this or that branch; universities raid one another for staff; promoters and bureaucrats dislocate tenants for urban redevelopment.

The Hope of Community

Neglected, such conditions must end up in total anomie, lack of meaningful relation to the environment and society. There seem to be two alternative remedies. One was proposed forty years ago by Le Corbusier: to centralize and homogenize completely, so that one dwelling place is exactly like another, with identical furniture, services, and surroundings. When all live in identical hotel rooms, mobility does not involve much dislocation. The other alternative is to build communities where meaningful voluntary association is again possible; that is, to decentralize. This has, of course, been the wistful aim of suburbanism, and it continually appears in the real estate advertisements. But a suburb is not a decentralist community; its purposes, way of life, and decisions are determined by business headquarters, the national standard of living, and the bureau of highways. The hope of community is in people deciding important matters for themselves.

Then a student raises a related objection: Decentralism is for small towns, it cannot work with big dense populations. But this objection has no merit. Decentralism is a kind of social organization; it does not involve geographical isolation, but a particular sociological use of geography.

In important respects, a city of five millions can be decentrally organized as many scores of unique communities in the framework of a busy metropolis.

Usually in modern urban administration, the various municipal functions — school, job-induction, post office, social work, health, police and court for misdemeanors, housing and rent control, election district, etc. — are divided into units only for the administrative convenience of City Hall. The districts do not coincide with one another nor with neighborhoods. A citizen with business or complaint must seek out the district office of each department, or perhaps go to City Hall. And correspondingly, there is no possible forum to discuss the co-ordination of the various functions except at the very top, with the Mayor or before the Council.

Decentralist organization would rather follow the actuality of living in an urban community, where housing, schooling, shopping, policing, social services, politics are integrally related. Each neighborhood should have a local City Hall. Such *arrondissements* could have considerable autonomy within the municipal administration that controls transit, sanitation, museums, etc., whatever is necessarily or conveniently centralized. Taxes could be collected centrally and much of the take divided among the neighborhoods to be budgeted locally.

For the average citizen, the convergence of all kinds of related businesses in one local center is not only convenient but must lead to more acquaintanceship and involvement. Poor people especially do not know their way around, are stymied by forms to fill out, and have no professional help; they are defeated by fighting City Hall and soon give up. Besides, each neighborhood has interlocking problems peculiar to itself. These can be reasonably confronted by citizens and local officials, but they are lost in the inner politics of central bureaucracies that have quite different axes to grind. A neighborhood should certainly police itself, according to its own mores, and avoid the present police brutality inevitable in trying to impose an unworkable city-wide conformity.

Urbanism

A neighborhood so constituted might learn to decide on its own redevelopment. In programs for urban renewal, the Federal government follows the traditional formula of balancing centralism and decentralism and asks for approval of plans by the local community. Cities therefore set up local "planning boards." But this works out as follows: Occasionally, middle-class residential neighborhoods can organize themselves to prevent any change whatever; poor people are entirely passive to the powers that be; usually, the boards are rubber stamps for City Hall and promoters. The say of a neighborhood in its destiny can be meaningful only if the neighborhood has begun to be conscious of itself as a community. For this, mere "consent" or "participation" is not enough; there must be a measure of real initiating and deciding, grounded in acquaintance and trust.

However, the question is not whether decentralization can work in dense urban populations, but how to make it work, for it is imperative. The increase of urban social disease and urban mental disease is fundamentally due to powerlessness, resignation, and withdrawal. People's only way to assert vitality is to develop symptoms. The central authorities try to cope as stern or hygienic caretakers; the citizens respond by becoming "community-dependent" — in jail, in the hospital, on relief; that is, they become chronic patients. With many, this has gone on for two or three generations.

Yet something further needs to be said about big dense populations. In my opinion, there is a limit of urban density and urban sprawl beyond which *no* form of social organization, centralist or decentralist, can cope. Urban crowding creates a peculiar climate of both too many social relations and a kind of sensory and emotional deprivation. Instead of contact and communication, there is noise and withdrawal. It is no different than among John Calhoun's over-crowded rodents who become confused and die. E.g. the density of population in Central Harlem, 67,000 persons per square mile, is nearly three times that of New York City as a whole. Even apart from the other unfavorable conditions of the Negroes, such crowding itself is pathological, overstimulating yet culturally impoverishing, destructive of solitude, excessively and brutally policed.

Our degree of urbanization is beyond reason. In this country we have the symptoms of a "population explosion" at the same time that vast and beautiful rural regions have become depopulated. In the present set-up, only big operators with migrant labor can make a go of farming, and the farm subsidies work almost entirely in favor of this group alone. Except for a few earnest but powerless voices, there is general agreement to let farming-as-a-way-of-life die out. Yet no effort whatever is made to find urban substitutes for the independence, multifarious skills, community spirit, and extended family that were rural values.

During the Great Depression, the Roosevelt administration made some effort to support subsistence farming, as a factor of social stability and to relieve both rural and urban misery. But with the return of prosperity, nothing further came of it. (Let me say that there was a shaggy decentralism in many parts of the early New Deal.)

Decentralism and "Human Nature"

A student hotly objects that decentralism is humanly unrealistic, it "puts too much faith in human nature" by relying on intrinsic motives like interest in the job and voluntary association. Another student mentions Rousseau, who is still academically out of fashion since his debunking by Professor Babbitt a generation ago. (Jefferson, too, is now getting his lumps.)

This objection is remarkably off-base. My experience is that most decentralists are crotchety and sceptical and tend rather to follow Aristotle than Rousseau. We must avoid concentration of power precisely because we *are* fallible; *quis custodiet custodes?* Democracy, Aristotle says, is to be preferred because it is the "least evil" form of government, since it divides power among many. I think the student states the moral issue upside down. The moral question is not whether men are "good enough" for a type of social organization, but whether the type of organization is useful to develop the potentialities of intelligence, grace and freedom in men.

More deeply, of course, the distrust of "human nature" is anxious conformism. One must save face, not make a mistake in any detail; so one clings to an assigned role. But unfortunately, the bigger the organization, the more face to save. For instance, we shall see that the government Peace Corps is many times as expensive as similar less official operations largely because an errant twenty-year-old well-digger might become an International Incident, so one cannot be too careful in selecting him. Convenience of supervision overrides performance. And the more "objective" the better; if the punch-card approves, no one is guilty. A fatal hallmark of decentralist enterprises is their variety in procedure and persons; how can one *know*, with a percentage validity, that these methods and persons are *right*?

Morally, all styles of social organization are self-proving, for people understand the rightness of what everybody in fact does. But different styles have different norms. The centralizing style makes for both petty conforming and admiration for bigness. The more routine and powerless people are, the more they are mesmerized by extrinsic proofs of production and power. An enterprise that is designed on a small scale for a particular need of particular people comes to be regarded as though it were nothing at all. To win attention and support, it must call itself a Pilot Project, promising mighty applications.

Nevertheless, still deeper than these neurotic confusions, there is, in my opinion, an authentic confusion in the face of unprecedented conditions of modern times, that makes for rigidity and fear of social experiment. A student says, "We could afford to experiment if it were not for the Chinese, the Cubans, the crime rate, the unemployment, the space race, the population explosion." The leap in technology, the galloping urbanization, nuclear weapons, the breakdown of the colonial system — all involve threats and dilemmas. The inevitable response of people is to rally to the style of strict control by experts. In emergencies, centralized organization seems to make sense and often does make sense. It is also comfortingly dictatorial.

Finally, the moral objection is stated also the opposite way: decentralizing is impossible not because people are incapable, but because the powers-that-be won't allow it. (This student is an Angry Young Man.) Granting that in some areas decentralization is workable, how could it possibly be brought about? We cannot expect central powers to delegate autonomy any more than we can expect the Nation-States to give up any of their sovereignty and grandeur. Indeed, the tendency is entirely in the other direction, toward bigger corporations, combinations and tie-ins, toward tighter scheduling and grading in education, toward increased standardization and the application of automatic and computer technology in every field, and of course toward the increase of power in Washington to become the greatest landlord, the greatest sponsor of research and the greatest policeman.

All this is undeniable. Yet the situation is not so black and white. There are also forces in the other direction. I must assume for instance that it is not a social accident that I am writing a book on the subject of decentralization.

Voluntary Associations

In principle, there are two ways in which an overcentralized system can become more mixed. Either voluntary associations form spontaneously because of pressing needs to which the central system is irrelevant or antipathetic; or the central authority itself chooses, or is forced, to build in decentral parts because its method simply is not working.

Certainly there are major social trends toward spontaneous do-it-yourself associations. We have already noticed the spontaneity, localism, and decentralist federation of the Negro civil rights movement, as opposed to the more conventional maneuvering of the Urban League and the older NAACP. But this is part of a general spread of paralegal demonstrating, boycotting, and show of power that clearly express dissent with formal procedures that are not effective. Nonviolent activism is peculiarly epidemic; it immediately provides something to do rather than being merely balked — a beautiful feature of it, perhaps, is to balk the authorities — yet it does not require forming political parties or organizing private armies. (When the nonviolence is authentic, indeed, its very action is decentralizing; it restores the opposition to being persons rather than personnel. Violence has the contrary effect.)

Do-It-Yourself can be parainstitutional if not overtly paralegal. Beat youth withdraw from the economy, Off-Broadway withdraws from Broadway. Students quit famous universities because they decide they are not being educated; then they form, for instance, the Northern Student Movement in order to tutor backward urban children; but then the Northern Student Movement decides that the public school curriculum is inadequate too, and the tutors will teach according to their own lights. Freedom Now sets up what amounts to a "para-party" in Mississippi.

But there is a similar tone within the political framework. Contrasted with older "reform" movements which were devoted to purging the bosses and grafters, the new urban reform movements rapidly constitute themselves *ad hoc* for a concrete purpose, usually to block outrageous encroachments of governments or big institutions. Unfortunately, they usually do not then have a counter-program; they stop with exercising a veto, lose steam, and eventually lose the issue anyway.

All this kind of ferment is what Arthur Waskow calls "creative disorder."

But also, in my opinion, the startling strength of know-nothing movements in the country is importantly due to justified dissatisfaction with the centralization, exactly as they claim when they reiterate the slogan "Government must not do what people can do for themselves." By "people" our reactionary friends seem mainly to mean corporations, which are not people, yet I do not think that liberals and progressives pay attention to the underlying gripe, the loss of self-determination. The liberals glibly repeat that the complex problems of modern times do not allow of simplistic solutions; but what is the use of solutions about which one has no say, and which finally are not the solutions of one's own problems?

I do not notice any significant disposition of central powers to decentralize themselves. Rather, their disposition, when the organization begins to creak, is to enlarge it further by adding new centralized bureaus and overseers, to stall by appointing committees without power, to disregard difficulties and hope that they will go away, to call hard cases "deviant" and put them out of circulation.

Nevertheless, there are actual examples to show how decentralization *can* be built in.

The management of a giant corporation — General Motors is the classical example — can shrewdly decide to delegate a measure of autonomy to its corporate parts, because more flexible enterprising is more profitable in the long run. Or a huge physical plant can be geographically dispersed and somewhat decentralized, to save on labor costs and get better tax breaks. Naturally these motives do nothing at all for the great majority of subordinates.

More interesting for our purposes is the multifarious application of industrial psychology. For the most part, the psychologists are decentralist and have taught the opposite wisdom to "scientific business management." Rather than subdividing the workman further, they have urged the efficiency of allowing more choice and leeway, asking for suggestions from below, increasing "belonging." To give a typical example: it has been found to be more productive in the long run for half a dozen workmen to assemble a big lathe from beginning to end and have the satisfaction of seeing it carried away, than to subdivide the operation on a line.

Needless to say, our industrial psychologists cannot pursue their instincts to the logical conclusion of workers' management. But questions of degree are not trivial. Consider the following example. In some areas of England it is traditional to work by a Gang or collective contract. (This has been studied by Professor Melman of Columbia University.) A group of workmen agree to complete in a certain period a certain quantity of piece work for which they are paid a sum of money divided equally. The capitalist provides the machinery and materials, but *everything else* — work rules, methods, schedule, hiring — is left to group decision. This arrangement has proved feasible in highly skilled work like building and in semi-skilled work on automobile assembly lines. The group may be half a dozen or a couple of thousand. Humanly, the arrangement has extraordinary advantages. Men exchange jobs and acquire many skills; they adjust the schedule to their convenience (or pleasures); they bring in and train apprentices; they invent labor-saving devices, since it is to their own advantage to increase efficiency; they cover for one another when sick or for special vacations. Obviously such a system, so amazingly at variance with our top-down regulation, timeclock discipline, labor union details and competitive spirit, is hard to build into most of our industry. Yet it would suit a lot of it and make a profound difference. Where would it suit? How could it be tailored?

An attempt to build in decentralization is at present occurring in the New York school system. Because of a combination of near-riots in poor neighborhoods, some spectacular run-of-the-mill scandals, and the post-Sputnik spotlight on upgrading, a new and pretty good Board has been appointed. Deciding that the system is overcentralized, these gentlemen have resuscitated twenty-five local districts — averaging forty thousand children each! — and appointed local

Boards with rather indefinite powers, to serve as liaison to the neighborhoods. But unlike the case of urban renewal planning boards mentioned above the intention *is* to delegate positive powers; and anyway, the remarkably strong-minded body of people who have been appointed to the local school boards have no intention of being rubber stamps. At present, there is a jockeying for position and power. The local boards are empowered to hold budget hearings and "suggest" allocation of money. What does this mean? Could they suggest to eliminate some of the curriculum and services and substitute others? Some local board members want to decentralize radically, making the field superintendents and the local boards nearly autonomous within the big system, as is reasonable, since the different neighborhoods have different conditions and therefore have different curricular, staff and service needs.

One of the Manhattan boards, curious to know what its sister-boards were doing, convened a meeting of the five Manhattan boards, and they agreed to exchange minutes. At once the central board protested and forbade such attempts at federation. "If you issue joint statements," they pointed out, "people will think that you speak for the school system." "What can you do about it?" asked the locals; "since you have called us into existence, we exist, and since we exist, we intend to act." I mention this incident not because it is important in itself, but because it is at the heart of the constitutional problem of centralization and decentralization.

These, then are *prima facie* objections raised by college students. Decentralization is disorderly and "anarchic." You cannot decentralize air-traffic-control and public health. What about automation? Decentralization is a peasant ideology. It makes for "States Rights" injustice. It is unworkable with big dense populations. It implies an unrealistic faith that human nature is good. It is impossible to go against the overwhelming trend toward bigness and power.

Discouragingly in such discussions, the students keep referring to "your system" or "the decentralist system." But I am not proposing a "system." It is hard to convince college students that it is improbable that there *could* be a single appropriate style of organization or economy to fit all the functions of society, any more than there could be a single mode of education ("going to school") that suits almost everybody, or that there is a "normal" behavior that is healthy for almost everybody.

It seems to me as follows. We are in a period of excessive centralization. It is demonstrable that in many functions this style is economically inefficient, technologically unnecessary and humanly damaging. Therefore we ought to adopt a political maxim: to decentralize where, how and how much is expedient. But where, how, and how much are empirical questions; they require research and experiment.

In the existing overcentralized climate of opinion, it is just this research and experiment that we are not getting. Among all the departments, agencies and commissions in Washington, I have not heard of one that deals with the organizational style of municipalities, social work, manufacturing, merchandizing or education, in terms of their technical and economic efficiency and their effects on persons. Therefore, I urge students who are going on to graduate work to choose their theses in this field.

The Sentiment of Powerlessness

1

Feeling that the present social style is stifling them, college students are interested in decentralist ideas as an alternative. There is not such interest among the voting citizens. In the political spectrum from Left to Right, all shades share the belief in top-down management. Liberals believe in more rather than less Federal intervention in this management; "conservatives" would rather leave it to the corporations, which are a kind of feudal baronies. (The term "conservative" in our politics tends to mean back to McKinley. Strict constitutionalists like Black are regarded as radical. And those would conserve the natural environment and human freedom to breathe and initiate are, at present, usually anarchists.)

A generation ago, intellectual liberals used to express enthusiasm for a "mixed economy." The model was Sweden which enjoyed, it was said, a mixture of welfare-State socialism, independent enterprise, corporate enterprise, a strong co-operative movement, and a stable balance of farm and city. In this mixture, the co-operatives, the independents, and the small farms were decentralist components, and they were a power against engulfment by State and corporations.

The mixed system is no longer mentioned. Not since the Populism of 1890 has this country had any spirit for producers' co-operatives. During the past thirty years consumers' co-operatives have lost headway, and even the service of consumer information, the consumers' union, has retrogressed and been left to the federal government. Everybody agrees, and legislates, to drive small farms out of existence. And there are no longer many independents, e.g., less than 2 percent of college graduates go into independent enterprises, but 35 percent into the corporations and an even greater number into government service and teaching in the public systems or great universities. Even the majority of professionals become "professional personnel."

Liberals do not now think that anybody is engulfed and needs a recourse to exercise initiative. Their strategy for helping the powerless is not to cut things down to size or open spaces to breathe, but to spend money on schools, welfare, retraining, area redevelopment, managed from above. The powerless become clients. Astoundingly, liberals no longer even talk about civil liberties, though there is end-less talk about civil rights. That is, one is entitled to due process within the central organization, but one is not protected in going one's own way.

The regulatory agencies, sponsored by the older liberalism, have become accommodations with the giant monopolies, rather than means of pluralizing. And of course liberal government has itself be-come a giant entrepreneur, in highways, housing, research and development, space exploration. Not to mention the sixty-billion-dol-lar budget for Defense, which is managed by whatever government, Democratic or Republican. (With a modest multiplier, this budget for Defense controls a quarter of the entire economy.)

Accordingly, there is a major new class of bureaucratized intellec-tuals, a kind of monkhood. These are the professors, sociologists, con-tracted researchers, diplomats, licensed social workers, consultants, think-factory hands, and other doctors of philosophy and profes-sional-personnel who provide the reasoning and rationalizations for the centralizing programs of liberal government.

2

Oddly, the rhetoric of independence and civil liberties is now spoken only by Big Business, at least by the branches of Big Business that are not immediate partners of government and operating on cost-plus. But the tone of Business rhetoric is no longer the social-Dar-winism of rugged individualism, but rather defensive complaint against the encroachment of the *other* entrepreneur. The usual sub-stance is the wish for lower taxes, less regulation, and the elimination of the corporation of Labor; often, however, one can detect a direct clash of rival combinations, e.g. Steel-Oil-Aircraft vs. Electronics-MIT-National Science Foundation.

This ancient war of the King and the Barons has little to do with decentralization in the meaning of this book, nor indeed with per-sonal liberty. Let me tell an anecdote. I was on a panel with the pub-lisher of the *National Review*, and he complained grievously about Mr. Kennedy's police harassment of the head of U.S. Steel. I was sym-pathetic, and I told him about a couple of Puerto Ricans in New York who were treated even worse, actually manhandled. But I could not get him interested in their case.

I doubt that at present, on balance, the more or less intervention of Federal government is unfavorable or favorable to free enterprise in any important human sense.

3

Nevertheless, although it is hypocritical, the conservative rhetoric about encroachment is important, perhaps dangerous, because it is true. All classes believe in the inevitability of top-down direction in one form or another, but people are also restive at their powerlessness. And this restiveness is especially acute in two great strata of the middle class, those who are losing out (including small farmers), and those who are precariously climbing, anxious suburbanites often educated beyond their capacities. These groups are inflamed by the anti-centralist rhetoric which they accept, personally, in its most extreme statements — anti-Negro, anti-urban, anti-sociological, and jingoist. They thus constitute a fascist threat, not in the name of Order but of Liberty! To be sure, they are not consistent. We are told that extremism in the defense of liberty is no vice; but progressive education or giving the accused a fair shake in court is not liberty but License.

By the usual irony of history, the big Business rhetoric of today is rather like the rhetoric of Populism, including its know-nothing excesses, that was invented just to break out of the centralizing trap of Big Business.

Conversely, the rhetoric of Liberalism has become paternalistic and moderate, and promises to lead us right to 1984.

To find how this extraordinary switch has come about, let us make a quick survey of American history from the beginning. Our theme is the growth among citizens of a feeling of powerlessness to initiate and decide.

4

When the American Revolution removed the British authority at the top, society remained mainly organized as a network of highly structured face-to-face communities and associations, and these were fairly autonomous. The structures were sometimes democratic; more often they were little clusters around an elite. There were town meetings, congregational parishes, yeoman families, masters and apprentices, masters and indentured servants, gentry families with hired help and slaves, professionals and their clients. Democratic or hierarchic, the groups were small, and on most matters people were in frequent personal contact with those who initiated and decided.

It is astoundingly likely, however, that with respect to the State or confederated government, during the first twenty-five or thirty years of the Republic these communities existed in a virtual community-anarchy. The franchise was heavily restricted by requirements of property, education, sex, religion, and color; but the interesting evidence is that very few of those who were enfranchised bothered to vote anyway, often only 1 or 2 percent of the population. Nevertheless, the general sentiment and rhetoric are intensely democratic, sometimes egalitarian.

No such anarchist picture appears in our histories; but, of course, they are written to highlight either the previous war or the breakdown of the Articles of Confederation or the *prospective* importance of the Federal government in the next century, or else particular major Federal actions, like the Northwest Ordinance, the Sedition Laws, or the Louisiana Purchase. It is not much mentioned, e.g., that for a couple of years Jefferson abolished the navy as useless; or that once Shays' Rebellion was dispersed, it was entirely condoned. (Jefferson to Madison: "A little rebellion now and then is a good thing …. This truth should render Republican governors so mild in their punishment of rebellions as not to discourage them.")

One has the impression that unless a man engaged in interstate or international commerce or was a creditor and had to do with lawyers, he was quite indifferent to what went on in government. Formally, the total sovereignty had devolved on the States; but how much addition of positive powers did this imply? Except for matters of high culture — where it was of major importance — the departure of the British seems to have left few gaps and simply removed unnecessary clogs to life. This is certainly the implication of Richard Henry Lee's complaint that, in 1787, a Constitution was entirely premature; all that was needed was the regulation of trade, of legal tender, and of fraudulent debtors and "men unfriendly to Republican equality."

5

Yet these "anarchist" communities were *not* non-political. Quite the contrary! Especially the independent elite regarded themselves as a band of citizen-friends born to make institutions, constitutions, or whatever. The rhetoric of the Declaration of Independence, and the act itself, were momentous just because they had this existential spontaneity; they initiated in the void, with a decent obligation to explain everything to mankind but no formal obligation to anything or anybody. Twenty-five years later, Jefferson's First Inaugural breathes exactly the same spirit, only more so. In the changed circumstances, it is personal, offhand, self-assured, like the remarks of a professor who has been elected temporary rector by his own faculty. No aura attaches to the Presidency. To be political, to govern, is an ordinary human act. (John Adams had tried to work up a little aura, and Jefferson didn't like it.)

In this view, political institutions are nothing but deliberate social experiments. In a beautiful passage, Madison explains the advantages of decentralism: each autonomous unit can experiment; if the experiment fails, only a small community is hurt, and the others can help out; if the experiment succeeds, it can be imitated to everybody's advantage. (It *is* a misfortune that the Federal system of States has not operated in this way. I can think of only a few radical experiments, in Minnesota, Wisconsin, Louisiana. If Upton Sinclair's EPIC program in California had come to power, it might have been the most interesting.)

To cement this easy assumption of a band of citizens who could experiment on their own and give mutual support, there were, of course, shared assumptions in moral philosophy and on the Nature of Man. There was an acceptance of human diversity, but a confidence, as is clear in *The Federalist*, that there need never be party divisions, though there would undoubtedly be "factions." Common reason, a common ultimate goal would provide coherence.

More deeply, people used to autonomy experienced no conflict between reason and feeling, or between objectivity and engagement. This led to a crucially important view of history, that existing conditions were *plastic* to human purposes. Problems were amenable to improvement by practical proposals, and these practical proposals would be put into effect by the meeting of minds. Typically, Washington and his friends were great canal planners. (Some of the canals, like the Ohio-Potomac, were never dug.) By the same token, past history was assiduously studied because of its moral lessons, as a source of examples for present action.

In this idyllic climate there was no thought of powerlessness and very little thought of coercion. Historical conditions were *for* men to act in, and men *could* act. So far as centralization and top-down direction were necessary, they were built into the system in a characteristic style: federation, limited sovereignty, multifarious checks and balances. The very calling of a constitutional convention, for example, implied that others could and would be called — perhaps "every twenty years," so that each generation could again make society. There is no rhetoric that "what we now do will last a thousand years."

The checks and balances are regarded by historians as compromises, between big States and small States, between monarchic Executive and popular Legislature, etc.; and of course, so they were. But more importantly, they expressed a positive theory about Human Nature: that each man is fired by special interests and is co-operative; he is reflective and executive; he is initiating and obedient to Law; he is conservative and progressive; he is individualistic and social. Naturally, in these polarities, some men or groups would opt strongly for one or another extreme, but these would constitute only transient factions.

6

As the country passed into the Jacksonian period, however, the face-to-face structured groups were steadily disrupted. Master-apprentice and indenture relations gave way first to paternal capitalism and then to the formation of a proletariat. With new technology, family-slavery and gentry-farming rapidly became field-slavery on big plantations. With the growth of urban population, there was cash-cropping on an increased scale. There was an increase of absentee ownership and abstract money, banking and investment.

In this disruption, the more powerful persons could combine in new functional associations, whether joint-stock corporations or lobbies, forming new centers. But the smaller people tended to become homogenized. The new immigrants, e.g. Negro or Irish, were "mere" labor.

There then began to be a sense of impersonal "objective" conditions. In the utilitarian mode, the rhetoric began to abound in statistics and in enthusiastic identification with rather abstract national goals and achievement, such as growth of population, territory, and wealth, and also with being part of a mighty interlocking system of division of labor, both craft and sectional. (Of course this rhetoric was largely true; the question is, "Under what conditions are people moved by it?") With the imposition of tariffs, manipulated currency, the terms of admission of new States, and pork-barrelling public works, people now had a vital stake in centralized politics and the community-anarchy was at an end. The more homogenized majority was able to force a nearly universal white adult male suffrage.

In the new abstract relations, there were irreconcilable conflicts, not to be settled by practical proposals meeting common agreement: class conflict, conflict of sections, conflict of city and country. Factions became permanent parties, looking for mass support in the wide suffrage, and the sense of history was entirely transformed. History was now an It that had to be pushed; it was the tendency of objective conditions which could be influenced to one's advantage by belonging to the victorious Party and sharing in the spoils. Correspondingly, compromise was no longer a reasoned positive solution but an avoidance of worse conflict. But nothing could really be settled.

Naturally, the division into only two mass parties, necessary to try to gain the upper hand, could not represent the actual manifold conflicts of interest. The more "popular" party might represent small debt-ridden farmers and urban workingmen, but it might also represent the country against the city, the South against the North. The more elite party might represent Industry and therefore urban jobs, but also rural stability and gentry. Inevitably, political rhetoric became blurred and phoney, and the patriotic rhetoric of cohesiveness tended to become symbolic and emotional, abounding in "our heritage" and in panegyric that the continent was broad.

Fatefully, government itself became an independent institution of society, rather than an existential act of ordinary citizens. Men "ran for office" as once the office had sought the man. The change in the attitude toward the Constitution is significant. There began to be a pedantry and aura of the text. It was no longer regarded as a man-made document that might be remade — though in fact it was continually being remade, e.g. by the Party system itself.

Government, especially the Presidency, assumed the curious dual role that we are used to. On the one hand, it was the victorious Party with a drive toward tyranny of the majority. But on the other, it was an impersonal arbiter among the irreconcilable conflicting groups. (Jackson: "There are no necessary evils in government. If it would confine itself to equal protection and shower its favors alike on the high and the low, it would be an unqualified blessing." Note that this was still the opinion of the popular Party, not the plutocrats.)

Finally, by the familiar psychological mechanism, with the increase of powerlessness, internal tension, and sectionalism there developed xenophobia and narrow patriotism, instead of the beautiful Enlightenment tolerance and internationalism of the preceding generation. The universal ideal of education of Jefferson and Madison lapsed into sectarian and elite colleges. The electorate divided into ethnic and religious blocs.

On the other hand, of course, it was an open society, with opportunity and space, and there were strong forces toward both community and personal freedom. There was the possibility, in some places transiently realized, of combining industrial and farm occupations, for no enclosures threw the farmers off the land. The combination could be capitalistic, as when textile mills hired surplus farm girls, or it could be communal, as in the Owenite or Fourierist experiments.

It is during this period that Tocqueville speaks with admiration of the disposition of Americans to form voluntary associations to perform every kind of function. But unfortunately, just those associations which might essentially have countervailed the new homogenizing conditions, e.g. craft unions and the intentional communities, proved abortive. Indeed, in some respects the freedom of the frontier and the expansion of wealth were misfortunes, since they provided easy safety valves. And the immigration provided industrial labor that was exploitable in a way that prosperous yeomen were not. Perhaps just at this time, at the beginning of modern industrial society, people with the original American character could have hammered out authentic institutions.

As it was, moral philosophy fell apart into three kinds of theories: Calhoun's "types of mankind," with irreconcilable interests and the need for a balancing strong authority; the egalitarianism without qualities that Tocqueville complains of; and the individualism of Emerson and Thoreau. This last is terribly prescient of the generations to come, when civilized society is regarded as coercive and corrupt, when the consensus is always in the wrong, and when a man must break away into the physical or moral wilderness in order to be free and noble.

7

The outcry of Populism marked the crisis in the feeling of loss of power, which is our theme. More than the beginnings of the modern labor movement during the same period, and certainly more than Reform politics, Populism clearly saw the closing trap of interlocking centralization. Like any war, the Civil War had centralized and over-capitalized. Now the free market was restrained by trusts and ever higher tariffs. As producers and consumers, the farmers were squeezed by railroads, packers, manufacturers. There were new immigration and accelerated urbanization. The political parties became entirely massified and distantly controlled, and there were alliances between government and the monopolies. To all this, the Populists responded with heroic self-reliance, and tragic paranoia and political confusion.

In my opinion, this was the last American political movement to face squarely the crucial dilemma of modern society: how to preserve practical democracy in high industrial conditions. For a couple of decades, Populism saw the answer: the Jacksonian Party democracy could not work; one had to start anew from below.

Inevitably, but unfortunately, the movement was agrarian, since only the farmers had a live sense of the practical independence they were losing. From its beginnings, the American workingmen's movement had accepted the role assigned to it by management, of being wage-slaves, and its demands were merely for shorter hours, higher pay, and safer and more dignified conditions; it was not syndicalist, seeking power, and it was not anarchist, seeking workers' management. To the extent that the labor movement was political, it looked to socialist collectivism, with top-down administration, though without competition and profits.

The rhetoric of Populism was apocalyptic; people were trapped in the Last Times. Let me cull from the Platform of 1892: "Our country finds itself confronted by conditions for which there is no precedent in the history of the world .... A vast conspiracy against mankind has been organized and is rapidly taking possession of the world. If not met and overthrown at once, it forebodes terrible social convulsions, the destruction of civilization .... These are the issues upon which not only our individual prosperity but the very existence of free institutions depend." Strikingly — e.g. in the Declaration of the National Grange, 1874 — the Constitutional appeal now went back to the Preamble, for all the rest had become suspect. Yet this rhetoric was not, in the end, exaggerated, for since that period the older democracy has indeed been dead, and the national States have mounted two World Wars and have a thousand overkill in nuclear bombs.

8

With the Apocalypse, there was an efflorescence of paranoia, especially in the form of suspicion of all strangers, who were the troops of the diabolic entrapment. Absentee owners were all Jews. Cheap immigrant labor was part of the plot. For a brief spell, Negroes were equally oppressed brothers, but very soon they became diabolically black. The East consisted of Cities of Sin; it poisoned the food with preservatives and made shoddy and obsolescent manufactures to bilk the honest. Following out the logic, it was necessary to complete a North-South waterway — in principle the St. Lawrence Seaway connected with the Mississippi and the Gulf of Mexico — to bypass the East altogether in overseas trade, and exclude it from the national economy!

Government, too, was part of the entrapment. Politics was dirty in its nature and no honest man would seek office. Like the labor movement of the same period, the Populists continually disclaimed the revolutionary politics that were implicit in their protest. Yet, at the same time, they clamored for nationalization of the railroads and utilities and some industries, for strengthening the civil service, for establishment of the Federal regulatory agencies, and for a graduated income tax to be dispensed from Washington. *These* demands became, of course, the platform of the lapse of Populism into Progressivism and modern Liberalism.

9

The relations between Populism and the labor movement were tragically askew, so that at this critical moment again it was impossible to form a united and successful movement to ease us into the twentieth century. The groups respected each other and expressed sympathy, but they could not co-operate. First, there was a superficial clash of interests, the workers in manufacturing and transport wanting higher wages and the farmers cheaper goods. More deeply, the farmers tended to include all urban workers in the hated circle of foreigners and people dependent and lackeys by nature. Also, though they believed fervently in co-operation, the Populist co-operatives did not resist using their own enterprises to gouge profits whenever they could, and this was contradictory to the truer socialism of the more extreme labor movement.

On the other hand, the labor movement was persistently wrong in principle. As it was set up, it could not be an instrument to struggle against the enclosing trap — and indeed we see, a half century later, that either in its bureaucratized or in its Statist form, labor-unionism has become a chief partner in centralization.

In Europe there had been a sharp conflict in unionism, between the centralizing Marxist and welfare-Statists and the decentralizing Proudhonists, Bakuninists, and Guild Socialists. Fundamentally, the decentralists wanted worker-management in one form or other. Their workers tended to belong especially to highly skilled, self-reliant, or daring occupations — watchmakers, artist-craftsmen, peasants, miners, lumbermen, seamen — and they felt that they could manage handsomely without top-down direction. They looked to a future of syndicalist federation as the organization of society. The Marxist and La Sallean unions, on the other hand, worked at routinized occupations in highly rationalized plants; they formed bureaucratic and centralized parties; and they looked to a future of top-down planning and administration. In my opinion, it was a disaster that this tendency (which was in the minority) gained control of the international labor movement, for the decentralist guilds and syndical federations would have countervailed the subsequent overcentralization.

It is possible — to make a pointless speculation — that in America a more daring labor theory, concentrating on worker-management and the co-operation of farm and factory, might have been more congenial to Populism. Certainly the most "anarchist" American labor organization, the IWW, did best on Populist soil. As it was, however, the Populists looked askance at the foreign socialists — intellectual Germans and Jews who had fled Europe in 1849 or from the Czar. Meantime, like the Populists themselves, the skilled craft-unionists sought their own short-range interest.

10

Despite paranoia, pettiness, and political confusion, the effort of the Populists is beyond praise, to reopen society, starting at the bottom, by the process of Do-It-Yourself. They excellently analyzed the costs of distribution and how to diminish them, the dangers of one-crop farming, the need to avoid "the credit system, the mortgage system, the fashion system," and how to substitute their own arbitration for litigation. In political theory, they pushed to abolish the Party system, for direct primaries, and popular initiative and referendum. These were consistent with their best inspiration, and are probably necessary for any modern workable democracy. (Of themselves, of course, they guarantee nothing.) With amazing co-operativeness and energy, each farm stringing its wire, they built their own phone systems, and even managed to construct short railroad lines. Their merchandizing co-operatives saved them 40 and 50 percent. They organized their own insurance.

With this went an emphasis on universal education of the practical kind. Populism inspired the best vocational high schools, the flowering of the land-grant colleges, and adult education. My feeling is that the functionalism of Sullivan and Wright, the pragmatic sociology of Mead and Veblen, and the progressive education of Dewey were nourished by the climate of Populism more than by the labor movement. They constitute the specifically American contribution to world philosophy, following and perfecting Jefferson and Emerson: the idea of humanizing industrialism and re-establishing community democracy among alienated and powerless masses.

11

Lapsing into Progressivism, Liberal Democracy, and the New Deal, the programs of Populism, the labor movement, and Debs socialism have, for the most part, become the law of the land; but in their effect they have been entirely transformed by becoming bureaucratized and administered from above. It is a remarkable proof, if proof were needed, that the method is more important than the content. These programs were designed to strengthen the hand of independent groups; they have succeeded in centrally organizing society more tightly and more in depth. Each step of the way — primaries, referendum, regulatory agencies, increasing the years of compulsory schooling, progressive income tax, muckraking, women's suffrage, right to organize, minimum wage, social security, etc., etc. — promised to be a revolutionary democratizing of society, and was so attacked and so championed. Yet all have cumulatively added up to the one interlocked system of big government, big corporations, big municipalities, big labor, big education, and big communications, in which all of us are pretty regimented and brainwashed, and in which direct initiative and deciding have become difficult or impossible.

In the past ten or fifteen years, especially during the Eisenhower and Kennedy Administrations, this *fait accompli* of centralization has dawned on the general consciousness. It has been the theme of dozens of books of social criticism. Yet the response to it has been entirely different from the apocalyptic frenzy of the Populists when the trap was closing. The present belief is that "under modern conditions," the trap is inevitable and we are powerless. This sentiment is itself an effect of accustomed powerlessness. One can no longer even imagine another State, not to speak of inventing means to it and trying to execute them.

What is the objective background? During the twentieth century, we have engaged in two world wars. It is said that Wilson hesitated to enter World War I because it would be necessary to subsidize corporations that would never cut back. He was right. The United States is now the chief imperialist power, with a vast permanent military and overcapitalized industries to support the role. The warring trusts have settled into a system of semi-monopolies, with fixed prices, for mutual security. The free market has turned into a synthetic creature of advertising. Government has entered into colossal alliances; in real estate, with municipalities and promoters; in agriculture, with giant croppers and grocery chains; in science and education, with the universities and high-technology corporations; in highways, with automobile manufacturers and oil men.

A sovereign citizenry is no longer even thought of. Let me quote two remarks of Franklin Roosevelt: "The day of the Politician is past; the day of the Enlightened Administrator has come" — the State had already withered away! — "The greatest duty of a statesman is to educate." What a remarkable change in American theory! Madison though that it was the democratic process itself that educated. But for Roosevelt there is an ongoing system expertly tended by administrators, and there is a mass of pupils who do not know how to fend for themselves — especially the "underprivileged." There have ceased to be prudent or angry citizens.

Since the New Deal paternalism, we have seen two strikingly different images of administration, Eisenhower's non-intervention and Kennedy's let's-get-a-move-on, yet social changes have had little to do with these differences. Automation, urbanization, Negro revolution, colonial revolution have developed according to their own laws. Government policy, so far as there is policy, resides mainly in the entrenched system of the Civil Service, Pentagon, Scientific Foundations, and proliferating Agencies that are hardly subject to political decision. There has been a great addition of school-monks, but they have been nicely organized into the same structure. All this grinds on, not incompetently, not without benevolence, and with surprisingly little peculation. (Significantly, it is only the secret, para-political agencies, FBI and CIA, that seem dangerous, because they *might* do something unforeseen.)

This machine runs, by and large, for its own sake. The real form of sovereignty is democracy-by-consent, with a post-political unanimity on the issues that are inherent in the system itself: the expanding GNP, the Cold War, the solution of problems by adding new agencies staffed by school-monks. Occasional moments of living politics occur when some condition becomes intolerable and there is an outcry. The political solution is to try to make it not intolerable by money, a new agency, or at least a commission of inquiry. Embarrassing or dissenting officials may be shifted to other departments; the seasoned never quit and nobody is fired.

It is said that governmental power has all gravitated to the Executive, away from the Congress who, like people, can only consent or balk. Extreme liberals are now hot to streamline Congress so it cannot even balk. But in the system we have been describing, the Executive also is not a governing person nor group of persons, any more than the baronial corporations are persons except as a fiction. During the activist Kennedy regime, frustration was continually expressed because, somehow, the Cabinet and the President himself were powerless. Just so the heads of giant corporations and of apparently autonomous universities claim that they are powerless to alter policies that they say they disapprove of. It is inherent in centralization that powerlessness spreads from the bottom to the top. There is certainly a structure of power in the country, but it seems to be a misnomer to call it a power *elite*.

It has become common to call this mighty interlocking organization the Establishment, usually with an ironical but comfortable satisfaction, as if America had come of age. This conception is ludicrous. The cultural baseness of the executives, whether in government, the universities, or broadcasting; the communal moronism of the city and regional planners; the qualitative deterioration of the standard of living; the frantic insecurity of the middle class; the reduction of the authority of Law to force — such things are the contrary of Establishment. The idea of an Establishment is to provide a tolerable setting in which the serious affairs of life can proceed unhampered, spontaneously, often eccentrically, within agreed limits of style. Instead, not unlike a garrison State, our organization invades, and dispirits, every detail of life; it discourages dissent and kills spontaneity. It does have a style — I myself fall into it — but I do not think I agree.

When people feel powerless, they no longer think there is practicable history. "Pragmatic," as used for instance by the Kennedy regime, comes to mean keeping the works going, without a goal outside itself, and finally without information outside itself. So, in both domestic and foreign affairs, history and policy consist of coping with unanticipated events, almost on a day-to-day basis. Here is a typical anecdote to illustrate what I mean: There was a crisis in Panama set off by a petty incident in a seething environment. Out of the files at the State Department came an accurate prediction of the very event, made six years before, and advising remedies; but of course at *that* time it was not "pragmatic" to act, for Panama was not part of the day's news that realistic politicians cope with. It was now too late to act on the good advice.

12

We thus come out with the paradoxes that we have sought to explain. The gentlemen of the Right, who invented the protective tariff and the trusts, now complain in Populist terms that liberty is encroached on. But liberal democrats, the old champions of *laissez faire*, come on like pillars of the Establishment, patrons of monasteries, and almsgivers to the poor, as if they were royalists. *They* have the responsibility to keep the show going. As Mr. Schlesinger put it, "One simply must govern."

Middle-class citizens withdraw from civic responsibility into suburban privacy, and leave the central city to segregation and blight. But poor Negroes and Puerto Ricans, bearded students, and Bohemian artists exercise citizenly initiative and engage in reform politics.

Confusion and Disorder

1

In the old anthropology there was an important proposition about how a tribe took on culture from its neighbors: If the cultural trait had to do with a new utility or technique, e.g. better seeds, a new plough, or making vessels out of clay, it was picked up readily and it diffused rapidly; but if the trait was moral, psychological, or religious, e.g. a change in taboo, kinship, child-rearing, or music, then its adoption was resisted and it diffused slowly. People want what is useful and lightens labor, but they refuse what makes them anxious and seems to threaten their moral integrity. Sometimes there may be an odd compromise: basket-weavers will pick up fired pottery, but they paint the old basket design on the new pots, for people are conservative about aesthetics.

Our supermarkets readily sell Danish ham and cheese, but we are much slower in buying the equally salubrious Danish ideas about pornography. The Japanese enthusiastically adopted Western technology but, at least up to World War II, they clung with remarkable tenacity to their ancient ideology, emperor-worship, and suicide.

The case is quite different when the new cultural trait is not picked up *by* the tribe but is imposed *on* the tribe, for instance by conquest, or by overwhelming technical and economic superiority of an advanced nation that cannot be resisted. Then the moral integrity of the tribe *is* shattered, it is "colonized." People are disoriented; they can no longer pick and choose what suits them and what they can assimilate at their own pace. Obviously there are then problems of de-colonization: the former colonized people have to find *themselves* again. (According to Fanon, in this process they have to become irrational and violent, so the forgotten can return from the unconscious.)

There is cultural imperialism as well as military imperialism. Even without military conquest, a technical culture appearing on the border may be so foreign that it totally disrupts tribal morale and way of life. Consider a people for whom the sentence "I'll come in due time" means "I'll come when the corn is yea high, if the moon is not in the third quarter which is bad luck in my clan." And suppose they take on an interlocked high technology where "in due time" means "8:30 a.m. by the clock," for in the division of labor and the interlocking of machinery everybody and everything has to mesh and start off together. Then the entire way of life, family pattern, eating habits, sexuality, and community will be disrupted. The technology cannot work without a drastic change in social organization, and the technology disrupts the existing pattern in order to create the necessary social organization. The people become "alienated." Some may die of depression.

2

I suggest that for a couple of hundred years, and suddenly at an accelerating rate, modern societies have colonized and disoriented themselves, imposing on themselves a technology, urbanization, and centralized social organization that they cannot morally and psychologically cope with.

The usual way of saying this is that our physical sciences and technology, have made giant strides but our social sciences, politics, and ethics have not kept pace. This is true but it is a misleading formulation. It implies that using the same attitude and methods but being busier about moral matters, we can catch up and restore the balance. But if advanced people have indeed been colonized by their own advances, they are confused and have lost their capacity to pick and choose what they can assimilate. We certainly manifest a remarkable rigidity in our social institutions, an inability to make inventive pragmatic adjustments. And perhaps worse, the sociology and politics that we do think up have the same technological, centralizing, and urban style that is causing our derangement. The remedies make things worse.

I need not spell out the evidence that people are confused. Here are four analogous items from one day's New York *Times.* There is an epidemic increase in gonorrhoea because a new strain has developed that is immune to antibiotics; but relying on that treatment, young people have not kept up the cautious habits of previous times. A new hybrid of corn is so efficient to breed that it has been universally adopted and no supply of other seeds was stored; but now the new strain proves to be liable to a disastrous and rapidly spreading blight. (These cases are identical with the Europeans wiping out the Aztecs and Polynesians by infecting them with diseases to which they were not immune; except that we are both the carriers and the victims.) In the general haste to introduce methadone in New York to get addicts off heroin, it is distributed without safeguards, and there are now a couple of thousand methadone addicts who never were heroin addicts. Lastly, a statistical study at Princeton Theological Seminary shows that seminarians will stop to succour a (planted) "man in need" if they are not late for an examination, but they will pass him by if they are late; so the Good Samaritan, who was lower class and no doubt did not have important engagements, had time for the man in needs, but the Priest and the Levite, who had important engagements, were in the high-hurry category.

Our lovely impulses have ugly results. I like to live in Hawaii because it's beautiful. But with the new franchises for the jets, 3 to 5 million others a year are going to come for the same reason I do; the native population is 800,000 and there's not much room. Similarly, it's a grand thing for kids to go on the road and see the world, and also for them to gang together in their tribes, making human togetherness their chief sacrament. But the mathematical result is that they turn Telegraph Avenue and Harvard Square into slums and they are a threat to the Yosemite Valley. It's not *necessarily* because adults are uptight that they don't want the ravening horde to descend. I don't know the answer to these problems. One can limit tourism by imposing a whopping airport and hotel tax, but that would exclude the lower middle class, who are poignantly appreciative tourists, to the advantage of the upper middle class who are so-so. Or are we supposed to give people at birth a limited number of tickets to the beauties of the world that they can visit?

Luckily, our confusion is such that evil predictions are also unreliable. For instance, from Huxley's *Brave New World* through Orwell's *1984* to Marcuse's *One-Dimensional Man*, it looked certain that we were headed for universal regimentation, drugged conformity, and brainwashing. But the present does not look that way; there are drugs, but the style is ragged and disorderly and likely to become more so. There are unruly crowds in almost every country. In America at least, the new generation is far less consumerist than the old, in spite of the TV ads — maybe because of the TV ads. Consider how in Czechoslovakia since 1947 the regime used every means of thought-control, the press, TV, schools, labor-unions, dragnet trials of dissenters; yet in 1968, Czech youth, brought up entirely in these circumstances, rose almost unanimously against the regime; they were — no doubt are — just biding their time.

My own view is that people cannot be "dehumanized"; they can just be made unhappy. Their apparent docility and conformity simply mean that, for the time being, they have no available alternative. Real brainwashing, internalizing Big Brother's voice, requires actual physical fright, not advertisements or propaganda. Unless a man's marrow freezes, he doesn't replace his own mind with somebody else's.

Our confusion is worldwide, and it is not interesting to assign blame for it. No doubt, centuries of bad policy, profits, power, Statism, racism, and wars have exacerbated the abuse of science, immodest technology, enclosure of the countryside and herding into cities, growth of bureaucracy, and wildly distorted social priorities. Nevertheless, there is no present evidence that any political regime or ideology is exempt from the plight of modern times. With few exceptions, the rates of excessive urbanization and the decay of rural life are higher in the "Third World" countries of Asia, Latin America, and Africa than in North America and Europe — and of course the technologically underdeveloped countries can afford it less. Shanghai, even without automobiles, is said to have as much smog as New York, and Mexico City, with scads of automobiles and dirty gasoline, is worse than either. The Hudson, the Rhine, and the Danube are polluted. Lake Superior and Lake Baikal are threatened. To make a vast sugar plantation of Cuba for the Russian market, it is necessary to DDT whole provinces, just as Americans use insecticides to make vast plantations for chain grocers. The delusion of compulsory schooling for extended years crosses every ideology. Episodes of youth dissent turn up in Spain, China, France, Egypt, the United States, Mexico, Czechoslovakia, Ceylon, you name it. In the past decade, the Americans have shared the honor of using advanced weapons to mow down hundreds of thousands with Indonesia, Nigeria, and now perhaps Pakistan. Even when "aid" has not been weapons, the United States, European nations, and Russia have all given aid to underdeveloped countries that has done more harm than good. Bureaucracy, Statism, and social-engineering are universal. Every nation belongs to one power-bloc or another, although this decreases everybody's security.

It is a sad picture. Yet the plausible — and charitable — and distressing explanation is not that modern people are wicked or perverse or stupid, any more than mankind has usually been, but that they are unusually confused. On the one hand, many of our problems are unprecedented; and on the other hand, disoriented people lose their pragmatic inventiveness and often even their common sense. There are new problems that would be deeply puzzling in the best of circumstances: How to maintain any stability and rootedness with the possibility of speedy travel that we have? How to go about one's business when there is so much instant world-wide communication? What to do with One World that has suddenly emerged? Since general war has finally gotten to be out of the question — it never did make sense — how to organize peace? What *is* the political constitution that, under modern conditions, can further individuality and community and collective justice? What is the right blend of centralization and decentralization? What to automate and what not to automate? Is there really overpopulation and if so, what then? What the devil to do with organ transplants and genetic transformation? Is there really a substitute for the Calvinist ethic? (In my opinion, the mass of mankind has always succeeded in integrating life only by *some* kind of productive activity in the environment, though not, of course, activity tied to making money or making a living.)

Problems of this philosophical depth could perhaps be faced and solved by a mankind that was in possession of its wits. They are honorable and interesting problems — not something to be indignant about. They are not problems like unjust war, social injustice, pollution, piling up armaments, mis-education and mandarinism, where indignation is in order; these are outrages and the right answer to them is clear-cut: stop doing it, period. But the right solution to the new honorable problems of civilization would make an amazingly different civilization. Even seriously working at such problems, experimentally and thoughtfully, would make a worthwhile and interesting civilization.

Unfortunately, just this mess of brand new problems and age-old outrages is faced by mankind not in possession of its wits but self-colonized and confused, because we have taken on but been unable to assimilate the quantum jumps of science, technology, urbanization, and complex social organization. And the matter is not helped by the prevalent sentiment among the young that "there is no time." Then confusion becomes quiet panic. In my opinion, the sentiment of immediate crisis has some justification but not as much as young people think. It is partly a rationalization for their own inability to bear frustration, unwillingness to learn anything, and the plain spite of the powerless. To be sure, *these* hang-ups, psychological hang-ups, are inevitable: the young have no world, and *that* is not their fault.

Let me repeat and make clear what I don't mean and what I do mean by this diagnosis. I do *not* mean that we can temporize about outrages like imperialist war, social injustice, pollution, and endless schooling. But I *do* mean that the most fundamental problems are due to modern times and are world-wide. I have not heard any traditional political or ideological answer to them. It confuses matters worse to single out the Americans as special devils. Nor are older people especially finks, hypocrites, plastic, and uptight, while the young are innocent, natural, frank, and morally courageous.

It is no doubt hard to engage vigorously in politics, to stop outrages, and especially activist politics, without having slogans to shout and clear-cut enemies to hate and abuse, and without taking sides in the Cold War. It is hard for a militant in the Movement to point out with the disapproval it deserves that the Panthers feed small children propaganda with free breakfast, or that China or North Korea have a Statist idolatry that turns your stomach, or that Cuba jails its anarchists, dissident poets, and queers (I happen to be all three). Yet it is necessary to be clear about such things and not tell half-truths, especially to oneself, or one becomes stupider oneself; and other people aren't fools and won't buy the rhetoric anyway.

3

This is the problem as I see it, but I don't know the answer, being confused myself, and worse as I get older and in poorer health — I am 60. Since I am asked, however, I can safely give the old prescription of Hippocrates: With a systemic disorder like confusion, the thing is to slow down, take it easy, let things fall apart and hopefully fall into place, until you catch up with yourself. Plain food, breathing exercises, afternoon siesta. Change of scene, preferably in the country. No new commitments, but don't increase guilt by neglecting what is necessary. Don't look for a miracle cure but gradually diminish tension and build up resistance all along the line. *Natura sanat non medicus*: nature heals, not the doctor.

In fact, the drift of my programmatic ideas, of which I have been so prolific, has always been toward withdrawal and simplification. In *Communitas*, my brother and I called it "neo-functionalism," the first principle of design is to ask if it is worthwhile to have the thing at all! Let me repeat half a dozen examples.

At present the right maxim of technology is to innovate nothing, unless it is an innovation that simplifies the technical system. If there is a choice of a solution, choose the alternative that cuts back; e.g. to diminish smog, it is better to ban private cars from the cities rather than to clean the engines. Design machines that are repairable by the user, to diminish dependency on middlemen. Prefer the technological style that avoids interlocking, so that a system can break down without wide catastrophe, e.g. the Dutch or Danish style of intensive agriculture. (Incidentally, it is absurd for people who want to do organic farming just for themselves and their families to import potato-beetles and praying-mantises so as not to use chemicals. This is ideology. Grow something else instead. If a raccoon eats 10 percent of my corn, I don't build a fence but plant another row.) Technology is not autonomous, though science is; it is a branch of moral philosophy, with the criteria of prudence, safety, modesty, common sense.

The first question about transportation is not private cars and highways vs. public transportation, but why the trip altogether. I have not heard this question asked either in Congress or in City Hall. Why must the workman live so far from the job? Could that be remedied? Why do I travel 2,000 miles to give a lecture for an hour? But let me say that I am grateful to the thousands of taxi-drivers, bus-drivers, pilots, and railroad engineers who have so far brought me home safe and rarely ever late.

Social organization is now usually overcentralized. People in an enterprise cannot know the process, initiate, make decisions, communicate face to face. The maxim is to decentralize wherever it can be done without too great loss of efficiency. Urban mini-schools and the rural little red schoolhouse instead of central schools, not to speak of educational parks. Indeed, as I showed in *People or Personnel*, in enterprises where the chief cost is people rather than fixed capital and raw materials, the small scale will always show savings of 300 percent or more; so-called economies of scale are eaten up by overhead and administration to glue the people together and hamstring their efforts. Keep in mind Borsodi's law that, even in manufacturing and processing, as the unit cost of production decreases, the cost of distribution rises, and at some point it catches up. Similarly the "external" costs of a big concentrated plant should be assigned to the manufacturing cost; e.g., the hours of commuting of workers, the roads they commute on, the housing problems and increase in rent that occur. The human advantages of decentralization, in initiative and face-to-face communication, often pay off in inventions and improvements.

In the United States, we can realistically aim a rural ratio of 20 percent, like Canada's, rather than the present 5 percent. I distrust the concept of New Towns as a way of thinning out the cities; they are fantastically expensive and repeat the urban style. It is better to build up the countryside and revive the old towns as regional centers. City and country thrive best in symbiosis, by their *difference*. I agree that for the foreseeable future small farmers in America cannot make a living by cash-farming; but it is possible to get money back to small farms, and encourage new subsistence farms, by using the country to do for the cities many things that the cities do very badly for themselves.

Many families on city welfare would prefer to live on the land, if they could get the same check. Many city parents would send their children to country schools for a year or two — city school costs run nearly twice country costs, and the money could be divided between the country school and the farmers who room-and-board the children. Many in old people's homes would certainly prefer to live on the farm or in the village. Ninety percent locked in insane asylums are harmless to themselves and others but cannot cope in the city; many of these would do well in freedom in the country, vast sums spent for urban renewal and rehousing, with little or no improvement of life, would provide drastic improvement of life for very many more if spent in the country. If more of us had country cousins, we could have better and cheaper vacations than we get at city-owned resorts.

With automobiles, power tools, and TV, rural life is at least as desirable as middle-class city life. Nevertheless, from age 15 to 30 it is boring to live in a rural area; I would try to get to the city where the action is. After 30 it is another story.

Note that I am proposing a rural ratio of 20 percent, not 98 percent. In general in these proposals for decentralization and dispersal, I am thinking not of global solutions but of 2 percent of this, 3 percent of that, 7 percent of the other. Perhaps 10 percent of children might opt to go to country schools for one year; 5 percent of old people; 2 percent of the insane; 20 percent of urban renewal money. The aim is not to find a "solution" but to de-tensify, erode, cut down to size the problems that have quite suddenly gotten out of hand. It is only a few percent difference that has caused power shortages, water shortages, traffic congestion, overcrowded clinics, overcrowded buses, garbage that cannot be hauled away, not enough housing vacancies so that people cannot move when it is convenient (this is a major reason for commuting to the job). Below a certain tipping point, city services can be performed and the city is livable; above that point, nothing works, costs rapidly mount, enlargement or replacement is ruinously expensive and disruptive, the city becomes unlivable, people who can afford it move to the suburbs, the tax base diminishes, the services become still worse. But if we can de-tensify by 2 percent of this and 3 percent of that, it might add up to 20 percent and we have an alternative option.

My brother says it is not necessary to go to the Columbia School of Architecture to remodel a farmhouse.

Schools are an intermediary between the young growing up and the world of activity that is for real. It is a poor society where the young cannot enter the active world directly and learn something; but they are denied access — really they are useless and being kept on ice, just as the old are pensioned off as soon as possible. Schools are now the chief public expense, more than $80 billion annually; even the Pentagon, paying for past, present, and future wars, spends only $65 billion. It is better to spend a lot of the school money to provide direct access into the world for the young. (There are dozens of ways of doing this, like apprenticeships, travel, community work, conservation jobs, hiring them in laboratories, design offices, theaters and TV studios, etc.) The high schools are especially worthless; the money should be put directly in the pockets of adolescents if they are doing anything useful for themselves or society — it costs $1,600 a year to keep a youth in a New York high school. The evidence is that there is no correlation between years of schooling and actual competence on most jobs; the schooling is a dispiriting waste, but necessary in order to get a paper credential. There should be access to the professions *before* going on to higher education rather than after; then a young person can case the situation, find out if it suits and what one needs to learn academically — often there is nothing — and then take the necessary courses with one's own motivation. The present mandarin obstacles to access are especially disastrous for poor youth, who can't afford to waste their time and don't have the school style, though they perform well enough on jobs that are for real. What poor people should be demanding for their children is not "quality education" and open enrollment, but a change in the licensing and hiring practices. Naturally, if I say this in a black neighborhood, I am called an elitist honky, but I am right nevertheless. I agree that poor people must have an equal right and opportunity to act as stupidly as everybody else; but I will not agree to hush up that it is stupid.

In giving technological aid to "underdeveloped" regions, what must be avoided is destroying the way of life and the community, creating inflation and instant urbanization, causing farms to be abandoned, piling up machinery that cannot be used because there are no skills and replacement parts, making the region dependent on imports priced on the world market. The answer is Intermediate Technology: the use of high science and modern analysis to devise techniques that use only native social organization, local raw materials, skills that exist or can be easily learned. The aim is to help people out of disease, starvation, and drudgery, but nothing more. They must then accumulate capital and take off at their own pace in their own style; there is no other way to avoid being culturally colonized. To be sure, this kind of foreign aid cannot serve to dump the donor's surplus or outmoded equipment; what is useful may be *too* old-fashioned. Nor is Intermediate Technology highly palatable to the receiving countries that have "rising aspirations." Simple folk want shiny goods; and their sophisticated political leaders, trained in Princeton, Cambridge, or Moscow, pander after the whole Western package, including a 12-lane boulevard from the port to the capital, a steel mill, a high school system that consumes a third of the national product, and a retinue at the United Nations that eats up the rest.

I have mentioned Fanon's thesis that the colonized must become narrow and violent, to cast off their self-hatred and affirm themselves. In our advanced self-colonized societies, we have seen a certain amount of this among the young, projecting onto their parents, and onto the System, the hated traits they feel in themselves. But of course this projection cannot succeed, the hatred cannot stick, because the parents are *not* different enough; they are equally confused, as well as being mostly decent human beings and usually dear. Instead, we have hit on a quite different way to eradicate the internalized enemy, namely disorder. Since Modern Times, the Establishment, etc. are keeping things in control, for the time being liberation means letting the cat out of the bag.

4

I am sure that the reader has by now gotten my idea, such as it is. So let me close with another kind of thought.

In the coming decade, our society must learn to tolerate disorder, and profit from it. Disorder will increase, not necessarily explosively but in the more interesting forms of erosion, raggedness, disobedience, institutions falling apart. Many more 12-year-olds will be truant. Some of the expanded neo-classic community colleges and state universities will become ghost towns. The cities will decay right on. The invisible people and pariahs will continue to come out of the walls, blacks, redskins, adolescents, women, gays, jailees. At long last we may give up trying to legislate morals, gambling, sex, drugs. We may even learn — but I doubt it, it seems to be against "human nature" — to stop putting undesirables in jail because there is no percentage in it, the process always creates more crime than it prevents. It may become difficult neatly to distinguish the employed and the unemployed — hopefully we will adopt the guaranteed income instead of welfare. The country will teem with communes and life-styles. And more and more pilgrims to rock festivals and Ivan Illich in Cuernavaca. Populist protests, crowds suddenly gathering on every kind of issue, will be an accepted method of politics. There will also be more crime-in-the-streets — and we had better remember that the kind of civil peace we have had for a few generations has been unique in history; at all other times and places people used to carry swords and lock themselves in at night.

I suspect that our trillion-dollar economy won't flourish as well when the system is not so highly tuned. But if the falling off is gradual, this could be a good thing. (Except for folk who simply didn't have enough to eat, the Great Depression was not a bad time to be young in — I was class of '31.)

To me as an anarchist and psychologist, it is promising when things fall apart. They have been meshed together too tightly and artificially. Maybe some things will fall into their natural parts and recombine into more natural wholes. "Chaos is order" is an old anarchist epigram. Anyway, as Freud pointed out, once contents have come out of repression, it is impossible to cram them back; any attempt to do so produces distortion and violence; you must let them run their course and find their own integration. Disorder as such is not dangerous — though it *can* be a nuisance if one is busy. When people are really vitally threatened, they respond with authentic anxiety and tone the noise down.

The real dangers are otherwise. On the one hand, there are those who want to re-establish Law and Order. On the other hand, there are crazies who foment disorder artificially, with some fantasy that they can direct it. Between them, these two groups are likely to cause a lot of unnecessary suffering.

Notes of a Neolithic Conservative

For green grass and clean rivers, children with bright eyes and good color whatever the color, people safe from being pushed around so they can be themselves — for a few things like these, I find I am pretty ready to think away all other political, economic, and technological advantages.

Conservatives at present seem to want to go back to the conditions that were obtained in the administration of McKinley. But when people are subject to universal social engineering and the biosphere itself is in danger, we need a more neolithic conservatism. So I like maxims such as "The right purpose of elementary schooling is to delay socialization" and "Innovate in order to simplify, otherwise as sparingly as possible."

Liberals want to progress, which means to up the rate of growth by political means. But if the background conditions are tolerable, society will probably progress anyway, for people have energy, desires, curiosity, and ingenuity. We see that all the resources of the State cannot educate a child, improve a neighborhood, give dignity to an oppressed man. Sometimes it can open opportunities for people to do for themselves; but mostly it should stop standing in the way and doing damage and wasting wealth. Political power may come out of the barrel of a gun, but as John L. Lewis said, "You don't dig coal with bayonets."

Edmund Burke had a good idea of conservatism, that existing community bonds are destroyed at peril; they are not readily replaced and society becomes superficial and government illegitimate. It takes the rising of a prophet or some other irrational cataclysm to create new community bonds. It is like a love affair or a marriage — unless there is severe moral disagreement or actual physical revulsion, it is wiser to stay with it and blow on the embers, than to be happily not in love or not married at all. The hard decisions, of course, come when people imagine that they are already in love elsewhere; but nations of people are rather cautious about this.

In his American policy, Burke was a good conservative; he was willing to give up everything else to conserve the community bonds. It is just here that phoney conservatives become trimmers and tokenists and talk about "virtual representation" or "maximum feasible participation of the poor," really protecting vested interests. A proof that the American Revolution was justified is that the British government did not take Burke's and Pitt's advice. Later, during the

French Revolution, Burke was a sentimentalist clinging to the bygone, for after Louis tried to go over to the invaders, there were no community bonds left to conserve.

The problem is to allay anxiety, avoid emergency, when dictatorship is inevitable and decent people sometimes commit enormities. There was the real emergency of Hitler, and we have not yet finished with the growth of the military-industrial complex that was rooted back there. But Woodrow Wilson foresaw the same with the war industries in 1916 and we did get out of it. So long as ancient Rome had vitality, it was able to dismiss its dictatorships. We, however, have trumped up the at least partly paranoiac emergency of the Cold War, now for more than twenty years. We might get out of even that.

But the worst is the metaphysical emergency of Modern Times: feeling powerless in immense social organization; desperately relying on technological means to solve problems caused by previous technological means; when urban areas are technically and fiscally unworkable, extrapolating and planning for their future growth. Then, "Nothing can be done."

I think it is first of all to escape being trapped that I improvise dumb-bunny alternatives to the way we do things. I can then show that the reasons men are not free are only political and psychological, not metaphysical. Unlike most other "social critics," I am rather scrupulous about not attacking unless I can think up an alternative or two, to avoid arousing metaphysical anxiety. Usually, indeed, I do not have critical feelings unless I first imagine something different and begin to improvise with it. With much of the business of our society, my intuition is to forget it.

Coleridge was the most philosophical of the conservatives writing in English: "To have citizens, we must first be sure we have produced men" — or conserved them. The context of this remark, in *The Constitution of the Church and State*, is his critique of the expropriation of the monasteries by Henry VIII. The property was rightly taken away from the Whore of Babylon, to stop the drain of wealth from England to Rome; but Coleridge argues that it should then have been consigned to other moral and cultural institutions, to produce men, rather than be thrown into the general economy. He makes the same point vividly in another passage, somewhere in *The Friend*. A Manchester economist had said that an isolated village that took no part in the national trade was of no importance. "What, sir," said Coleridge, "are seven hundred Christian souls of no importance?" The English factory towns destroyed people for the economy. We increasingly do not even need people for the economy.

As a man of letters, I am finally most like Coleridge (with a dash of Matthew Arnold when the vulgarity of liberalism gets me by the throat). Maybe what we have in common is our obsessional needs, his drug addiction, and my frustrated homosexuality. These keep us in touch with animal hunger, so we are not overly impressed by progress and the Gross National Product, nor credentials and status. For addicts and other starving people the world has got to come across in kind. It doesn't.

My homosexual acts have made me a nigger, subject to arbitrary brutality and debased when my out-going impulse is not taken for granted as a right. Nobody (except small children) has a claim to be loved, but there is a way of rejecting someone that accords him his right to exist and be himself and is the next best thing to accepting him. I have rarely enjoyed this treatment.

Stokely Carmichael once told me and Allen Ginsberg that our homosexual need was not like being black because we could always conceal it and pass. That is, he showed us the same lack of imagination that people show to niggers. Incidentally, this dialogue took place on (British) national television.

A vital nigger can respond with various kinds of spite, depending on his character. He can be ready to destroy everything, since there is no world to lose. Or he might develop an in-group fanaticism of his own kind. In my case, being a nigger seems to inspire me to want a more elementary humanity, wilder, less structured, more variegated. The thing is to have a National Liberation Front that does not end up in a Nation-State, but abolishes the boundaries. This was what Gandhi and Buber wanted, but they were shelved.

Usually we ought to diminish social anxiety, but to break down arbitrary boundaries we have to risk heightening social anxiety. Some boundaries, of course, are just the limits of our interests and people beyond them are indifferent or exotic. But as soon as we begin to notice a boundary *between* us and others, we project our own unacceptable traits on those across the boundary, and they are foreigners, heretics, untouchables, persons exploited as things. By their very existence, they threaten or temp us, and we must squelch them, patronize them, or with missionary zeal make them shape up.

The excluded or repressed are always right in their rebellion, for they stand for our future wholeness. And their demands must always seem wrongheaded, their style uncalled for, and their actions a violation of due process. But as in any psychotherapy, the problem is to tolerate anxiety and stay with it, rather than to panic and be in an emergency.

Curiously, the half-baked and noisy writing of the young is hopeful in this respect just because it is so dreadful. It is embarrassed or brazen rather than panicky. It is a kind of folk art of urban confusion, and where there is a folk art there might get to be a high art. It is not advance-guard, for they don't know enough to have an edge to leap from. It is not even eclectic but a farrago of misunderstood style. But it *is* without some previous boundaries. There is something in its tribalism, as they call it. It is somewhat a folk international. And it is boring, like all folk art; a little bit goes a long way.

Lord Acton, who understood conservatism, praises the character — George Washington was a good example — that is conservative in disposition but resolute in the disruptive action that has to be performed. A good surgeon minimizes postoperative shock and at once resumes as a physician, saying, "Nature heals, not the doctor." The advantage of a conservative, even back-tracking, disposition in a successful revolutionary is to diminish the danger of takeover by new bosses who invariably are rife with plans. After the American Revolution, the conservative disposition of the chief leaders blessed us with those twenty-five years of quasi-anarchy in national affairs, during which we learned whatever has made the American experiment worthwhile. "It's a free country, you can't make me" — every immigrant child learned to say it for over a century. The same would have occurred in the French Revolution if they had enjoyed our geographic isolation from invasion; the first French revolutionary leaders were the reverse of Jacobin. Danton wanted to go back to his wine and girls. But a defect of Leninist revolutions is that, from the beginning, they are made by Leninists. They have ideas.

I myself have a conservative, maybe timid, disposition; yet I trust, as I have said, that the present regime in America will get a lot more roughing up than it has, from the young who resent being processed; from the blacks who have been left out; from housewives and others who buy real goods with hard money at inflationary prices hiked by expense accounts and government subsidies; from professionals demanding their autonomy, rather than being treated as personnel of the front office; not to speak of every live person in jeopardy because of the bombs and CBW. Our system can stand, and profit by, plenty of interruption of business as usual. It is not such a delicate Swiss watch as all that. The danger is not in the loosening of the machine, but in its tightening up by panic repression.

It is true that because of massive urbanization and interlocking technologies, advanced countries are vulnerable to catastrophic disruption, and this creates a perceptible anxiety. But there is far more likelihood of breakdown from the respectable ambitions of Eastern Airlines and Consolidated Edison than from the Sabotage of revolutionaries. Nevertheless, I think the revolutionary rhetoric should be nonviolent, as by and large the actions have been, though there are bound to be fringes of violence.

In a modern massive complex society, it is said, any rapid global "revolutionary" or "Utopian" change can be incalculably destructive. I agree; but I wish people would remember that we have continually introduced big rapid changes that have in fact produced incalculable shock. Consider, in the past generation, the TV, mass higher schooling, the complex of cars, roads, and suburbanization, mass air travel, the complex of plantations, chain grocers, and forced urbanization; not to speak of the meteoric rise of the military industries and the Vietnam war and the draft. In all these, there has been a big factor of willful decision; these they have not been natural processes or inevitable catastrophes. And we have not begun to compound with the problems caused by those Utopian changes. Rather, in what seems an amazingly brief time, we have come to a political, cultural, and religious crisis that must be called prerevolutionary, and all because of a few willful fools.

There is also authentic confusion, however. Worldwide, we are going through a rapidly stepped-up collectivization which is, in my opinion, inevitable. I have just been watching the first lunar landing, and the impression of collectivity is overwhelming. We do not know how to cope with the dilemmas of it. The only prudent course is to try piecemeal to defend and extend the areas of liberty, locally, on the job, in the mores. Any violent collective change would be certainly totalitarian, whatever the ideology.

Needless to say, I myself hanker after and push global institutional changes: drastic cutback of the military industries, of the school system, and of the penal system; giving the city streets back to the children by banning the cars, and the cities back to the citizens by neighborhood communications and rural reconstruction; guaranteed income and a sector of free appropriation. I look for the kind of apprentice system that would produce workers' management, and the kind of guild association that would affirm authentic professionalism. The effects of these changes are also incalculable; it is hard to think through the consequences in our society that would flow from any and all of them. But I believe that in the fairly short run they would be stabilizing rather than explosive.

In any advanced society there is bound to be a mixture of enterprises run collectively and those run by individuals and small companies; and either kind of management will either try to be busy and growing or conservatively content to satisfy needs. There are always "socialism" and "free enterprise," "production for profit" and "production for use." The interesting political question is what is the right proportion and location of these factors in the particular society at the particular time. Safety from tyranny, flexibility of innovation, the possibility of countervailing power, all these political things depend on this balance. But cost efficiency also depends on it: "For any set of technological and social conditions, there is probably a rough optimum proportion of types of enterprise, or better, limits of unbalance beyond which the System gives sharply diminishing returns. A [good] mixed system would remain within the efficient range."

It is astonishing that nobody wants to explore this subject anymore. When I was young, it used to be a respectable liberal ideology called the Scandinavian Way. Now if I say that a mixture is inevitable and desirable, it is dismissed as "common sense," meaning a trivial platitude.

Since I am often on Canadian TV and radio, I tell it to the Canadians. If they would cut the American corporations down to size, it would cost them three or four years of unemployment and austerity, but then, in my opinion, Canada could become the most livable nation in the world, like Denmark but rich in resources and space and heterogenous population, with its own corporations, free businesses, and co-operatives, a reasonable amount of socialism, a sector of communism or guaranteed income as is suitable to affluent productivity, plenty of farmers, cities not yet too big, plenty of scientists and academics, a decent traditional bureaucracy, a nonaligned foreign policy. A great modern nation not yet too far gone in modern mistakes. There would be a flood of excellent immigrants from the south.

In one of his later books, *The Third World War*, C. Wright Mills had a foolish proposition far below his usual strong sense. The concentration of decision-making in our interlocking institutions, he argued, makes possible big changes for the better if the decision-makers can be rightly influenced — he seemed to be thinking of John Kennedy. But it is dubious if any administrator indeed has the kind of power to make an important change of policy; by 1961, the Kennedy people complained that they could not. And even if it would and could make policy, concentrated power can't produce human results anyway; it freezes what it touches. However, there is perhaps a different kind of truth in Mill's idea. The interlocking of institutions, the concentration of decision-making, and mass communications are the things that render people powerless, including the decision-makers; yet because of these same things, if freedom-loving people, honest professionals, or any other resolute group, indeed fight it out on their own issues, the odds are against them but their action is bound to have resonance and influence. In a reckless sentence in *Growing Up Absurd* I said, "One has the persistent thought that if ten thousand people in all walks of life will stand up on their two feet and talk out and insist, we shall get back our country" — damned if I don't still think so, with more evidence than I had then.

The right style in planning is to eliminate the intermediary, that which is neither use, nor making for use. We ought to cut down commutation, transport, administration, overhead, communications, hanging around waiting. On the other hand, there are very similar functions that we ought to encourage, like travel and trade, brokering, amenity, conversation, and loitering; the things that make up the busy and idle city, celebrated by Jane Jacobs. The difference seems to be that in logistics, systems, and communications, the soul is on ice until the intermediary activity is over with; in traffic, brokering and conversation, people are thrown with others and something might turn up. It is the difference between urbanism that imperially imposes its pattern on city and country both and the city planning for city squares and shops and contrasting rural life.

It was the genius of American pragmatism, our great contribution to world philosophy, to show that the means define and color the ends, to find value in operations and materials, to dignify workmanship and the workday, to make consummation less isolated, more in-process-forward, to be growth as well as good. But in recent decades there has occurred an astonishing reversal: the tendency of American philosophy, e.g. analytic logic or cybernetics, has been to drain value from both making and use, from either the working and materials or moral and psychological goods, and to define precisely by the intermediary, logistics, system, and communications; what Max Weber called rationalization. Then the medium is all the message there is. The pragmatists added to value, especially in everyday affairs.

Systems analysis has drained value, except for a few moments of collective achievement. Its planning refines and streamlines the intermediary as if for its own sake; it adds constraints without enriching life. If computation makes no difference to the data or the outcome — "Garbage in, garbage out" — then, to a pragmatist, the computation adds to the garbage. In fact, the computation abstracts from the data what it can handle, and constrains the result to what it can answer. Certainly cybernetics could be enriching, as psychiatry or as ecology,

but it has not yet been so — an exception has been the work of
Bateson.

It is interesting to notice the change in the style of scientific explanation. At the turn of the century they spoke of development,
struggle, coping, the logic of inquiry. Now they emphasize code,
homeostasis, feedback, the logic of structure.

A decade ago it was claimed that there was an end to ideology, for
the problems of modern society have to be coped with pragmatically,
functionally, piecemeal. This seems to have been a poor prediction,
considering the deafening revival of Marxist-Leninist rhetoric and
Law and Order rhetoric. Yet it was true, but not in the sense in which it
was offered. The ideological rhetoric is pretty irrelevant; but the pragmatic, functional, and piecemeal approach has not, as was expected,
consigned our problems to the province of experts, administrators and
engineers, but has thrown them to the dissenters. Relevant new
thought has not been administrative and technological, but existentialist, ethical and tactical. Administrators and planners write books
about the universities and cities, extrapolating from the trends — and
asking for funds; but history does not hasten to go in their direction.

Rather, pragmatism has come to be interpreted to include the
character of the agents as part of the problem to be solved; it is
psychoanalytic; there is stress on engagement. (Incidentally, it is good
Jamesian pragmatism.) Functionalism has come to mean criticizing
the program and the function itself, asking who wants to do it and
why, and is it humanly worth doing. Piecemeal issues have gotten entangled with the political action of the people affected by them. Instead of becoming more administrative as expected, affairs are
becoming more political. The premises of expertise and planning are
called into question. The credentials of the board of trustees are
scrutinized. Professionalism is a dirty word. Terms like "commitment," "dialogue," "confrontation," "community," "do your thing"
are indeed anti-ideological — and sometimes they do not connote
much other thought either; but they are surely not what *The End of
Ideology* had in mind. And it turns out that they are relevant to the
conditions of complex modern societies.

An advantage I have had over many others — I don't know
whether by luck or by character — is that I have never had to do, nor
forced myself to do, what was utterly alien to me. I was good at school
work and liked it. From age fifteen I never had a job that was altogether useless, or harmful, or mere busywork, or that did not use
some of my powers, so that I could try to do a good job in my own
style. This does not mean that I did what I wanted. Sometimes the

work was unpleasant or boring and it was almost never what I should have been used for. I was poor, without connections, bisexual, and socially inept, so that I was always driven by need and had to take what turned up, without choices. But I could not do — and I did not consider as a possibility — anything that I would not somewhat identify with. If somebody had offered me a stupid job at good pay, I could hardly have refused, but this never happened. I always worked hard in a way that made sense to myself — and sometimes got fired.

It is devastating that this is not the common condition. If people go through motions that do not make sense to them and do not have their allegiance, just for wages or other extrinsic rewards, there is an end to common sense and self-respect. Character is made by the behaviors we initiate; if we initiate what we do not mean, we get sick. And as we see, the accumulation of such motions that are not continually checked up as meant can produce calamities.

The more time I spend on politics — it is not much time but it is more than I have — is a fair example of how I work at what is mine but is onerous and boring. As a conservative anarchist, I believe that to seek for Power is otiose, yet I want to derange as little as possible the powers that be; I am eager to sign off as soon as conditions are tolerable, so people can go back to the things that matter, their professions, sports, and friendships. Naturally, politics should not be for me. In principle I agree with the hippies. They become political when they are indignant, as at the war or racist laws, and they also have to work at power and politics in order to protect their own business and community, e.g. against police harassment; but otherwise they rightly judge that radicals are in a bag.

But I am political because of an idiotic concept of myself as a man of letters: I am that kind of writer who must first have done his duty as a citizen, father, and so forth. Inevitably, my disastrous model is John Milton — and it's a poor state to be waiting to go blind in order to be free to write a big poem. But at least thereby, I write with a good conscience. I do not have to be a political poet.

In normal fiscal conditions, the way for free citizens to check the government has been to grant or refuse taxes, usually through the parliament, but if both the parliament and government are illegitimate, by individual refusal. At present, some are refusing their federal taxes, or 70 percent of the amount, in protest against the armaments and, of course, the Vietnam war. (They estimate the military budget as about 70 percent of the total.)

I agree with the principle of refusal, yet, except for the surtax and the telephone tax, I pay the taxes because of a moral scruple: in the present fiscal set-up, the kind of money I get is not really pay for my work, is not mine, but belongs to the very System I object to. I have a comfortable income. I well deserve an adequate one and a little more; I worked hard till forty-five years of age, and brought up children, on an income in the lowest tenth of the population; nor have I found that my late-come wealth has changed my thought, work, or even much my standard of living. But most of my money is "soft" money, from the military economy and the wasteful superstructure, and I cannot see how I am justified in keeping Caesar's share from dribbling back to him through my hands. For instance, I am paid a large sum to give a lecture — mainly because I am a "name" and they want to make their series prestigious; the lecture series is financed by a Foundation; and you do not need to scratch hard to find military-industrial corporations supporting that Foundation — perhaps as a tax dodge! I give the lecture innocently enough; I am probably not the only one who can give it, but I do my best and say my say. It would not help to refuse the money, or 70 percent of it, since by Parkinson's Law that all the soft money will be spent, the money will certainly be spent.

I wouldn't know how to estimate the pay that I get for hard work in hard money, on which I would feel justified in refusing the tax because it is mine to give or refuse, but it cannot be much of the whole. There is a hypothesis that in our society pay is inversely proportional to effort. The idea, I guess, is that big money accrues from being in the System, and the higher you are in the System, the less you move your ass. But empirically this is not accurate. Top managers and professionals do work hard for long hours for high pay; those on a thirty-six-hour week work much less, for varying pay; farmers, hospital orderlies, dishwashers, and others work very hard for miserable pay; some students work hard and it costs them money. Unemployable people do not work, for inadequate pay. In my individual experience there has been no relation whatever between effort and pay. For twenty years I averaged a few hundred dollars a year for good writing that I now make good royalties on; I work hard for a possibly useful cause and lay out fare and a contribution, or I do the same work at a state college for a handsome honorarium and expenses. My editor takes me to costly lunches on the firm, and the food is poor. Third class on planes is often the most luxurious because if the plane is not full you can remove the seat arms and stretch out.

The lack of correlations between effort and pay must be profoundly confusing and perhaps disgusting to the naive young. In my opinion, it is unfortunate at present but promising for the future:

it creates the moral attitude, "It's only money," and politically, a soft-money affluent society can easily come to include a sector of communism in the form of guaranteed income or free appropriation or both.

The telephone tax, however, was explicitly a war tax and my wife and I don't pay it, getting the spiteful satisfaction that it costs the government a couple of hundred dollars (of the taxpayers'— our — money) to collect $1.58. We also have refused the 10 percent surtax, which rose directly out of the Vietnam war. This tax for this war is like the ship tax that Charles I exacted for his Irish War that John Hamden refused. The FBI seems to be breathing down our necks, but if they arrest me I'll bring up that shining precedent — and they'll be sorry that they picked on me. (No, they have attached the money at the bank.)

In otherwise friendly reviews and expostulatory fan mail from young people, I read that there are three things wrong with my social thinking: I go in for tinkering; I don't tell how to bring about what I propose; I am a "romantic" and want to go back to the past. Let me consider these criticism in turn.

My proposed little reforms and improvements are meaningless, it is said, because I do not attack the System itself, usually monopoly capitalism; and I am given the philological information that "radical" means "going to the root," whereas I hack at the branches. To answer this, I have tried to show that in a complex society which is a network rather than a monolith with a head, a piecemeal approach can be effective; it is the safest, least likely to produce ruinous consequences of either repression or "success"; it involves people where they are competent, or could become competent, and so creates citizens, which is better than "politicizing"; it more easily dissolves the metaphysical despair that nothing can be done. And since, in my opinion, the aim of politics is to produce not a good society but a tolerable one, it is best to try to cut abuses down to manageable size; the best solutions are usually not global but a little of this and a little of that.

More important, in the confusing conditions of modern times, so bristling with dilemmas, I don't know what is the root. I have not heard of any formula, e.g., "Socialism," that answers the root questions. If I were a citizen of a communist country, I should no doubt be getting into (more) trouble by tinkering with "bourgeois" improvements. Since all actual societies are, and have to be, mixtures of socialism, market economy, etc., the problem in any society is to get a more judicious mixture, and this *might* be most attainable by tinkering.

A second criticism is that I don't explain how to bring about the nice things I propose. The chief reason for this, of course, is that I don't know how or I would proclaim it. Put it this way: I have been a pacifist for thirty years, and ... But ignorance is rarely an excuse. What my critics really object to is that I accept my not knowing too easily, as if the actuality of change were unimportant, when in fact people are wretched and dying.

As I have explained, I do not have the character for politics. I cannot lead or easily be led, and I am dubious about the ability of parties and government to accomplish any positive good — and which of these is cause, which is effect? — therefore, I do not put my mind to questions of manipulation and power, I do not belong to a party, and therefore I have no thoughts. Belief and commitment are necessary in order to have relevant ideas. Nevertheless, somebody has to make sense, and I am often willing to oblige, as a man of letters, as part of the division of labor, so to speak.

I do agree with my critics that there cannot be social thought without political action; and if I violate this rule, I ought to stop. Unless it is high poetry, Utopian thinking is boring. "Neutral" sociology is morally repugnant and bad science. An essential part of any sociological inquiry is having a practical effect, otherwise the problem is badly defined: people are being taken as objects rather than human beings, and the inquirer himself is not all there.

For the humanistic problems that I mostly work at, however, the sense of powerlessness, the loss of history, vulgarity, the lack of magnanimity, alienation, the maladaptation of organism and environment — and these are political problems — maybe there are no other "strategies" than literature, dialogue, and trying to be a useful citizen oneself.

I am not a "romantic"; what puts my liberal and radical critics off is that I am a conservative, a conservationist. I do use the past; the question is how.

I get a kind of insight (for myself) from the genetic method, from seeing how a habit or institution has developed to its present form; but I really do understand that its positive value and meaning are in its present action, coping with present conditions. Freud, for instance, was in error when he sometimes spoke as if a man had a child inside of him, or a vertebrate had an annelid worm inside. Each specified individual behaves as the whole that it has become; and every stage of life, as Dewey used to insist, has its own problems and ways of coping.

The criticism of the genetic fallacy, however, does not apply to the *negative*, to the *lapses* in the present, which can often be remedied only by taking into account some simplicities of the past. The case is analogous to localizing an organic function, e.g., seeing. As Kurt Goldstein used to point out, we cannot localize seeing in the eye or the brain — it is a function of the whole organism in its environment. But a *failure* of sight may well be localized in the cornea, the optic nerve, etc. We cannot explain speech by the psychosexual history of an infant; it is a person's way of being in the world. But a speech defect, e.g., lisping, may well come from inhibited biting because of imperfect weaning. This is, of course, what Freud knew as a clinician when he was not being metapsychological.

My books are full of one-paragraph or two-page "histories" — of the concept of alienation, the system of welfare, suburbanization, compulsory schooling, the anthropology of neurosis, university administration, citizenly powerlessness, missed revolutions, etc., etc. In every case my purpose is to show that a coerced or unauthentic settling of a conflict has left an unfinished situation to the next generation, and the difficulty becomes more complex in the new conditions. Then it is useful to remember the simpler state before things went wrong; it is hopelessly archaic as a present response, but it has vitality and may suggest a new program involving a renewed conflict. This is the therapeutic use of history. As Ben Nelson has said, the point of history is to keep old (defeated) causes alive. Of course, this reasoning presupposes that there is a nature of things, including human nature, whose right development can be violated. There is.

An unauthentic solution complicates, produces a monster. An authentic solution neither simplifies nor complicates, but produces a new configuration, a species, adapted to the on-going situation. There is a human nature, and it is characteristic of that nature to go on making itself ever different. This is the humanistic use of history, to remind of man's various ways of being great. So we have become mathematical, tragical, political, loyal, romantic, civil-libertarian, universalist, experimental-scientific, collectivist, etc., etc. — these too accumulate and become a mighty heavy burden. There is no laying any of it down.

I went down to Dartmouth to lead some seminars of American Telephone and Telegraph executives who were being groomed to be vice-presidents. They wanted to know how to get on with the young people, since they would have to employ them, or try. (Why do I go? Ah, why do I go? It's not for money and it's not out of vanity. I go because they ask me. Since I used to gripe bitterly when I was left out of the world, how can I gracelessly decline when I am invited in?)

I had three suggestions. First, citing my usual evidence of the irrelevance of school grades and diplomas, I urged them to hire black and Puerto Rican dropouts, who would learn on the job as well as anybody else, whereas to require academic credentials would put them at a disadvantage. Not to my surprise, the executives were agreeable to this idea. (There were twenty-five of them, no blacks and no women.) It was do-good and no disadvantage to them as practical administrators. One said that he was already hiring dropouts and it had worked out very well.

Secondly, I pointed out that dialogue across the generation gap was quite impossible for them, and their present tactics of youth projects and special training would be taken as, and were co-optation. Yet people who will not talk to one another can get together by working together on a useful job that they both care about, like fixing the car. And draft counselling, I offered, was something that the best of the young cared strongly about; the telephone company could provide valuable and interesting help in this, for instance the retrieval and dissemination of information: and all this was most respectable and American, since every kid should know his rights. Not to my surprise, the executives were not enthusiastic about this proposal. But they saw the point — and had to agree — and would certainly not follow up.

My third idea, however, they did not seem to know what to do with. I told them that Ralph Nadar was going around the schools urging the engineering students to come on like professionals, and to stand up to the front desk when asked for unprofessional work. In my opinion, an important move for such integrity would be for the young engineers to organize for defence of the profession, and strike or boycott if necessary: a model was the American Association of University Professors in its heyday, fifty years ago. I urged the executives to encourage such organization; it would make the telephone company a better telephone company, more serviceable to the community; and young people would cease to regard engineers as finks. To my surprise, the prospective vice-presidents of AT&T seemed to be embarrassed. (We were all pleasant people and very friendly.) I take it that *this* — somewhere here — is the issue.

I am pleased to notice how again and again I have returned to the freedoms, duties, and opportunities of earnest professionals. It means that I am thinking from where I breathe.

PIERRE-JOSEPH PROUDHON
A Biography
2nd revised edition

The first full-scale English-language biography of the prominent 19th century social thinker and "father of anarchism."

…essential reading for a true appreciation of economic history and thought.
Small Press

295 pages, index
Paperback ISBN: 0-921689-08-X $17.99
Hardcover ISBN: 0-921689-09-8 $35.99

BAKUNIN
The Philosophy of Freedom
Brian Morris

This book confirms Bakunin was a holistic thinker; that his anarchism was dominated by a desire to achieve a unity of theory and practice within the reality of a given historical social order and that he opposed all the dualism which Western culture had bequeathed.

159 pages, index
Paperback ISBN: 1-895431-66-2 $18.99
Hardcover ISBN: 1-895431-67-0 $37.99

BAKUNIN ON ANARCHISM
Sam Dolgoff, ed.

4th printing
The best available in English. Bakunin's insights into power and freedom, the new classes of specialists, are refreshing, original and often still unsurpassed in clarity and vision.
Noam Chomsky

453 pages
Paperback ISBN: 0-919619-06-1 $18.99
Hardcover ISBN: 0-919619-05-3 $37.99

FREEDOM AND AUTHORITY
William R. McKercher

Freedom and Authority traces the intellectual heritage of the libertarian tradition. It clarifies the distinctions between Marxist and Bakuninist thought as well as the distinctions between libertarian thought, and such ideologies as anarchim and socialism.

300 pages, bibliography
Paperback ISBN: 0-921689-30-6 $16.99
Hardcover ISBN: 0-921689-31-4 $36.99

BLACK ROSE BOOKS

has also published the following books of related interests

Manufacturing Consent: Noam Chomsky and the Media,
edited by Mark Achbar
Political Ecology, *by Dimitrios Roussopoulos*
The Legacy of the New Left, *by Dimitrios Roussopoulos*
Civilization and its Discontented, *by John Laffey*
Feminism, *edited by Angela Miles and Geraldine Finn*
Women and Counter-Power, *edited by Yolande Cohen*
Finding Our Way: Rethinking Eco-Feminist Politics, *by Janet Biehl*
Post-Scarcity Anarchism, *by Murray Bookchin*
Urbanization Without Cities, *by Murray Bookchin*
Toward an Ecological Society, *by Murray Bookchin*
Pierre-Joseph Proudhon: A Biography, *by George Woodcock*
William Godwin: A Biographical Study, *by George Woodcock*
The Modern State: An Anarchist Analysis, *by Frank Harrison*
The State, *by Franz Oppenheimer*
The Politics of Obedience, The Discourse of Voluntary Servitude,
by Etienne de la Boétie
The Anarchist Moment: Reflections on Culture, Nature and Power,
by John Clark
The Irrational in Politics, *by Maurice Brinton*
1984 and After, *edited by Marsha Hewitt and Dimitrios Roussopoulos*
The Anarchist Papers, *edited by Dimitrios Roussopoulos*
The Radical Papers, *edited by Dimitrios Roussopoulos*
The Radical Papers 2, *edited by Dimitrios Roussopoulos*
The Anarchist Papers, edited by Dimitrios Roussopoulos
The Anarchist Papers 2, edited by Dimitrios Roussopoulos
The Anarchist Papers 3, edited by Dimitrios Roussopoulos

THE COLLECTED WORKS OF PETER KROPOTKIN
*Memoirs of a Revolutionist; The Great French Revolution; Mutual Aid; The
Conquest of Bread; Russian Literature; In Russian and French Prisons; Words
of a Rebel; Ethics; Fields, Factories and Workshops; Fugitive Writings;
Evolution and Environment*

Send for our free catalogue of books
BLACK ROSE BOOKS
C.P. 1258, Succ. Place du Parc
Montréal, Québec
H2W 2R3

Printed by the workers of
Les Éditions Marquis
Montmagny, Québec
for Black Rose Books Ltd. ⊛